LAMSON OF THE GETTYSBURG

LAMSON OF THE GETTYSBURG

— • ◆ • —

THE CIVIL WAR LETTERS
OF LIEUTENANT ROSWELL H. LAMSON,
U.S. NAVY

EDITED BY

James M. McPherson
Patricia R. McPherson

New York   Oxford
Oxford University Press
1997

Oxford University Press

Oxford   New York
Athens   Aukland   Bangkok   Bogotá   Bombay
Buenos Aires   Calcutta   Cape Town   Dar es Salaam
Delhi   Florence   Hong Kong   Istanbul   Karachi
Kuala Lumpur   Madras   Madrid   Melbourne
Mexico City   Nairobi   Paris   Singapore
Taipei   Tokyo   Toronto   Warsaw

and associated companies in
Berlin   Ibadan

Published by Oxford University Press
198 Madison Avenue, New York, New York 10016

Oxford is a registered trademark of Oxford University Press

Library of Congress Cataloging-in-Publication Data

Lamson, Roswell Hawks.
Lamson of the Gettysburg : the Civil War letters of
Lieutenant Roswell H. Lamson, U.S. Navy /
edited by James M. McPherson and Patricia R. McPherson.
p.   cm.   Includes index.
ISBN 0-19-511698-4
1. Lamson, Roswell Hawks—Correspondence.
2. United States. Navy—Officers—Correspondence.   3. Gettysburg (Ship)
4. United States—History—Civil War, 1861–1865—Naval operations.
5. United States—History—Civil War, 1861–1865—Personal narratives.
6. United States. Navy—Biography.   7. Oregon—Biography.
I. McPherson, Patricia R.   II. McPherson, James M.   III. Title.
E595.G48L36   1997   973.7'5—dc21   97-11129

1   3   5   7   9   8   6   4   2

Printed in the United States of America
on acid-free paper

To

SHELDON MEYER

Valued Editor
and Friend

CONTENTS

MAPS

PREFACE

P RESIDENT ABRAHAM LINCOLN used public letters to make
important pronouncements in the same way that a modern president uses televised news conferences. On August 26, 1863,
Lincoln sent such a letter to a political rally in his home state of
Illinois. This rally occurred at a time when things were going well for
the North in the Civil War. The recent victory at Gettysburg, the
capture of Vicksburg, and other Union advances had turned the war
around after a series of discouraging Northern defeats earlier in the
year. In a passage that contained several vivid images, Lincoln sum-
marized these achievements. "The Father of Waters again goes unvexed
to the sea," he said of the Mississippi River, now entirely under Union
control. Lincoln thanked the armies for their victories, and added: "Nor
must Uncle Sam's Web-feet be forgotten. At all the watery margins
they have been present. Not only on the deep sea, the broad bay, and
the rapid river, but also up the narrow muddy bayou, and wherever
the ground was a little damp, they have been, and made their tracks."[1]

Uncle Sam's Web-feet were, of course, the United States Navy.
From rivers that penetrated deep into the Confederate heartland to the

---

1. Lincoln to James C. Conkling, Aug. 26, 1863, in Roy P. Basler, ed., *The Collected Works of Abraham Lincoln*, 9 vols. (New Brunswick, N.J., 1953–55), VI: 409–10.

port cities captured by naval attacks or blockaded by patrolling warships, the Union navy played a crucial part in the Anaconda strategy that was strangling the Confederacy. Sailors welcomed Lincoln's praise of their contribution as an overdue recognition of the navy's importance in the war effort. The great battles fought by armies captured public attention during the war and have likewise attracted the lion's share of historical writing ever since. In one respect this was not unreasonable, for of the 2,200,000 men who fought for the Union, only 115,000 served in the navy.

Yet the navy's contribution to Northern victory was far greater than implied by its 5 percent of Union personnel. Warships maintained an increasingly effective blockade of Confederate ports, cutting their trade to less than one-third of the antebellum volume at a time when the Confederacy needed a large expansion of imports to supply its armies. The Union navy also protected coastal shipping lanes and inland rivers essential to logistical support of Northern armies operating in the South. Most important, army–navy task forces won some of the most significant Northern victories of the war: Fort Donelson, Roanoke Island, Vicksburg, Port Hudson, Mobile Bay, and Fort Fisher. And the navy won some remarkable battles and captured forts or cities all by itself: Hatteras Inlet, Port Royal Sound, Fort Henry, New Orleans, and Memphis.

Historians have begun to appreciate the crucial role of the Union navy in the war's outcome as well as the significant innovations by the overmatched Confederate navy in such areas as ironclad rams, naval mines ("torpedoes"), torpedo boats, and the first submarine to sink an enemy ship. Every student of the Civil War is familiar with such figures as David Glasgow Farragut, Andrew Hull Foote, and David Dixon Porter on the Union side, and Raphael Semmes, Franklin Buchanan, and James D. Bulloch on the Confederate side. Some are aware that Lieutenant William B. Cushing was the youngest naval officer ever to receive the Thanks of Congress (then a higher award than the medal of honor) for his daring feat of sinking the feared Confederate ironclad ram CSS *Albemarle* in 1864.

But few of even the most dedicated Civil War buffs have heard of Roswell Hawks Lamson. We readily confess that we knew nothing of him until we encountered the extraordinary collection of his letters at—of all places—our own university library. Yet Lamson, a friend of Cushing, had a reputation equal to his as one of the most bold and skillful young officers in the Union navy. Lamson commanded more ships and flotillas than any other officer of his age or rank in the service, climaxed by his captaincy of the navy's fastest ship in 1864, the USS *Gettysburg*. As commander of the "Torpedo and Picket Division" on the James River in May–June 1864, with the duty of clearing the river of Confederate mines, he pioneered techniques in the dangerous new naval mission of minesweeping.

Lamson always seemed to be where the action was in the naval war on the South Atlantic coast: he was captain of the big deck guns on the USS *Wabash* that did the most damage to enemy forts at Hatteras Inlet and Port Royal; he was the officer who took command of the CSS *Planter* in May 1862 when slaves led by Robert Smalls ran her past Confederate fortifications in Charleston harbor and delivered her to the Union blockading fleet; he commanded a gunboat fleet on the Nansemond River that helped stop James Longstreet's advance on Norfolk in the Suffolk campaign of April 1863; he skippered the ship that towed the USS *Louisiana* packed with more than 200 tons of gunpowder under the guns of Fort Fisher in December 1864; and he led a contingent of seventy men from the USS *Gettysburg* in the January 15, 1865, attack on the sea-face parapets of Fort Fisher, where he was wounded.

Lamson described all of these actions and others in letters to Catherine Buckingham, his cousin and fiancée, and to his cousin Flora Lamson. These letters also provide the best portrayal of blockade duty in the Civil War that we have ever read. We first encountered these letters in the Special Collections of Firestone Library at Princeton University when we were doing research for the book *For Cause and Comrades: Why Men Fought in the Civil War* (New York, 1997). In the course of this research we read more than 25,000 letters written by some 800 Civil War soldiers and sailors. Few sets of letters equal and none surpass those of Lamson for richness of description, scope of coverage, or keenness of perception and analysis. An extra bonus, rare in Civil War collections, are letters *to* Lamson from his fiancée, which offer fascinating glimpses of life on the home front.

Several excellent editions of Civil War letters have been published in recent years. Nearly all of them were written by army officers or soldiers. In this epistolary outpouring the navy has not received its due. This edition of Roswell Lamson's letters will help redress that imbalance. They are, quite simply, the best Civil War navy letters we have ever read or expect to read. And we are delighted to share them herein with a larger audience.

If Lamson has been forgotten by Civil War historians, he was not forgotten by the U.S. Navy. In 1908 a ship in the new class described as "Torpedo Boat Destroyer" was named the USS *Lamson*. She fought in World War I and was decommissioned in 1919. In that same year the keel of a new destroyer USS *Lamson* was laid down, to be replaced in 1936 by the third USS *Lamson*, which fought in the North Atlantic during World War II. The letters that follow make it clear why the Navy chose to honor Lamson in this way.

Princeton, New Jersey   J. M. Mc.
February 1997   P. R. Mc.

ACKNOWLEDGMENTS

LIBRARIANS AND archivists at five institutions offered assistance and courtesies without which this book could not have been completed. At Firestone Library, Princeton University, Alice Clark efficiently and cheerfully made copies of materials we requested from the Lamson Papers. Donald Skemer, curator of manuscripts, and Margaret Sherry, reference librarian and archivist, also provided crucial assistance. Unless otherwise noted, all letters reproduced in this volume are from the Roswell H. Lamson Papers in the Manuscripts Division, Department of Rare Books and Special Collections, Princeton University Library, and are published with permission of the Princeton University Library. Photographs from the Lamson Papers and the Blair and Lee Family Papers are also published with permission of Princeton University Library.

At the Huntington Library in San Marino, California, Robert C. Ritchie, Carolyn Powell, and Elsa Sink assisted with many of the important little things that facilitated research for the annotations. At the Oregon Historical Society in Portland the chief librarian Louis Flannery, the executive director Chet Orloff, and project archivist Todd Welch helped us track down items relating to Lamson's life in Oregon. Olive Johnson of the Yamhill County Historical Society in Lafayette, Oregon, provided additional material on Lamson's years in Oregon.

And Mark Hayes of the Naval Historical Center in Washington helped us find photographs of the USS *Gettysburg* and the three USS *Lamson*s, which are published with permission of the Naval Historical Center.

We spent a rewarding afternoon with Kenneth Lamson and Barbara Lamson Woodstock, Roswell Lamson's great-grandnephew and great-great-grandniece. Both live near the farm in Oregon where Roswell grew up, part of which is still owned by Jeremiah Lamson's descendants. With them we rambled over the Lamson homestead, visited the Willamina cemetery where Roswell's parents and two of his children are buried, and reviewed family genealogy. The experience was fascinating and helpful, and we express our gratitude to the Lamsons for their generosity. With the help of Arlene Clemens we found the graves of Roswell and Kate Lamson and four of their children in Portland's Riverview Cemetery. And, of course, we wish to thank our daughter Joanna Erika McPherson for taking such good care of the house while we spent all these rewarding hours with Roswell and Kate 3000 miles from home.

A NOTE ON

EDITORIAL METHOD

THE LAMSON COLLECTION is large. Most of it consists of correspondence between Roswell Lamson and Catherine ("Kate") Buckingham from November 1860 until their marriage seven years later. Because it was easier for Kate to preserve Roswell's letters at home than for him to preserve hers on shipboard, there are at least twice as many of his letters than hers. In addition to these letters, the collection includes several letters from Roswell's father and a few from his mother and other persons, letterbooks containing copies of Roswell's business correspondence when he worked for his uncle's manufacturing company from 1867 to 1870, some other official correspondence, miscellaneous items, and copies of Roswell's wartime letters to Flora Lamson.

To reproduce all of this material would make a volume of a thousand pages. Much of it is of little value or interest; some of it is repetitive. The focus of this book is on Lamson's wartime activities as a Union navy officer. This focus is therefore the main criterion for the selection of letters to be reproduced and for the internal editing of these letters to eliminate extraneous and repetitious material. Much of the correspondence between Roswell and Kate refers to personal and domestic concerns; we have included just enough of such material to provide a word picture of their personalities and their relationship. Jeremiah's few letters are reprinted almost in full because of the rare glimpses they offer of Oregon during the war.

We debated whether to include the letters to Flora in this book. They are edited copies made by Lamson himself, probably in the 1890s, rather than the actual letters. Lamson deleted all personal material from these copies, indicating such deletions by his own form of ellipses. We have no way of knowing whether he also silently altered anything he had written thirty years earlier. Yet many of these letters contain rich and valuable descriptions of naval actions in 1861 and 1862, when the letters to Kate were infrequent—or perhaps were not all preserved. Had we not included some of the letters to Flora, the chapters for these years would be thin indeed. Comparisons of letters to Kate with copies of those to Flora that were written on or near the same date describing the same events show great similarities, sometimes even identical phrasing, which gives us confidence that Lamson did not alter the letters to Flora when he copied them. Whenever letters to the two women described the same events or offered similar observations, we reproduce the letters to Kate.

The letters are reprinted here as written with respect to spelling, capitalization, paragraphing, and most punctuation. We have silently provided periods where the authors penned dashes or nothing at all between sentences. Roswell had a tendency to use semicolons when he should have used colons or commas; we have silently corrected his usage. His letters *i*, *e*, and *a* had a tendency to look alike; we have given him the benefit of the doubt and spelled such words correctly. Deletions of sentences or parts of sentences are indicated in the usual way by ellipses. In no instance do we alter the meaning of a letter by such deletions, whose sole purpose is to eliminate unimportant or irrelevant material. To save space we have also omitted the salutations and valedictions of all letters. Each letter is headed by the name of the writer and recipient and the date and place of writing. We have retained the personal flavor of most of these letters by heading them with first names: "Roswell to Kate," "Roswell to Flora," and so on.

Roswell's middle name sometimes appears as "Hawkes." His mother's maiden name, however, was Hawks, so we assume that is the correct form and have therefore used it here.

Each chapter and some sections within chapters are headed by brief introductions to set the background and context for the letters, which themselves carry most of the narrative. To avoid excessive editorial intrusions, we have kept the annotations to the minimum necessary to identify persons, events, or places that might be unfamiliar to readers.

LAMSON OF THE GETTYSBURG

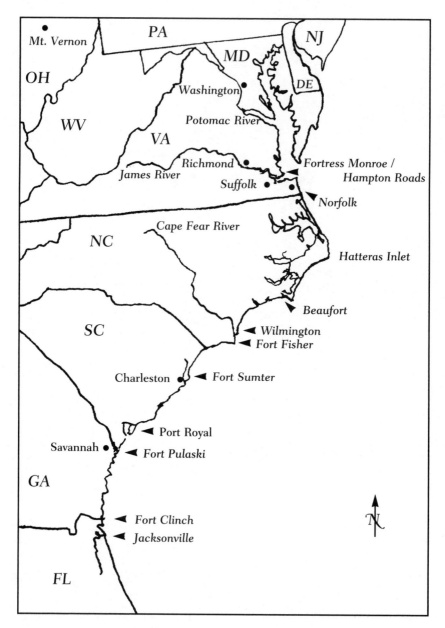

The South Atlantic Coast

PROLOGUE

ROSWELL HAWKS LAMSON was a child of the frontier. Like so many American naval officers in World War II who came from the Midwest, Lamson spent his early years far from salt water. But perhaps the sea was in his blood. His father Jeremiah Lamson was born in Massachusetts, the descendant of a long line of New England Yankees, some of them seafarers, whose progenitor William Lamson settled at Ipswich in 1634. Roswell's mother, née Helen Maria Hawks, was the daughter of Presbyterian clergyman Roswell Hawks. Young Roswell Lamson probably acquired his love of books and learning from his mother and from his maternal grandfather, who helped found Mount Holyoke College. Two of his grand-uncles were, respectively, president of the College of New Jersey (Princeton) and Williams College.

Jeremiah Lamson and Helen Hawks were married in Massachusetts on March 14, 1837. They promptly became part of New England's nineteenth-century westward migration, moving to Iowa Territory where one of their first actions was to conceive Roswell, who was born on the Lamson farm near Burlington on March 29, 1838. Jeremiah prospered on the fertile soil of the Mississippi Valley, but soon after Iowa achieved statehood in 1846 the migration fever hit him again. In the spring of 1847 he packed his wife, nine-year-old Roswell, and six-

3

year-old Henry with all their belongings into three wagons drawn by thirteen yoke of oxen and headed west on the Oregon Trail. One of Jeremiah and Helen's first actions after arriving in Oregon Territory in September 1847 was to conceive Dorinda, born the following July. The Lamsons initially settled near Astoria, not far from where the Lewis and Clark expedition wintered in 1805–6, and where young Roswell probably got his first glimpse of the sea.

In the spring of 1848 the Lamsons took up residence on a 640-acre claim near Willamina, fifty miles southwest of Portland, which Jeremiah had bought from a pioneer settler for $200. A Democrat, Jeremiah served several terms in the territorial legislature and four years as a county judge in Yamhill County. A fourth child, Edward, was born in 1850. Jeremiah must have been a good farmer, for he added to his holdings and eventually owned 2500 acres. Judging from his spelling in the wartime letters to Roswell reprinted in this volume, Jeremiah had a minimal education. But he sent Roswell and subsequently the other children to the best school in the territory, Oregon Institute, in the capital city of Salem. There on March 13, 1854, Roswell H. Lamson gave the "Salutatory Address."[1]

During the next four years young Roswell seems to have worked on his father's farm and perhaps continued his education under his mother's tutelage. (Whether he absorbed his father's political opinions is less clear. By 1860, as appears from his letters, Roswell was an antislavery Republican, perhaps having been influenced in that direction by uncles in Ohio and Massachusetts during vacations from the Naval Academy.) In 1855, serious fighting with Indians broke out in Oregon Territory and in Washington Territory, which had been detached from Oregon in 1853. The Yakima Indians and other Native American nations retaliated against the intrusion of white settlers with hit-and-run raids that escalated into pitched battles with companies of U.S. Regulars and territorial volunteers during the winter of 1855–56. Seventeen-year-old Roswell Lamson, large and mature for his age, enlisted in the Second Washington Volunteers and saw action in northeastern Oregon during the spring of 1856.

Discharged in September 1856 after the Indians had been subdued, Roswell returned to the farm—but not to contemplation of life in his father's footsteps. Using his political influence, Jeremiah secured Roswell an appointment to the Naval Academy at Annapolis in 1858.

1. *Oregon Statesman,* March 14, 1854.

Thence Roswell traveled that summer, retracing the overland trip of eleven years earlier rather than going around the Horn by sea. At this stage of his life Roswell was much more familiar with horses than with ships. On his way to Annapolis, he stopped to visit his aunt Marion Hawks Buckingham in Mount Vernon, Ohio, where he met his cousin Eastburne Buckingham, a young man of about his own age with whom Roswell became friendly and to whom the first letter reproduced in this book was written.

Whether Roswell's fifteen-year-old cousin Kate (Catherine) made any impression on him does not appear in the record. He saw Kate again in Mount Vernon during his summer vacation in 1860 and began corresponding with her as "My Dear Friend" that fall. But he also corresponded with his cousin Flora Lamson (three years older than Kate), whom he had met on visits to Uncle Ebenezer Goodnow Lamson, his father's younger brother, in Shelburne Falls, Massachusetts. For two years Roswell's letters to Flora were equally warm and apparently more frequent than letters to Kate. There are hints in Lamson's papers that his first love may have been Cousin Flora. Before the fall of 1862 no evidence of strong affection for Kate appears in his correspondence. But during a Christmas furlough that year he and Kate bespoke their love for each other and became engaged. Roswell continued his correspondence, now less frequent, with "Dear Cousin Flora" but repeatedly assured an apparently jealous Kate that she was his one and only true love. Their engagement lasted five years, for the war and Lamson's postwar tour of duty in Europe postponed their marriage until 1867. Flora never married.

CHAPTER 1

I SHALL STAND

BY THE UNION

OCTOBER 1858–AUGUST 1861

O NLY A FEW letters written by Lamson during his three years at the Naval Academy have survived. His class and the first class (the fourth-year class) were commissioned directly into the navy when the Civil War began in 1861. Lamson was assigned as a midshipman on the USS *Wabash*, a 46-gun steam frigate built in 1855. Like most steam warships of that transitional era, whether driven by a screw propeller (as the *Wabash* was) or by paddle wheels, the *Wabash* was also fitted with spars to carry sails for cruising in order to save fuel or in case of engine failure. On April 19, 1861, President Lincoln proclaimed a blockade of Confederate ports. As soon as she could be gotten ready for sea, the *Wabash* joined the blockade fleet off Charleston.

———•———

Roswell to Eastburne P. Buckingham

U.S. Naval Academy
Annapolis
Oct. 25, 1858

I suppose by this time you are as busy with your studies as I am with mine. We have to work all the time—drilling when not studying.

I like [it] fully as well as I expected I should and as I did not come here to play I do not mind the confinement or hard work. . . . Last week we were arranged in sections from the "class Reports" of last month. In Mathematics I am no. 1, and in Ethics no. 2. I have been obliged to study almost day and night for besides those who had been here a year several came direct from college and having had better advantages were better prepared than myself. I shall have to study to keep my place but I'll give them a hard struggle for it. The one above me in Ethics is quite low in Mathematics and that counts more than anything here.[1] I have often thought of my pleasant visit at Mt. Vernon and I only regret that I cannot see any of my friends for two long years.

I have not time to be homesick but I sometimes think of the mountains I have wandered over so free and I cannot help sighing as I look at the walls which I can pass but once in two weeks. If I could spring upon one of my ponies at such a time I should be tempted to make a dash for the mountains again.

There is a wildnes[s] a fascination about mountain life that one knows nothing of until they have felt it and then it is never forgotten.

After you have led your party across the Rocky Mts. you will miss their wild grandeur and the adventure incident to such a trip. Perhaps I shall be ready to cross them again by that time I hope so at least. But this will be my home for four years and then "A home on the roaring deep."

The examinations at entering were rigid especially the Physical but I passed without difficulty.

1. Lamson eventually finished second in his class of 1862, just behind his best friend at the Naval Academy, Samuel W. Preston. His class studied their fourth-year textbooks while on active war duty and took their final examinations when opportunity was available in 1862. The class of 1862 had numbered 62 when it entered in 1858. Thirty of them had dropped out or had been washed out before April 1861; six more resigned between April 19 and 25, 1861, to join the Confederate navy. In addition, seven other men who had started with the class of 1862 served in the Confederate navy.

Roswell to Katie

U.S. Naval Academy
Nov. 25, 1860

. . . There is a good deal of political excitement among the students, and as most all of our crew are warm Southroners, we do not agree very well as to what is right, and what wrong. They proposed to show me clearly that the Bible and the Constitution both recognize slavery as *right*; but of course they could not make any headway on that tack, and wound up their argument with the assertion of their entire ability to "whip the Northerners five to one." Capt. Blake[1] addressed a few remarks to the Battalion reminding us that what ever occurred we were *sworn to defend the Constitution*, and forbidding political discussions at the mess-tables. I hope and trust that our glorious union may be preserved, but the feeling of Southroners is so *implacably* hostile to the North and they have really so many causes of complaint that no one can be surprised if the worst comes. All Southroners here will resign as soon as their states secede. For myself I shall stand by the Union as long as there is a plank afloat or a stitch of canvas that will draw and *then* if I can be of *no service here*, I will go to join Garibaldi.[2]

On Election day I was sent out surveying in charge of a Section of our class so I could not go to vote for Lincoln. He received one vote in the city. . . .

Roswell to Flora

U.S. Naval Academy
January (no day) 1861

. . . Christmas we had a suspension of duties from morning till evening parade. I went to Church in the morning and spent the rest of

1. Captain George Smith Blake (1803–1871), a 42-year veteran of the U.S. Navy, superintendent of the Naval Academy from 1857 to 1865.
2. Guiseppe Garibaldi (1807–1882), the Italian patriot and general commanding the forces fighting for Italian unification.

the day in quarters. We had a nice Christmas dinner over which the Steward presided with all his dignity, although evidently shocked at the unmilitary merriment that reigned unrebuked at the mess tables. In fact we had a jolly time. . . .

On Monday Forrest[1] and I were both sent to the hospital with sore throat. New year's day was dull enough I assure you. We were not sick enough to appreciate being shut up all day and we could see the "Fellows" calling at the officers quarters and walking around the grounds making the most of their short liberty. . . .

Things are getting rather exciting down here in a political way, and it is the opinion of most that a peaceable secession is impossible. Is it to be that this beautiful land is to experience the dreadful horrors of civil war. Heaven forbid—but if it must come my humble services shall be on the side of the right, the Union, and the North, as long as there is a plank afloat. Southerners here wish to make slavery national instead of local and to perpetuate it by Constitutional guarantee; on that point the flag must be nailed to the mast. The Midshipmen are resigning as fast as their states go out of the Union and many of them have accepted commissions in the Southern military; some of them are on board the gunboats at Charleston where their training at the heavy guns is of use to them. . . .

Our chaplain prays every day for the Union and that all citizens may have equal rights in all parts of the Country. I do not know whether he includes taking slaves into the territories or not. . . .

Roswell to Katie

U.S. Naval Academy
January 15, 1861

. . . I was a little amused at your political comments but I am afraid the North do not know how bitter is the hatred the Southroners bear them. I am afraid you deceive yourself if you think they will "be glad enough to come back." It is truly appaling to every patriotic heart to view the government that has protected our liberties and made us such

---

1. Morreau Forrest, a native of Maryland and a close friend of Lamson. Forrest remained loyal to the Union, graduated third in the class of 1862 just behind Lamson, and went on to a distinguished war record in the Union navy.

a glorious example to the world torn asunder, and its people on the brink of civil war. And if war does come it will be one of the most terrible the world ever saw. I pray Heaven to avert so terrible a calamity, but if the worst does come my humble services shall be on the side of the North and the Union, which I think without doubt the side of the *right*; though politically they (the North) have not always done the South justice.

Movements are going on here so quietly that they are noticed by few but which show that we are to be ready for action at any moment. With scarcely anyone being aware of it the Constitution[1] has been watered and provisioned for sea, the light artillery battery and boat howitzers embarked, ostensibly for practice but most of them have been *stowed below*; the ammunition transferred from the Battery magazine to the ships, and the vessel put in as complete order as possible. A store ship is expected soon with guns to replace those in our Battery which are worn out, when she will throw just a few 68 pdrs and 11 inch shell guns on board for *practice*. Of course the officers keep their own counsel, but it is plain to me that we are to be ready to take the Constitution out as soon as her safety requires it and I learn from good authority that our class and the first class will be sent on board in such an emergency. These preparations are absolutely necessary as those in this vicinity in favor of Secession are extremely anxious to get possession of her. The seceding states have no navy as yet though they are purchasing merchant vessels for that purpose, and the possession of a new first class frigate with the prestige of Old Ironsides would please them exceedingly.[2] Fort Madison, too, on the opposite bank of the Severn commands the harbor; and a battery of heavy guns thrown in it would prevent the ship's going out unless previously prepared.

This movement will certainly be necessary when this state secedes if not before and we are then to be sent to the vessels of the Home Squadron. . . .

1. The most famous ship in the U.S. Navy, the USS *Constitution*, was a 50-gun sailing frigate built in 1797. It earned the sobriquet "Old Ironsides" by withstanding the fire of British warships and sinking two of them in the War of 1812. In 1860 the *Constitution* was a training ship at the Naval Academy.

2. There were genuine reasons for this fear. Although the *Constitution* was obsolete, its armament was not, and as Lamson notes, possession of the ship would confer great prestige on the Confederacy by linking the new nation with the old nation's heroic traditions. Tidewater Maryland south of Baltimore, where Annapolis is located, was a hotbed of pro-Confederate sentiments.

Roswell to Katie

U.S. Naval Academy
March 10, 1861

. . . How did you like the Inaugural?[1] I think it is just the thing: let us know if we have a government or not, and if we have not allow it to be trampled upon, and the honor of its flag covered with insult by traitors. A number of Southeren fellows have resigned recently but there are a good many here yet, who denounce the government as everything that is despotic and bad. I tell them if they have no sense of gratitude for the *many* benefits they are receiving from the government they yet should remember their oath and that as long as they wear its uniform their own honor is connected with it; for of all things that would dishonor an *American* it would be to serve a government such as they represent ours to be.

Almost all who resign enter the Southern service. Three are respectively 1st 2d & 3rd lieutenants of the War Steamer Savannah.[2]

There are some honorable exceptions to those mentioned first among whom is Forrest.

We had a terrible storm during yesterday and the day before several fishing craft were blown ashore. Old Ironsides is accustomed to such things and only seemed to want a little more sea room. During the evening I walked down to the sea wall to listen to the music made by the wind in her rigging which was converted into a monster Aeolian harp only its strains had a kind of hoarse fierceness.

We have Howitzer drill now instead of Zouave, but to keep up the practice I run a mile every morning before parade.[3] . . .

---

1. Abraham Lincoln's inaugural address on March 4, 1861, held out an olive branch of peace to the seven seceded states that had already formed the Confederate States of America, but expressed the new president's firm determination to preserve the Union—which those seven states perceived as a threat of "coercion."

2. The CSS *Savannah* was a 400-ton sidewheel steamboat built in 1856 and converted in 1861 to a gunboat carrying one 32-pounder. In 1863 it was renamed the *Oconee* and converted to a blockade runner; it foundered in a gale at sea on August 19, 1863. Not to be confused with the CSS *Savannah*, an ironclad ram built in 1863 and burned in December 1864 to prevent its capture by Sherman's army when it entered the city of Savannah.

3. Howitzers were field artillery cannons carried on ships or gunboats; they could

Roswell to Flora

U.S. Naval Academy
March 22, 1861

. . . When I knew you were in Washington I cast many wistful glances at the Walls, and did wish myself beyond them most intensely. . . . I should have enjoyed the opera with you very much. . . . I fully reciprocate your patriotic sentiments, and as for the "flag," why I hope to live and die under it and shall be most happy if I can contribute even in a small degree to its prosperity and glory. Everything here is in statu quo, we are awaiting the development of events, all ready to take the Constitution to sea if necessary, in the meantime pursuing our studies and duties as usual. If there is not further trouble we shall go to sea in the sloop of war Plymouth[1] in June.

Roswell to Flora

U.S. Naval Academy
April 19, 1861

. . . We had our last drill in the battery on Saturday and the remainder of our heavy guns were immediately transferred to the Constitution (Old Ironsides); only our small arms and the battery of Dahlgren boat howitzers being kept ashore. Last evening Capt Blake received information that an attack was contemplated soon on the ship from Baltimore or Norfolk or both. Our Company and two howitzer crews were immediately ordered under arms for guard duty. Signal

---

be landed on shore to be used in land operations. The Zouave drill was an athletic form of infantry skirmish drill modeled on that of the French colonial soldiers in North Africa known as Zouaves. The colorful Zouave uniforms and the showy drill were popular in the United States at the beginning of the Civil War.

1. A 20-gun sailing ship built in 1843 and used as a training vessel at the Naval Academy in 1859–60, the USS Plymouth was scuttled by the U.S. Navy at Norfolk on April 20, 1861, to prevent her capture by Virginia militia. The Confederates raised her but scuttled the hulk again on May 10, 1862, when they evacuated Norfolk.

lights were observed but we were not molested. A strong guard is kept all the time both ashore and on board and a number of the guns are trained to sweep the long narrow bridge connecting the ship with the shore. . . . They will not catch us napping and will meet with a reception they will remember. The Academy grounds are many times too extensive for so small a force as ours to defend but we can hold the ship against almost any assaulting force and we are determined to do it. Tonight we have a guard boat out in the bay on the watch for boats coming up from Norfolk. All not on duty have their arms in their rooms ready for service.

It is sad, sad to think that we are obliged to arm ourselves against our Countrymen and I cannot tell you how heartsick I feel when I look at my arms and think I will probably be obliged to use them against those who till recently I regarded as brothers. But as long as there's a star in the flag I stand by it. I have seen a little fighting without any flag and now if it must come I'll not flinch under it. It rejoices me to know that you and those I hold most dear will be out of the way of danger. Pray to Heaven my dear Cousin that if possible this great danger may be averted from our Country. But if it must come we will meet it as Americans, true and loyal, who must always be more than a match for traitors. Capt Blake has given me the command of a Company of the Cadets.

An order has just been passed that any Midshipman can resign and leave immediately and the acceptances of their resignations will be forwarded to them. Over a dozen have gone to the Commandant's office for this purpose. Some allowance is to be made for those whose friends and homes are in the South but shame on the others—they are my enemies from this time. . . .

Roswell to Katie

> On Board the USS
> *Constitution*
> Off Brooklyn Navy Yard
> May 4, 1861

. . . You are of course acquainted with the events that have brought us here but I hope have not heard any of the "yarns" about our fights

with "secessionists," being taken and rescued by the gallant Mass. 8th.[1]
We were in eminent danger of attack *before* the arrival of the volunteers, but our defensive *action* was limited to the firing of one rifle into
a boat load of armed men who attempted to pass our wharf in the
night without heaving to, as ordered. They assured us they were peaceable citizens and of course we could not detain them they landed above
the Academy and tore up the railroad track. The first Mass. volunteers
arrived in the night our guard boat out in the bay threw up rockets
and we beat to quarters thinking the "Secesh" were coming. The next
morning we hove up one of the Constitution's anchors slipped her
other cables and the steamer that brought the troops hauled her over
the bar. It was with no common feelings of pleasure that we saw her
float in deep water, and knew that she was safe for all we feared was
heavy guns on the adjacent heights, where a strong force was watching
us. About 10,000 men had landed when we received orders to embark
and bring the ship to this place. You may perhaps imagine how sad it
was to leave a place to which we were so much attached and which
had so many pleasant associations connected with it, to break up our
home, and part from the officers to whom we were much attached.

We marched into the Mess Hall to supper for the last time, and
afterwards formed in front of the Recitation Hall when a number of
the ladies of the Academy bid us good bye; the volunteers formed two
lines to the wharf. When we reached the steamer that was to take us
on board the Constitution we were halted, when Capt. Rodgers[2] said
he had a few words to say to us before we parted, but his eyes filled
and his voice trembled so he could only say *"Be true to the flag" "Be
true to the flag"* "God bless you all." "Good bye." He is a good man and

---

1. The 8th Massachusetts militia arrived at Annapolis by steamboat on April 22 on
its way to the defense of the capital. This regiment repaired the railroad from Annapolis
to Washington, which Confederate sympathizers had torn up, thereby opening a route
over which several thousand Northern troops traveled to Washington after other Confederate sympathizers in Baltimore had attacked the 6th Massachusetts on April 19
and subsequently blocked direct rail access to Washington through Baltimore. The
Constitution left Annapolis on April 25 for New York and ultimately Newport, where
the Naval Academy was relocated from 1861 to 1865 to avoid the perceived danger
of its seizure by Maryland secessionists.

2. Lieutenant (not yet Captain) C. R. Perry Rodgers was Commandant of Midshipmen at the Naval Academy. He subsequently commanded several warships in operations along the South Atlantic coast, including the USS *Wabash* in the Port Royal
campaign, described by Lamson in the letters of Nov. 4–6 and Nov. 8, below.

a high minded officer, and we loved him very much. The fellows stood
it bravely till Capt. R. spoke but then though there was not a sniffle
in the ranks or a muscle moved yet the tears *would* run. One of the
volunteer officers sang out, "Three cheers for the Midshipmen" which
were given with a will. After we embarked we gave three cheers for
Capt. R. three for the troops, and *for old friendship's sake* three for
those of our number who intending to resign were requested not to go
on board. Some of my best friends were among them. This will be a
sad *sad* war. It will be more painful to strike than to be struck. Heaven
help us for feeling must not interfere with duty. What a doom awaits
the traitors that have wrought such unhappiness for our country. We
got under way on the 26th ult. in tow of the R. R. Cuyler[1] and anchored off Castle Williams last Sun. evening came up to the Navy
Yard on Mon. where we are awaiting orders. The Union Defense Committee of N.Y. have done all they could to have the Academy established at Newport which from all we have learned will probably be
done.

We are told by officers from Washington that our class and the first
have been reported fully competent to do sea duty and that we will be
ordered on service. It is needless to say that we most earnestly desire
it I should be most heartily ashamed that those who owe the government so much besides their allegiance as Americans should be moored
in the gay harbor of Newport when our country needs all who are
acquainted with Naval or Military Tactics, and that for the sake of the
last year's course which we will promise to make good at our final
examination. We may go to Newport and be ordered on duty from
there. The officers on the Niagara[2] and at the Navy Yard say they
cannot get along without us.

I received a letter yesterday asking me to take command of a company of light Artillery forming at Shelburne Falls, Mass. Uncle has
promised them an outfit if the government cannot equip them immediately. I should like that very much but volunteer corps are only
temporary, and promotion will be very rapid in the Navy as soon as we
pass our examinations. I should be tempted to resign and go any how

1. A screw-propeller steamship, the *R. R. Cuyler* was built in 1859, chartered by
the navy (then purchased in August 1861), and converted into a 10-gun warship that
captured several Confederate blockade runners.

2. A 35-gun steam frigate built in 1854, the USS *Niagara* participated in the capture
several blockade runners during the war.

if there was not such a good prospect of our being called into service here where we are more needed. . . .

It does my heart good to go into the city and see the stars and stripes floating everywhere especially to see them hung from all the churches. At Annapolis it was painful to hear men openly expressing their hatred of the most liberal government the world ever saw, and be in a position where you could not resent it, but here there is but one feeling of true loyalty, which extends all over the "North," at least.

The ladies all wear the "Red White & Blue" and it is cheering beyond expression to see the interest they take in those who are going to the defense of our government. Any man would fight with *such* supporters.

If there ever was a time when true hearts and strong arms should rally to the defense of the liberty that cost so much, it is now; and nobly has American patriotism responded to the call.

Roswell to Flora

New York
May 11, 1861

. . . We sailed as expected on Tuesday evening (in the Constitution) and came to anchor off Fort Adams, Newport R.I. Wednesday afternoon. Thursday at 3 pm we received our orders and I reached here yesterday morning and reported to Commodore Breese[1] who ordered me to the Frigate Wabash, the ship I admired so much you will remember, and one of the finest ships in the Navy. Capt Mercer[2] had already applied for me. We are very busy at the Navy Yard getting our outfits &c. . . .

1. Commodore Samuel Livingston Breese (1794–1870), a 51-year veteran of the navy who commanded the naval base in New York.

2. The pride of the navy, the USS *Wabash* (built 1855) was a 46-gun steam frigate that played a large role in the Civil War, part of which is detailed in several of Lamson's subsequent letters. She was commanded in 1861 by Samuel Mercer (–1862), a Maryland-born veteran officer who had been in the U.S. Navy since 1815.

Roswell to Flora

> USS *Wabash*
> Brooklyn Navy Yard
> May 17, 1861

. . . We are so busy fitting the ship for sea that we do not have time even to take our meals. Yesterday we went into commission and received our crew (about 800 men) on board. . . . I have not a single doubt of the result of the struggle though I perhaps may not see it. Justice and right must triumph and soldiers and sailors cannot but fight well who have so much sympathy shown for them at home. The remembrance of the fair hands that provide for them and of the soft eyes that watch them would be enough even in a bad cause. . . .

Roswell to Flora

> USS *Wabash*
> New York
> May 23, 1861

. . . Yesterday evening we cast off from the wharf and hauled into the stream—we are lying off the Battery. Tomorrow we take on board our powder. We are doing our utmost to organize the crew, and get ready for action. We are to run into the Chesapeake as we go down and if they are ready, lend them a hand in forcing a way up to Norfolk; after which we will probably go to Fort Pickens[1] or to the Mouth of the Mississippi—where the hardest work is to be done I hope. So far from avoiding the "howitzer boats" I shall ask for the command of one, and no doubt will get it—our only aim now must be to do the most good. We are getting our mess under way nicely, though at first we made a few trifling mistakes, such as putting butter in the soap dishes &c. but our servants are improving under our excellent training, though they say they never did things that way before and I do not think they

---

1. A large fort on an island built to protect the harbor and navy yard at Pensacola, Florida. Confederates had seized Pensacola but Fort Pickens remained in Union hands.

ever did. We have a good laugh over every mistake and inconvenience. I think our cook could beat even Aunt Libby making "scouse."[1] . . .

Roswell to Aunt Polly
(Mrs. E. G. Lamson of
Shelburne Falls, Mass.)

USS *Wabash*
New York Harbor
May 26, 1861

. . . Wednesday we cast off from the Navy Yard wharf and hauled out into the stream where we are now lying. We have our crew pretty well organized, our stores, ammunition and armaments all on board. We sail Tuesday morning. Day before yesterday we took on board 30 tons of powder for the great guns alone, besides about 2000 loaded shells. The officers all say that we are going where the hardest work will be done and I only hope it will turn out so. I have a rough, tough set of real "old salts" in the forecastle who will give a good account of themselves if we only have a chance. . . . We have our mess arrangements going in good shape now. We have a steward, a pretty good cook, a boy to wait on table; and a man each to take care of our hammocks. . . .

Roswell to Flora

USS *Wabash*
Off Fortress Monroe, Va.[2]
June 15, 1861

. . . We made Cape Henry this morning and ran in and anchored off the fort at 10:30 a.m. Unless it is decided to attack Norfolk soon we will sail for Charleston tomorrow morning. Our ship is in excellent

1. Scouse was a sailor's stew of sea-biscuit, potatoes, vegetables, and meat if available.

2. A large fort commanding the mouth of the James River where it empties into Chesapeake Bay. Fortress Monroe remained in Union hands and was the principle base for the Atlantic blockading fleet in the first year of the war.

order and we are getting along fine drilling the men &c though we are kept as busy as possible yet. We sailed from N.Y. on Thursday about noon. The Cumberland[1] and several other men of war are lying near us. We fired a salute to Commodore Pendergast[2] when we came in, which he returned and as we passed his ship running up to our berth they cheered us and the band played "Hail Columbia." The fort shows its rows of teeth as usual and with the exception of a large number of sentries on the walls looks as in more peaceable times. The white tents of the soldiers look quite picturesque. Everything is quiet, both parties are preparing so that when the shock does come it will be more terrible. If there is a chance for a fight here within any reasonable time I hope you will hear of us; otherwise, we are anxious to get further south for while lying here we can do but little as there is a sufficient force for all blockading purposes.

Roswell to Flora

USS *Wabash*
Off Charleston, S.C.
June 27, 1861

. . . We have been cruising about off the harbor since we arrived occasionally running in to get a sight of the forts, but we draw too much water to get very near. When we have nothing else to do we amuse ourselves fishing, shooting sharks, and watching the shells from the forts burst and throw up the water. . . . Our mess is noted the merriest in the ship. . . . I have some good friends here among the old forecastlemen. Rough brawny weatherbeaten old tars, but honest and brave men who never require an order to be repeated; and with hearts big enough to ballast a ship of the line. I do like them and I think they like me, for they always seem eager to do any little thing for me that they can do. But with the good we have got some of the most rascally cutthroats I ever fell in with. They are getting straightened out though.

1. The USS *Cumberland* was a 44-gun sailing frigate launched in 1842; on March 8, 1862, it was one of the two Union warships sunk by the famous ironclad CSS *Virginia* (the former USS *Merrimack*).
2. Garrett Jesse Pendergast (1802–62), a 49-year navy veteran who was Flag Officer of the home fleet with his headquarters on the USS *Cumberland*.

My hammock man swings my hammock to a nicety and keeps it always snow white. . . . I wish you could see us sit down to dinner and see some of the funny dishes we have. My health is excellent and we are in good spirits, and only anxious for news and to get nearer the enemy. . . .

Roswell to Flora

> USS *Wabash*
> Blockading off Charleston, S.C.
> June 29, 1861

. . . Day before yesterday a little before sundown the black clouds came rolling up from the South & West in vast masses in the Western sky. The sun shining through apertures in the clouds gave them a most gorgeous appearance and occasionally glancing from the frowning walls of Sumpter seemed the lingering halos of Anderson's glory.[1] The wind came at first in fitful gusts moaning through the rigging, increasing as the darkness set in till the storm king raged in all his fury, howling through rigging and around mastheads and playing wild freaks with everything not perfectly secured. We had just beat to evening quarters as usual, and I had just reached the forecastle when the rain came down in torrents driven along the deck with such force that it was almost impossible to stand without holding on to the rigging. We secured our guns, the retreat was beat and I went off on the quarterdeck. The gale was at its height, the wind lifting off the tops of the waves and dashing them against and around us with the greatest fury. The topsail yards could scarcely be seen from the deck so dense was the rain and the showers of spray blown over us. The First Lieut ordered me to take a quartermaster and a drift-lead and go into the main chains and see if she was drifting towards the shoals. The quartermaster got into the chains with the leads and lashed himself to the main shrouds while I climbed higher up so that I could see the line better. The lead

---

1. Major Robert Anderson (1805–71) commanded the Union garrison at Fort Sumter in Charleston Bay when the Confederates opened fire on the fort April 12, 1861, thereby beginning the Civil War. His courageous defense against the odds had made him a hero in the North. "Sumpter" was a common misspelling of Sumter.

soon showed that she was walking away with the mudhook, though we had our best bower out, but it was in vain. I sang out "She drifts, Sir," so I was obliged to get down on deck again which was a more difficult operation than holding on while up, for the wind pressed me against the rigging so that I was in no danger of falling. I reported to the Lieut and returned when I heard him bellowing through the trumpet "Stand clear of the starboard cable—veer away." As we veered more chain the ship rode more easily, her head being less dragged down into the water and she stopped drifting. It was perfectly fascinating to listen to the wild roar of the winds through the lower rigging and the higher notes among the small taut ropes aloft mingled with the dash of the waves. The lightening which played around us and actually seemed to envelope us added to the scene which for a few moments was indescribably grand. I was sorry when ordered to come down, for under the bulwarks the scene lost much of the wildness which added to the pleasure. . . .

Father (Jeremiah D. Lamson) to Roswell

Willamina, Oregon
July 6, 1861

Yours of May 19th is received. We have written you often but it seems you have not received our last letters. You will see by my last letters that your course meets my approbation and I can truly say that I glory in having a son who is willing to risk life and all he has in this world in defence of *our country*. It is melencholy to think that you are called to fight against citizens of our country, but he that raises his hand to destroy the best government in the world, if a brother or forein foe he must and should be subdued at all hazards. It matters not what are the causes that have produced the unhapy state of affairs in our country no one has a wright to take one stept in word or deed to destroy it, and he that does it deserves the death of a trator. When the news came to Oregon that Gen. Lanes son John had resigned and joined the rebel army, Oregon was taken by surprise, and the question was asked if you would go to[o] (knowing our partiality for Gen Lane) I told them no if you did I would disown you as a son.[1]

1. Joseph Lane (1801–81) was born in North Carolina, moved to Indiana, fought in the Mexican War where he rose to the rank of brigadier general, and served as governor

Those who knew you joined with me in saying that you would be found standing by the Stars and stripes.

Go on and do your duty, as a loyal subject to the best government in the world and may God protect you from all harm. Gen. Lane has returned to Oregon he says he goes for the Union, but his simpathies are evidently to[o] much for the South. Oregon goes almost to a man for the Union. . . .

New gold mines have been found in the Nez Perce country, I think they are good many all going and the gold is beginning to come in. I hope they will make times better, but it is still hard times here, cows are not worth more than from $1 to $8 and all things in proportion. Henry is still at home but will soon move out to his own place. Edward is allso at home Dorinda is at Salem we are all well. So far the season is wet the crops look fine grass good, our barn is full of last years crop of hay I am building to put this years crop in. . . .

Roswell to Katie

> USS *Wabash*
> Off Charleston, S.C.
> July 10, 1861

. . . Our crew contains a large number of merchant seamen whom we are just beginning to get divided in some thing like a war ship. They all take [an interest] in the gun and everything belonging to it keeping everything as bright and neat as possible and woe to the luck-less jack from any other part of the ship that sits or stands on it or stows his "diddie box" on the gun sliders. They pride themselves on being called the best drilled crew in the ship at "the gun," rifles or broadsword.

They are rough men but brave even to recklessness and most of them *honest*. I cannot help but like them and the happiest times I have are when on duty among them on the forecastle. Jack is a singular

---

of Oregon Territory (1849–54) and as territorial delegate to Congress (1854–59). When Oregon became a state in 1859 he was elected as one of its senators. In 1860 Lane ran for vice president on the Southern-Rights Democratic ticket with John C. Breck-inridge. Joseph's son John Lane became a cavalry colonel in the Confederate army.

being but if you once get his confidence he will never leave you in the lurch. . . .

Since our arrival we have been lying off the entrance to the harbor—as near as our draft of water will permit, and occasionally cruising for short distances along the coast.

The Vandalia[1] a sloop of war and the Union gun boat are here.

We have taken a number of prizes and warned off several vessels ignorant of the blockade.

We are under banked fires all the time and ready to get under way instantly. The commerce of the port is completely cut off.

The other day we made out a large ship standing in which we took to be the Jamestown,[2] but she soon pulled away with everything that would draw to get under the guns of the batteries on Sullivan's Island. We signalled the Union[3] to give chase and soon after, the batteries opened on her and "all hands up anchor" ran through our ship and we were soon standing in to her assistance. The strange sail finding herself under our bow shell guns hove to when we sent an officer on board to bring her out. She proved to be a Spaniard from Barcelona papers allright and professedly ignorant of the blockade. We entertain no doubt but she was trying to run in to fit out as a privateer. We were in hopes on the forecastle to get a shot at the batteries with our 10 inch pivot gun but were disappointed. . . .

Roswell to Flora

USS *Wabash*
Off Charleston, S.C.
Aug. 2, 1861

. . . This morning a large ship hove in sight from the Northward which soon proved to be the Roanoke, Flag officer Pendergast from Hampton Roads with letters for us and orders to proceed to that place

1. A 25-gun sailing ship built in 1828 that helped capture four blockade runners in 1861.
2. A 20-gun sailing sloop of war built in 1844.
3. A screw propeller steamship chartered by the navy in May 1861 and converted into a gunboat for blockade duty; decommissioned in December 1861.

for supplies.[1] I knew your letters as soon as I got my eye on them; they seemed like the well remembered faces of dear friends and you may be sure I was not long in making a prize of them. I soon retreated to a quiet part of my own dominion on the spar deck and you cannot imagine how much pleasure their perusal gave me. . . .

Roswell to Flora

> USS *Wabash*
> At Sea
> Lat 33 14' N Long 77 55' W
> Aug. 3, 1861

Last night about 12 o'clock we gave chase to a sail and were roused from our "dreaming sacks" by the "beat to quarters." As we came down she hove to athwart our bows and so that we ran foul of her, her Lead booms running in on our forecastle, where for a few minutes there was nothing heard but the crash of spars and snapping of rigging. The wreck of her headrigging caught on our waist-anchor and the First Lieut sent me with a part of my division to clear it. The ships had fallen alongside of each other and were thumping as though they would knock everything to pieces. With our battle axes we cut all the rigging adrift when the ships separated. We sent a boat on board the strange sail which proved to be the gunboat Seminole.[2]

This morning we chased a large schooner to windward and fired a blank cartridge to make her heave-to, but being a fast sailer she kept on her course till a shell from my pivot gun went skipping over the water when she hove-to she proved to be from New York loaded with sugar and having a crew of "pirates"[3] on board, and also three of her

1. The USS *Roanoke* was a 46-gun steam frigate launched in 1855 that helped capture four blockade runners in 1861. She was decommissioned in March 1862 for conversion into the triple-turreted ironclad USS *Roanoke*. Pendergast had transferred his flag to this vessel for the voyage to Charleston.

2. The screw steamer USS *Seminole* (launched in 1859) carried five or six guns; the hazards of chasing supposed blockade runners in the dark of the moon are illustrated by this collision between two Union warships.

3. At the outbreak of the war, Confederate President Jefferson Davis offered letters of marque and reprisal to Southerners or others who wished to fit out armed ships as

original crew who were quite rejoiced as you may imagine. The "pirates" had thrown their flag overboard. This afternoon we made a large brig to windward, and showed English colors, when she immediately replied by hoisting the English ensign. We brought her to and I went on board with Lieut [John S.] Barnes who took her papers and Captain and returned to the Wabash leaving me on board. About the same time we sighted a large steamer and the Wabash filled-away to find out who she was. She proved to be the steamer Rhode Island[1] with letters and stores for us. It was quite dark before they sent a prize crew on board the schooner and a boat to take me back to the Wabash.

Hampton Roads
August 6, 1861

We came to anchor off the fort this morning.[2] I have been on boat duty ever since and have not had a minute to finish my letter.

---

privateers to prey on Union merchant vessels. The Northern term for the crews of these privateers was "pirates."

1. A sidewheel steamer built in 1860 and purchased by the navy in 1861 to be converted into a four-gun warship; its name was changed from *Eagle* to USS *Rhode Island*.

2. The fort referred to was Fortress Monroe, which commanded the anchorage in Hampton Roads. The *Wabash* had returned to fit out for the expedition against Hatteras Inlet, described in the next chapter.

CHAPTER 2

IF THEY WILL ONLY
GIVE US A CHANCE

AUGUST 1861–FEBRUARY 1862

I N JUNE 1861 Secretary of the Navy Gideon Welles appointed a
naval strategy board. Its first priority was to make the blockade
more efficient. As Lamson points out in several letters included
in this book, the task of blockading 3500 miles of Southern coastline
containing a dozen major ports and scores of minor ones where cargo
could be landed was a formidable one. In July 1861 the naval strategy
board made two important decisions: Union forces would seize as many
such ports and harbors as possible in order to deny them to blockade
runners, and the navy would convert some of these harbors into additional bases for the Atlantic and Gulf blockade fleets so that they
did not waste so much time steaming back and forth to Hampton
Roads and Key West for coal and supplies.

The *Wabash* returned to Hampton Roads in early August 1861 to
fit out for the first expedition, an attack on Forts Clark and Hatteras
guarding Hatteras Inlet, midway along the 200-mile line of barrier islands protecting North Carolina's Pamlico Sound and Albemarle
Sound, inland seas with rail and canal connections to the interior. This
transport network served as Richmond's back door to the Atlantic, the
front door having been closed by Union control of Hampton Roads at
the mouth of the James River. Numerous blockade runners passed in
and out of Hatteras Inlet during the war's early months. The North

Carolina sounds also served as a haven for privateers that dashed through the inlets to capture unwary Northern merchant vessels. Control of this inlet and the sounds became the goal of a combined army–navy task force of seven warships and two transport steamers carrying 900 soldiers.

———•••———

Roswell to Flora

> USS *Wabash*
> Hampton Roads
> Aug. 7, 1861

. . . Two of our Midshipmen are going home sick, which gives the rest of us more to do. We are coaling and getting ready for sea as fast as possible though it is uncertain where we will go. . . .

I take your "lecture" as you call it in all the kindness in which it was intended. But my dear Cousin, I hardly deserve your sencure [censure] as I still adhere to my old temperance principles. You know things strike people differently depending on habit and education. I have been so much among men who drank that had I not also witnessed some awful effects of it I should forget to consider it in any degree wrong, but rather as an evidence of good-fellowship. Perhaps the way in which I spoke of it may be accounted for by this fact. I have occasionally tasted whiskey, but never drank a glass in my life. It is too common on board a man of war to offer "something to drink" to visitors who of course are at perfect liberty to indulge or not; in fact it is almost a universal custom, though I am glad to say there are many officers who never drink. There is another custom of "keeping Saturday night," which tends to keep up the old habit of the solace of drinking. It is customary on Saturday night for all the officers to meet together for a social time—conversation, music, and songs and the wineglass enlivens the hours; friends are talked of, and there is such a strange facination about it that many find it difficult to refrain. The last toast is always to "wives and sweethearts," and is always drunk standing in silence.

I have never seen many Naval officers under the influence of liquor but I saw an instance a few days ago that I shall never forget. On the night of the 3rd we were startled by that most dreadful of all sensations at sea the shock of the ship striking on a reef. It was my watch on deck, and as I went close to the First Lieut. [Thomas C. Corbin] to get an order to reverse the engines I caught the smell of liquor and I saw from his actions that he was partially at least under its influence. I forgot the great danger of our situation, everything but the fact that an officer at least partially intoxicated was in command of the deck at such a time. No my dear Cousin never fear that I will tamper with whiskey. We had struck in the dangerous Frying Pan Shoals off Cape Fear. After hard work we succeeded in getting clear about half past one o'clock and I went below. . . .

Roswell to Flora

USS *Wabash*
Hampton Roads
Aug. 8, 1861

When I went on deck last night the town of Hampton was in flames, and this morning only blackened chimneys and charred ruins are visible except a female seminary which is untouched. It was a sad sight to see an American village burning, but the blame rests on those accursed traitors who have caused it.[1] It is said we are to haul up river and give them some shell; we earnestly hope we may have the chance. I do wish they would send us somewhere that will give us a better chance to do something more for our country. . . .

How much I would give to see you all before we are ordered away again. But I hope I am perfectly willing to give up everything even life itself to defend that liberty which our fore-fathers gained at such cost. It must not be said that their decendants were unable to retain it, and there is no danger if polititians could just have a little patriotism. They have made bad work so far, but we are able to drive the traitors off the continent if soldiers and not polititians are allowed to direct the movement. . . .

1. Hampton was a village three miles west of Fortress Monroe. Confederate forces under Brigadier-General John B. Magruder burned it on August 7 to prevent it from being used as a haven by runaway slaves. Union occupation forces rebuilt the town and it *did* become a community of "contrabands" (freed slaves); after the war Hampton Insititute was founded there.

Roswell to Flora

USS *Wabash*
Hampton Roads
Aug. 18, 1861

. . . I assure you I feel proud of our "blue jackets" when I go ashore with any of them, so neat and orderly, and such stout brawny looking fellows. I heard an Army officer say he would rather lead them than any other men in the world. He said he accompanied a boat expedition from our ships to destroy some schooners up one of the creeks near here. The boats grounded before reaching the schooners which were beached, and the first thing he saw was the blue devils in the water and in a few moments clambering up the sides of the schooners while the "Secesh" stood off on the other tack. . . .

Our crew is well drilled now to act both afloat and ashore and are eager for a fight for the stars and stripes. If we can only get a chance. . . .

I have just heard from home [Oregon]; the first time for six months, Father says "I would not have you anywhere else for the world." So you see I've nothing to think of but to do my duty. . . .

Roswell to Katie

USS *Wabash*
Hampton Roads
Aug. 19, 1861

It is some time since I have written to you, but much longer since I have had the pleasure of receiving a letter from you. . . .

I see much in the papers about the "inefficiency" of the blockade but I do not see how people can expect it to be otherwise with the comparatively small naval force at our command and the great extent of sea coast. And the Department at Washington seem to make poor use of even the small force they have at command and to have but little idea of what men of war are. Last week they sent a "Gun Boat" here that the Com'dre is afraid to send to *sea at all;* and yet she cost a large amount. It is the opinion of most officers who see our ship that the "Wabash" can whip any thing afloat except such iron casted frigates as the "Gloire"[1] but we cannot guard a long line of coast, *particularly off a port where we cannot get within several miles of the shore except at certain points,* small craft hug the shore to the Northward and Southward well knowing that our draft of water will not permit us to approach them within even the long range of our guns, and at night run the risk of getting to sea. The Navy Department must know of these things so obvious to all connected with the "blockade," and yet they took away the only gun boat of light draft we had, which we could send in within gun shot of the shore.

We have a crew of about 600 men well drilled at the great guns, and as infantry and all eager to show their devotion to the stars and stripes.

Now if they will only give us a chance.

I have command of the "Forecastle Division" consisting of six broadside guns, 8 inch shell and the foreward 10 inch pivot gun so far the only gun of our batteries which has spoken to the "rebels." I have also a boat, and "boarding crew."

I have been on boat duty for the last week and have been on shore several times. Day before yesterday I went to Gen. Butler's[2] quarters to make arrangements for sending our prisoners to Balto. Gen. Wool[3] had just arrived and he (Gen. B.) seemed in a most unamiable mood. Every one here seems much pleased at the change. Afterwards took the prisoners on board the Balto. steamer; two fellows I could not help feeling sorry for them.

Five of our Mess left yesterday, three for other ships and two home on sick leave so we have only three left. Fortunately we are all of the same class which makes it more pleasant. One of our lieutenants was dismissed from the Navy since we have been here for coming on deck

1. The world's first ironclad warship, which went into service for the French navy in 1859.

2. Benjamin F. Butler (1818–93), a Massachusetts Democratic politician commissioned as a major general of volunteers at the war's outset because of his political connections. His war record revealed him to be a better politician than military commander.

3. A 76-year-old brigadier general in the regular army (thus outranking Butler) who had fought in the War of 1812 and the Mexican War, John E. Wool became senior commander of Union army forces at Fortress Monroe in August 1861, superseding Butler.

drunk and the other night while on duty on board a coal ship I had serious difficulty with the capt. who was drunk and armed. The first Lieut. sent me an order to "put him in double irons" if he made any more trouble; so much for liquor, the reef on which *so many* sailors shipwreck.

Every Sunday I think of you at Mt. Vernon and do wish I could enjoy another of those quiet Sabbaths. Even our service on Sunday is liable to many interruptions and the remainder of the day seems almost like any other day: Parade, Quarters, &c. But there is consolation in the thought that wherever we may be if in the path of *duty* we may hope for the blessing of him who is Lord also of the Sabbath.

Pray for me, my sweet friend, that His blessing may be with me in calm and in storm, and that I may be enabled to *know* and *do* my *whole duty....*

I saw some of the wounded at Great Bethel hospital what a shame that such brave men should be subject to leaders who make such mistakes. Our government will yet be forced to learn from the Rebels to employ their military knowledge and experience when it can be of service, instead of placing ignorant politicians in *command.*[1]

The courses pursued by Lincoln and Davis in this respect are very different and the results are what would naturally follow. The *good cause* will triumph, though, there is no doubt of *that....*

Roswell to Flora

> USS *Wabash*
> Hampton Roads
> Aug. 25, 1861

...You see we have not gone to sea yet though we are all ready and have been waiting orders several days. Quite a strong naval force is collecting here, some say to destroy batteries in the Potomac, others for blockading the coast of North Carolina. The latter is the most probable. We have painted our ships and I wish you could see in what

---

1. A reference to the "battle" of Big Bethel (sometimes called Great Bethel or Bethel Church) near Hampton on June 10, 1861, in which a Union force poorly handled by General Butler had been easily repulsed by the Confederates at the cost of 76 Northern casualties.

beautiful order everything is outboard and inboard. Now if they will only give us a chance. . . . I wish I could write oftener and longer to you but my time is very much occupied, and I am trying to study as much as possible.[1]

Roswell to Flora

> USS *Wabash*
> Off Cape Hatteras
> Aug. 27, 1861

. . . We sailed from Hampton Roads yesterday having in company the Minnesota, Pawnee, Monticello, Harriet Lane, and Steamboats George Peabody and Adelaide having on board 1000 or 1500 [900] troops under command of General B. F. Butler, the whole under command of Commodore Stringham.[2] Today we fell in with the sloop of war Cumberland (sailing vessel) which was taken in tow by the Harriet Lane. The fleet is now at anchor off the "Stormy Cape," and we are making every preparation to attack their batteries tomorrow morning. The batteries are at the mouth of one of the inlets running into Pamlico Sound. . . . Today I drilled my division at the broadside and pivot guns and they all seem as eager for a fight as men can be. This afternoon I directed them to grind their cutlasses, when one brawny fellow came up to me and said "shall I grind both edges of my cutlass, Sir?" . . . I hope to get in the first shot from the forward pivot gun and the first shell shall go in your name.

1. Although commissioned as a midshipman in May 1861, Lamson still needed to pass a series of examinations in order to graduate from the Naval Academy. See his letter of Sept. 8, 1862.

2. Commodore Silas H. Stringham (1797–1869) had been in the navy since 1809. The ships named by Lamson were: USS *Minnesota* (launched 1855), 47-gun steam frigate, a sister ship to the *Wabash*; USS *Pawnee* (launched 1859), 10-gun steam sloop of war; USS *Monticello* (built 1859), a merchant screw steamer leased by the navy in 1861 and armed with three guns; and USS *Harriet Lane* (built 1857), a sidewheel steamer in revenue cutter service, transferred to the navy in March 1861, and armed with five guns. The *George Peabody* and *Adelaide* were merchant steamers chartered by the navy to carry the troops.

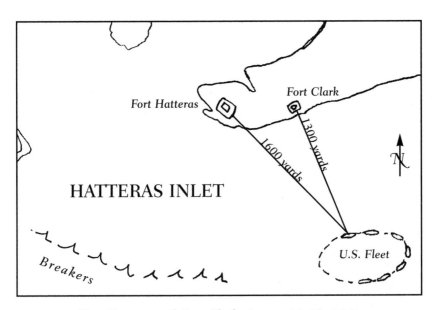

Fort Hatteras and Fort Clark, August 28–29, 1861

Aug. 28, 9:00 p.m.

This morning we turned out at four o'clock and soon after received orders to take the Cumberland in tow and stand in for the batteries. The boats containing troops commenced to land them several miles from the forts. . . . About eight a.m. we came in sight of the batteries which were on the north side of the Inlet. There were two, one water battery near the beach and a large fort a little further in. . . . At nine o'clock we "beat to quarters" and cleared for action. When I reported my division (Forecastle division—one 10 inch pivot gun—eight broadside 8 inch guns) all ready, the Captain said he wished me to direct the 10 inch pivot gun myself, and he ordered Lieut Matthews to direct the after pivot gun. We were now drawing within range of the water battery and could see their camp and tents just behind it. At nine forty the order came bellowing through the trumpet "Fire as soon as your gun will bear, Sir." "Aye Aye Sir," and as I had already estimated the distance and trained the gun I sent them the first shell "with the compliments of Miss Flora." They immediately returned with their rifled guns sending the shot whizzing and singing around us and we opened with our after pivot gun and in a few minutes with our gun deck battery. My shell struck their battery, burst just within it and totally destroyed one of their board houses. The Captain sent a messenger boy to tell me "That was capital, fire as fast as accuracy will permit." The Cumberland now opened astern of us and the Minnesota still further astern. We lay in nearly the same position for half an hour, during which time there was an incessant roar of guns from the ships answered from both batteries, which sent rifled shot whistling through our rigging and all around us and two came crashing into us. Every shot they fired was directed at the Wabash hoping to disable us and thus disable the Cumberland, which we were towing. As we were drifting too near the breakers we steamed ahead, turned around and came back nearer than before, the other ships doing the same. For a few minutes the firing was very heavy, the secession flag being shot away three or four times, when at one fifty pm. it was hauled down altogether on the water battery and a few of our men who had landed ran forward and planted the stars and stripes in the battery. As soon as the enemy's flag came down they retreated into the fort. The officers all told me that I shot away the flag the first time. As there was every appearance of a storm the Commodore ordered us to tow the Cumberland to sea where she made sail and left us unimpeded in our movements. We stood back for the batteries and found the little Monticello hammering away most gallantly her rigging and yards cut up and one of her boats shot away. The Commodore hailed and ordered us to go to her assistance, which we did, but it was so rough we could not get in for the breakers nearer than long range, and the flagship [the *Minnesota*] signalled the fleet to haul off a safe distance and to anchor for the night. . . . The firing just before they ran from their battery was very severe, the pivot guns throwing almost every shell right in their midst, and we had calculated time and distance so accurately that they almost all burst as soon as they struck. As the Captain had ordered me, I took the place of the "Captain of the gun" and fired it myself. . . . The men all acted like "tars" and only seemed anxious to get closer to the batteries.

Aug. 29 evening

We called all hands at four this morning, got breakfast, and beat to quarters at 6:45. The flagship made signal "Engage battery careful not to fire into captured battery." We immediately stood in as near as the breakers would permit. The Susquehanna[1] opened fire and we followed with the pivot guns. The Susquehanna steamed past the battery and we hove to abreast of it and opened our gun deck battery. . . . It was soon evident that the gun deck guns did not reach the fort at all, and the Commodore signalled "Use pivot guns only." . . . It was terrible to watch the large shells as they came down into the fort bursting almost as soon as they struck, scatter sand and tents, dismounting guns and tearing everything but the bombproof covers to pieces. In less than an hour the enemy was driven from their guns and their heaviest gun, a 10 inch gun, dismounted. For a long time we fired a shell every three minutes from the forward gun, and it was nothing but a continual bursting of shells around, over and among them. About half past eleven o'clock the officers aloft reported "They are fleeing from the fort to the extreme point of the beach." One of the Lieutenants pointed them out to me and I trained my gun on them and fired, turning away for I did not wish to see the effect. The shell struck the sand right among them, and instantly exploded. They ran back into the fort, their flag was hauled down, and a white one raised, which was greeted by a cheer from all the ships. There was no more firing. The last shell killed one man and wounded fourteen—so they have told me since. I cannot help crying when I think of them. . . . Oh how I wish the men who caused this war could have been in the battery instead of these deceived, misguided men who fought so bravely for what they believed their dearest rights. No one who saw them fight would doubt the sincerity of their belief in the justice of their cause. As soon as the white flag was shown General Butler went on shore (he did not land with his men), but the commanding officer refused to surrender to him saying he "would surrender to the men that whipped him." He came on board the Minnesota and surrendered his sword to Commodore Stringham. . . .

I wish you could hear some of the compliments paid me on the way my pivot gun was fought. . . . After the action I went on board the flagship for orders and the first thing the officers asked me was who trained the Wabash's bow pivot gun. They said it made the finest shots they ever saw. During the action my men would jump on the gun carriage, pat the gun affectionately, and bestow all kinds of praise on it. With their sleeves rolled up, their arms and faces blackened and

---

1. An 18-gun sidewheel steam warship launched in 1850.

grimed with powder they looked savage enough. I was frequently obliged to call fresh men from the guns not in use, the pivot gun's crew being exhausted. . . .

———•———

THE CAPTURE OF Forts Hatteras and Clark gave the Union army a toehold in North Carolina. In February 1862 another army-navy task force launched a campaign that gained control of Pamlico and Albemarle Sounds and captured several North Carolina coastal cities, including Beaufort, which became a coaling station for the North Atlantic Blockading Squadron that patrolled the coast of North Carolina and Virginia. In September 1861 the *Wabash* returned to blockade duty off Charleston for several weeks, and was then ordered to New York to prepare for a new expedition. The naval strategy board had decided to attack the forts guarding the entrance to Port Royal Sound, South Carolina, about midway between Charleston and Savannah and one of the best natural harbors on the South Atlantic coast with enough deep water to float all the navies of the world. If successful, the navy intended to make Port Royal the base for the South Atlantic Blockading Squadron responsible for patrolling the coast of South Carolina, Georgia, and Florida. The Navy Department named Commodore Samuel Francis Du Pont (1803–65) to be flag officer of the fleet being assembled in New York for this expedition. It was the largest American naval fleet ever put together to that time: 17 warships, 25 colliers, and 33 transports carrying 12,000 infantry and 600 marines. Du Pont earned the Thanks of Congress and won promotion to the rank of rear admiral for his success at Port Royal, described in the following letters.

———•———

Roswell to Flora

USS *Wabash*
New York
Oct. 9, 1861

. . . We arrived last evening, being ordered North to repair and refit and to take on board Commodore Samuel F. Dupont and staff. I wanted to write you yesterday but have been on duty ever since we anchored. We are to be the flagship of the expedition fitting out, and earnestly hope to strike another blow for the Union. We will probably remain here a week though we have received no orders yet. I received another proof of the kindness of yourself and Uncle and Aunt today, in two letters and a large box with a cargo such as only a Yankee girl could stow. . . .

Roswell to Flora

> USS *Wabash*
> At Sea
> Oct. 17, 1861—evening

. . . I did feel very sad after bidding you and Cousin Lottie goodbye till I got on board again and whistled "Once more on the deck I stand," to keep up my spirits. How kind and good it was in you both to come so far just to see me. My heart thanks you as my words cannot. As we passed Fort Hamilton[1] I was on the lookout for you with a glass and distinctly saw your parasols and handkerchiefs. You stood on the left of the first flagstaff. I waved my handkerchief in reply and stood up on the rail. I was attending to the signals at the time but watched you as long as you could be seen. We are steaming down the coast and will probably reach Hampton Roads tomorrow morning. Today I have been trying the range of our Parrott gun[2] and drilling my division at small arms. The fleet are all following in the "Second order of Steaming." We are still ignorant of where we are going but we are making every preparation to land as large a force as possible, which indicates Charleston. Wherever it may be I hope we may be able to do something for liberty and our Country—something towards ending this unhappy war. I have no fears of the result—we must conquer or sink alongside of them.

1. One of the forts guarding New York harbor.
2. Named for their inventor Robert P. Parrott, Parrott guns were muzzle-loading rifled cannon with a wrought-iron band around the breech to help them withstand the explosive force of the gunpowder.

Roswell to Flora

Hampton Roads
Oct. 19, 1861

We reached this place yesterday and found Commodore Goldsborough's[1] flagship Minnesota and a number of other vessels at anchor. We are getting ready as fast as possible but when the expedition will sail I am unable to say, probably Monday. We are organizing our forces for landing. I am to command a company from my division with some engineers and citizen officers as volunteers. I hope we will be the first ashore. This morning the rebels fired a few shells at the fleet from Sewall's point.[2] My rifled pivot gun has come on board and is a splendid piece. I am to select a crew of picked men for it. How I wish I could see you all at the Falls before we sail. . . .

Roswell to Flora

USS *Wabash*
Off Fortress Monroe
Oct. 25, 1861

. . . You see we have not sailed yet, and you may think it takes us a long time to get ready, but we have been waiting for the transports. We would have sailed today but for the old superstition of sailors about sailing on Friday. We have organized our men for landing, and landed them on the beach for drill. I command a company of infantry—the color company—mostly from my division. The old tars know how to handle their arms and they manoeuvre tolerably well—order them to "Board" and they'll go through anything. We have been busy night and day and will go to sea tomorrow—glad enough to get away too. Forrest is here in one of the gunboats. This morning Commodore Dupont sent

1. Louis M. Goldsborough (1805–73), a veteran of the U.S. navy since he had entered as a midshipman in 1812.

2. The Confederates controlled the south bank of the James River at this time and had established a seacoast battery on this point opposite Fortress Monroe. The fort was out of their range but Union ships in Hampton Roads sometimes tempted their marksmanship.

for Roland, Robertson and myself and gave us our promotion as Acting Masters in consideration he said, of the reports we received for the Hatteras affair, and of the services we have rendered since we left New York.[1] As you may imagine we are quite pleased and feel determined to gild our shoulder straps before this expedition is over, if fortune only gives us a chance. Our promotion gives us precedence in rank over all of the citizen appointments that have been made.[2] Capt Rodgers and all the officers have expressed themselves very much pleased with it. I have one of the new Parrott rifled guns added to my division. Gen'l Sherman[3] and staff came on board tonight by invitation of the Commodore and will go in the Wabash. The Gen'l is a very pleasant man indeed. We will have by far the largest fleet ever collected in American waters—about 50 ships men-of-war and transports. I shall keep this letter open till we get outside the capes, finish it in pencil on deck, and send it in by the pilot.

Off Cape Henry Light Va.
Tuesday morning Oct. 29

The fleet got under way at daylight this morning much to our gratification. We will soon know where we are bound and I hope you will soon hear that we have accomplished something to compensate for the defeats our cause has suffered. . . .

Roswell to Flora

USS *Wabash*
Off Port Royal S.C.
9:30 p.m. Nov. 4, 1861

. . . We had an extremely stormy passage down the coast. Hatteras favoring us with one of the severest gales I have ever experienced.

1. John Henry Rowland and James Patterson Robertson, fellow members with Lamson and Forrest of the class of 1862 at the Naval Academy.

2. Because of the huge expansion of the navy in wartime, many officers with experience as merchant seamen were appointed to navy rank during the war, but as in the army, professional officers outranked volunteer officers of the same nominal rank.

3. Brigadier-General Thomas West Sherman (1813–79), commander of the army troops in the Port Royal campaign. Not to be confused with the more famous William Tecumseh Sherman.

Many of our transports and supply ships were unseaworthy and we were obliged to make every effort to keep them afloat. It was very sad to see so many vessels hoisting signals of distress. Some were dismasted some had their engines crippled by their heavy rolling, some sprung a leak until our fleet presented quite a different appearance from what it did when we came out of Hampton Roads; indeed some of the vessels were almost wrecks, though so far we have heard of only one (steamer Governor[1] with Marines) that went down, a few men only being lost.

We arrived off this place last night and came to anchor as near the entrance as we could with safety. Today we have been as busy as possible surveying the channels, all the buoys and marks being removed. I left the ship early this morning with a boat and was sent to take soundings in one of the reefs, the Vixen with Capt Davis[2] on board tracing and buoying the channel. Some of the small gunboats protected us from rebel steamers. We were near enough to see their tents on shore. We finished a little after dark this evening, having exchanged a dozen or so shots with three of the rebel steamers. For lunch I had a slice of the nice fruitcake you sent me as did Robertson (the Middie you were talking with at the landing). We got quite a satisfactory survey of the channel leading to the mouth of the bay on each side of which is a battery—apparently very heavy ones.[3]

Nov. 6 evening

Yesterday we got the Wabash and the rest of the fleet over the outer bar and anchored just off the entrance to the bay and almost within gun shot of one of the forts. We sent down and unbent our royals and top gallant sails and top gallant masts and sent everything below, cleared the ship for action and stood in for the batteries; but unfortunately we ran aground and as night was coming on came to anchor

1. A sidewheel steamer designed for inland waters.

2. The USS *Vixen* was a sidewheel steamer built in 1845 and purchased by the navy in August 1861 for conversion to a two-gun gunboat; Charles H. Davis (1807–77) was fleet captain of the Port Royal expedition under Flag Officer Du Pont.

3. The entrance of Port Royal Sound was protected by Fort Beauregard on the north side and Fort Walker on the south. Together they could bring 43 big guns to bear on ships trying to enter the sound.

again. Today has been too stormy but it is calm this evening and every-thing promises a fight tomorrow.

I wish you could see our ship tonight—not so neat and trim as before but like a giant ready for the fight. Our boats are all out and towing astern to keep them from getting smashed and to be ready for landing; and all those preparations made that show to a sailors eye complete readiness. Before we started in yesterday Capt Rodgers in-spected every part of the ship and then sent for all the officers and calling us around him explained all his plans and added "I shall lay her as near the battery as possible, be careful to guard against fire." He said he expected we would have a very hot time. You will be glad to know that the Wabash is to lead the van, and I have no doubt that I shall open the ball with the forward pivot gun. One has only to look at Capt Rodgers as he walks around the ship to see that the Wabash will be where the most work is to be done—where the flagship ought to be. As he talked to us there was a solemness in what he said that impressed everyone, and as I scanned the faces of the officers around me and saw their compressed lips, fingers clutched around their sword hilts and calm, determined looks I knew the Wabash would do her duty. It was a thrilling scene that I would not have been absent from but it was impossible to prevent a smile as one of the Lieutenants asked dolefully and Sotto voce "Isn't the cake and wine coming around."

We must beat them tomorrow and I have no doubt but we will do it though probably many of us will not hear the cheer of victory. Every man should feel the highest personal responsibility to do his duty to the last extremity, and see the "Stars and Stripes" flying over the rebel forts or sink in the effort to place them there. I hope you will hear that the Navy has shown its old devotion to the old flag. I have the greatest confidence in our men, and as I stand on the forecastle and see the stouthearted old tars around me I feel a thrill I would not give for anything else in the world. I may never have another opportunity to thank you and my dear friends for all your kindness to me, but the remembrance of it is in my heart and will remain there till its last beat. Your friendship has given me more pleasure than you can know who have never wandered so far from friends and home. I know of but one way in which I can make any return and that is by doing my duty to the Country we both love so much, and I pray God for strength and courage to perform that duty cheerfully, and if I fall I only hope it will be said, He did his duty and fell like an American Sailor.

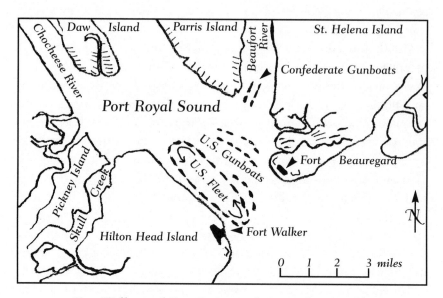

Fort Walker and Fort Beauregard, November 7, 1861

Roswell to Flora

Flagship USS *Wabash*
Off Hilton Head Battery
Nov. 8, 1861

. . . Yesterday morning we got under way and stood in to attack the forts on Bay Point and Hilton Head, the Wabash leading the van and followed by the Susquehanna, and 12 other vessels. As soon as we came within range the Bay Point fort opened on us and I gave them the first shot in reply from the forward pivot gun. We were soon warmly engaged, Capt Rodgers laying the ship close under the guns of the largest fort, (Walker) where we lay for a long time. The whistle and whiz and crash of shot and shell being literally incessant. They had very heavy guns. Shell guns, Columbiads and rifled and they cut us up in spars, rigging and hull pretty severely. There was a perfect thunder from our broadsides which is described by the lookers on in the transports as terrific and which finally silenced their batteries and drove them out in a manner that would have done credit to Bull Run. They fled in all directions leaving some of the guns loaded, their arms, tents

&c. One of the shell guns of my division was dismounted by a shot which killed the Captain of the gun and wounded 3 others. Part of the time we lay between the two batteries receiving the fire from both and giving it to them in return from starboard and port. It was the grandest sight I ever saw; the gallant frigate thundering away with both her batteries followed closely by the Susquehanna which will ever be dear to all of us for the way she supported us. The other vessels were not so near us but did finely and many of them are considerably damaged.

As soon as the rebels ran from Fort Walker we landed our marines and 50 sailors and took possession, substituting the glorious Stars and Stripes for the secession flag that was floating. We captured a few prisoners and when we asked one of them why he did not run too he replied "I have been in the Service. I was trying to make a 42 pounder bear on you." We took at least 20 officers swords. The other fort (Beauregard) was evacuated soon after and we took possession. After the batteries were taken we signalled the transports to come up and Gen'l Sherman landed with his troops and Fort Walker was turned over to him. Capt Rodgers complimented the spar deck divisions very highly on the accuracy of their firing.

This afternoon that saddest of all calls rang through the ship: "All hands—bury the dead." After the usual services on the gun deck a procession of boats was formed, the band leading, playing the dead march, then our first cutter containing the remains of the gun captain, his gun's crew and myself; his messmates followed, and the other dead seven men and one officer. As we left the ship the fleet lowered their flags to halfmast. We buried them in a beautiful spot underneath some large trees. Brave fellows, they will never answer to their muster again, but they died as American Sailors would wish to die, fighting for their Country. There were many wet faces as we fired the last volley over their graves. When my time does come I hope I may die as they have died, under the flag, and be buried within sound of the ocean.

There is a small battery near here which we are to take soon and I hope this success will be followed up vigorously till the war is ended. Several shot struck very near me, and the decks were so covered with fragments and splinters that we had to sweep them out of the way of the guns, but He who watches even the sparrows fall protected me—I hope to be of some service to my Country. . . .

Father (Jeremiah Lamson) to Roswell

Willamina, Ore.
Nov. 21, 1861

Yours off Hatteras Inlet Aug. 30th is the last received. One of the family write you almost every mail but I suppose you do not receive our letters as regular as we receive yours but I hope you will continue to wright often. I feel that I am called to make a great sacrifice to offer up the services and perhaps the life of a *dearly beloved son* on the alter of my country, but when I think of the great object to be obtained viz, the restoration to peace and prosperity of our once happy but now distracted country, I try to submit, and to say with you, that He who takes care of us will watch over you, and my prayer to God is that your life may be preserved and that you may again be permitted to return to your parental home and to your many friends in Oregon.

I hope you will not unnessarily expose yourself to dainger, but go only where duty calls you.

It seems that our country has no lack of men who are willing to take the field in defence of our Government but there is a great lack of good and competent men to take the command.

Great numbers without discipline and skilfull commanders tends to weaken rather than strenthen us. I firmly believe that at the battle of Bulls Run with one half of the men that we had there under good discipline led by good officers we should have been succesfull, at any rate our defeat could not have been as great.

Times continue dull in Oregon, no sale of anything for cash. I think the gold mines east of the Cascade mountains will make times better here next summer I think of taking a drove of cattle there.

Henry lives on the Putty place and is farming and takeing care of his new boy Dorinda and Edward are at Salem, but will come home soon.

We receive many letters from friends in the states all speak well of you. What pay do you get now and is it sufficient to pay your expenses.[1]

---

1. With the rank of acting master, Lamson's pay was $1,500 per year when at sea and $1,200 when on shore duty. When he was promoted to lieutenant in August 1862 his sea-duty salary increased to $1,875 and shore-duty pay to $1,500.

Write us all about what takes place with you from time to time on your cruises and of your engagements with the enemy if you have anny, do not think that we get all the news in the papers annything comming from you is better than if it come in the papers. You have not sent us your likeness since you left home can you not do it.

Roswell to Flora

USS *Wabash*
Port Royal, S.C.
Nov. 24, 1861

. . . I am glad you thought of us during the storm. I was doing duty as Flag Lieutenant and had to be on deck at all hours night and day making and answering signals, till the severity of the storm completely scattered our proud fleet leaving us only one ship in sight. There were anxious hearts in the Wabash, not on our own account, but on account of the hundreds of men embarked on half seaworthy vessels, that were making signals of distress all around us. Commodore Du Pont was always cheerful but I could detect his anxiety in the low tones in which he sometimes asked me if I was sure I had read the signals alright. . . .

There is one thing I must tell you though illustrative of the discipline of the service. When the "Governor" carrying Major Reynolds Battalion of Marines was nearly sinking some officer asked the Major what should be done. "Form the men by Companies" replied the Major, anxious that it should be done according to the "tactics." Seven of the brave fellows were lost—the rest were saved by the Frigate Sabine.[1] During the storm the command of the Governor was taken from the Captain and given to a midshipman who was on board as a passenger. . . .

We are all impatient now, awaiting the arrival of the Bienville[2] with powder, when we will start immediately on another expedition where

1. A 48-gun sailing frigate laid down in 1823 but not completed and launched until 1855.

2. A sidewheel merchant steamer built in 1860 and purchased by the navy in 1861 for conversion to an eight-gun gunboat.

I do not yet know—but we expect fighting ashore and we are improving the delay in drilling our battalion of blue jackets ashore on Bay Point. . . .

A little way back in the country are orange groves with plenty of oranges. . . .

When we were coming down on Fort Walker the last time we had orders to elevate for 500 yards and the Commodore told Capt Rodgers to lay the ship within that distance of the fort and "keep her there till we take them or sink." Capt Davis our Fleet Captain is a splendid man and a fine officer. I feel proud of the service when I see Du Pont, Davis, and C.R.P. Rodgers on deck. . . .

During the battle I saw an old salt running about the forecastle holding one arm with his other hand, and twisting his face in to all kinds of shapes. I asked him what was the matter—"Oh nothing, Sir, only a splinter's damaged one of my flippers a bit." I told him he had better go below, but he said he would be back at his gun in a minute. Seeing that he was not able to do anything I ordered him below, but he soon came back up with his arm dressed saying they might shiver all his timbers but he was going to see it out anyhow. They paid particular attention to the bow pivot gun, fourteen shot and shell striking that part of the ship. We did not allow any cheering from the fleet, but when the transports came up after the battle the soldiers seemed perfectly wild. Fernandina, Brunswick and St. Augustine are spoken of as our next points of attack.[1] We hope to be at them soon again and Capt Rodgers assures us that we shall not be idle long.

---

1. Lamson's information was more accurate than such rumors usually were, though these expeditions did not take place as soon as he expected. The navy captured Fernandina, Florida, on March 3, 1862; Brunswick, Georgia, on March 9; and St. Augustine, Florida, on March 11, denying these small ports to blockade runners.

Roswell to Flora

USS *Wabash*
Port Royal, S.C.
Dec. 12, 1861

. . . Two of your kind letters remain unanswered, not through neglect of mine, but because I have not had any time for the last few days to write even to you. Fleet Captain Davis detailed me on special duty connected with the other vessels of the fleet, and I have just returned to my usual duty on board the Wabash. . . .

Last week I went with Capt Davis to make a reconnaissance towards Beaufort and vicinity in the gunboat Seneca,[1] having in tow one of our howitzer boats to protect our landing party. It was a warm bright day and we had a very pleasant time. General Stevens'[2] brigade had just occupied Beaufort and we spent some time wandering around the place and looking into the deserted houses. You know it was the residence of the very elite of South Carolina, and the headquarters of secession, being worse in this respect than even Charleston. Here lived the Rhetts, Barnwells, Stewarts, Elliots, Haywards, and a host of others of the wealthiest and most aristocratic families of the South; men who had sworn to shed the last drop of their blood to defend the "sacred soil" from the "cursed Yankees," and who averred that they preferred gunpowder to any other food. The place might contain 4000 inhabitants and is situated on Port Royal Island about 15 miles up Beaufort River. The inlets around it must have been beautiful boating grounds for the lads and lassies in the "piping times of peace." We went into St Paul's church which is a very finely finished building though quite plain on the outside. One of our officers played the organ which made me think of "Auld Lang Syne." After reading the names in the prayer books we left, carefully fastening the doors. It was really sad to see a church thus deserted. Afterwards we went into some of the principal

1. One of a class of four-gun warships popularly known as "90-day gunboats" built quickly of unseasoned timber in 1861, the USS *Seneca* fought through the whole war from Port Royal in November 1861 to Fort Fisher in January 1865. She also helped capture two blockade runners.

2. Brigadier-General Isaac Ingalls Stevens (1818–62). On September 1, 1862, he was killed in the battle of Chantilly near Washington.

houses most of which had been completely ransacked and things torn to pieces generally.[1]

Just below the town is a strong earthwork with a trench, for defending the land and water approach. It had five heavy guns which were taken to Fort Walker the day before the fight. The parapet is beautifully decorated with diamond shaped sods and this battery must have been the admiration of the chivalry of Beaufort.

Capt Ammen[2] of the Seneca and a number of his officers were with us and we had a real jolly pleasant time. At dusk we landed on Parris Island at the Old Spanish redoubt, throwing our howitzer and crew ashore. This is an old fortification built about three centuries ago by one of the colonies of French Hugeonots sent out by Coligny under Ribault to protect themselves from the Spaniards.[3] It was several times taken and retaken in those bloody fights between the colonists of the two nations. It is built of lime and shells forming what is called "coquinae" and is in a good state of preservation. We had a beautiful moonlight night coming down and as the gunboat cut through the still water it was difficult to conceive that we are in the midst of a civil war. I thought of you and of all my friends, and wished that you could be with me as I with you. Finally the lights of the fleet hove in sight, and soon the Wabash loomed up majestically among the small craft, and casting off from the Seneca we were soon on board,—just in time for me to keep my watch. . . .

Some rebel officers who came down some time since with a flag of truce said to some of our army officers "We cannot stand the Naval gunnery, but, gentlemen we hope to meet *you* on the mainland." They

---

1. When the Union navy fought its way into Port Royal Sound, all the planters and the families on the sea island long-staple cotton plantations escaped inland, leaving behind nearly 10,000 slaves, some of whom looted the homes in Beaufort owned by these wealthy planters.

2. Daniel Ammen (1820–98), whose formal rank at this time was still lieutenant. Ammen later wrote *The Navy in the Civil War: The Atlantic Coast* (1885), which contained a good chapter on the Port Royal campaign.

3. Comte de Coligny (Gaspard de Chatillon) (1519–72), an Admiral of France and a convert to Protestantism, sent several ships under Captain John Ribault (1520–65) to the New World in an unsuccessful attempt to establish a Huguenot colony along the South Atlantic coast. Ribault was murdered by Spaniards in 1565 in Florida; Coligny was murdered in 1572 at the St. Bartholomew Day's Massacre in France.

said the broadsides from the Wabash were terrible beyond description. . . .

Roswell to Flora

USS *Wabash*
Port Royal
Dec. 25, 1861

. . . Although I cannot hear it, yet I feel a "happy Christmas" from
you all. I had the deck last night and I pictured you all at the
"Falls"[1] enjoying Christmas eve. We sent out a foraging party yesterday who purchased pigs, poultry &c from the darkies at the plantations. So we shall have a good dinner today. It is a bright morning
and our noble frigate looks as neat and trim as a Yankee Girl in a
morning dress, and everybody is as happy as the remembrance of
home, friends wives and sweet-hearts will allow. Some of the old
quartermasters, who are always privileged characters came down and
wished us a "Merry Christmas" this morning and I wished my division the same at quarters. The Wabash minstrels will perform this
evening for the amusement of the officers and crew. I wish you
could see Jack in theatricals. Our Christmas is saddened by a mel-
ancholy accident that occurred yesterday; a man of my division fell
through the hatches into the fire room, and has just slipped his cables for that unknown sea from which no one returns. Poor fellow—
he was a good man and a brave sailor. . . .

Roswell to Flora

USS *Wabash*
Port Royal
Jan. 23, 1862

. . . One thing, however of much importance to me—I have a state-
room in the Wardroom (commissioned officers quarters), one of the

1. Shelburne Falls, Massachusetts.

neatest, nicest, snuggest little berths you ever saw. . . . I have been
entitled to mess in the Wardroom ever since my promotion (from Midshipman to Master) but preferred waiting until rooms were vacant.
Midshipmen do not have rooms but swing in hammocks. So we are
prepared to appreciate the luxury of a room, and then it is in the
Wabash and afloat on wide deep sea. . . . I have command of a howitzer
boat[1] now. . . .

Roswell to Flora

> USS *Wabash*
> Port Royal
> Feb. 3, 1862

My class have applied for our final examination, which we are
fully able to pass, and which will insure our speedy promotion to be
Lieutenants. The Commodore says we must be promoted. This is
climbing up fast for some of our Lieutenants were 12 years and even
more before they were promoted to our present rank of Masters. A
Lieutenant in the Navy ranks with a Captain or Major in the Army
depending on the age of his commission. We certainly ought to
make every effort to improve ourselves and without thinking of personal comfort or sacrifice, do our duty with unflinching devotion and
fidelity. . . .

Going to war is not going on a pleasure excursion to the men, and
should not be made such to the officers, as it would be if they could
take their families along. You may think I am rather harsh and I have
no doubt but the militia officers would think so, but I know how men
feel about such things and I have seen the very same thing and with
only bad results. You know I am perfectly devoted to the ladies—at
home and in time of peace—but on duty an officer should be devoted
to his duty and the last thing he should think of or provide for should
be himself. . . .

---

1. A ship's boat powered by oarsmen carrying a small-caliber cannon (equivalent to
a field artillery piece) for operations in shallow waters.

The Hartford came in yesterday bearing the flag of Flag Officer Farragut of the Gulf Squadron.[1] As he is senior to our Commodore we shifted our pennant from blue to red.

---

1. David Glasgow Farragut (1801–70) entered the navy as a midshipman in 1810. Despite his Tennessee birth and his Virginia-born wife, he remained loyal to the service in which he had spent 51 years when war broke out in 1861. Appointed flag officer of the fleet sent out to capture New Orleans, he was rewarded with appointment as the first rear admiral in the history of the U.S. Navy for his success in that campaign. Farragut kept the 24-gun steam sloop of war USS *Hartford* (launched in 1858) as his flagship throughout the war; it was on this vessel that he had himself lashed to the rigging and shouted "Damn the Torpedoes! Full speed ahead!" during the battle of Mobile Bay on August 5, 1864.

CHAPTER 3

I WISH THE NAVY
COULD DO MORE

FEBRUARY–NOVEMBER 1862

F OR SEVERAL MONTHS after the victory of Port Royal Sound, Union forces consolidated their control of the South Carolina and Georgia sea islands stretching from Charleston to Savannah and established a large naval base in the region. While missionaries and teachers came from the North to begin the famous "Port Royal experiment" to educate the 10,000 freed slaves left behind when their owners fled to the mainland and to raise cotton by free rather than slave labor, the navy launched a series of strikes southward along the coast to capture additional ports and estuaries to deny them to blockade runners. These naval actions were more successful than the army's attempt to move northward through the islands against Charleston, which was frustrated by Confederate victory in the battle of Secessionville (June 16, 1862) on James Island a dozen miles from Charleston.

As spring turned into a hot and enervating summer, Lamson chafed at the navy's inability to do more to reverse a dispiriting series of Union defeats taking place hundreds of miles away in Virginia and Tennessee. The South Atlantic coast seemed to have become a backwater of the war, and Lamson welcomed the orders to return north in November 1862.

Roswell to Flora

Port Royal
Feb. 24, 1862

I have not heard from you since my last and probably will not til our return from our expedition which we have been preparing for some time and which is at last ready. We should have sailed today but for Westerly winds which drove so much water out of the harbor that we were afraid of touching on the bar. I do not know certainly where we are going but somewhere to the Southward; and it is said we will visit several places before we see Port Royal again. Our landing parties are all ready and we hope to have a chance to do Something for the glorious cause of Union and Liberty. I was given command of three companies of infantry (bluejackets) and had them ready for landing when it was decided to strengthen our armed boats crews and land a smaller force of infantry. This evening Capt Rodgers gave me one of the launches with the rifled howitzer. I like the change for the howitzer boats will be more certain of getting alongside the rebels, and sooner. I have a splendid boats crew—picked men—whom I have perfect confidence in. At noon on Saturday the 22nd we fired a salute of 21 guns, all the ships in the harbor joining; and in the afternoon the Flag Officer "received."[1] It was my deck watch and I had enough to do I assure you receiving the visitors on board. In the evening the Wabash Minstrels performed on the gun deck to an admiring audience from the other ships & from the forces on shore. . . .

Roswell to Flora

USS *Wabash*
Off Fernandina, Florida
March 4, 1862

We have taken Fernandina and St. Marys, and the Stars and Stripes are again waving over Fort Clinch.[2]

1. To celebrate Washington's birthday.
2. Fort Clinch was located on Amelia Island at the mouth of the St. Mary's River,

I have just returned on board having been absent since last Sunday morning, during which time I have not had a "square meal" and scarcely any sleep, and am suffering from a contusion of the right foot and ancle caused by an accidental gun shot. . . .

Owing to very bad weather we did not arrive off St. Andrew's Sound till the morning of the 1st inst.

At daylight the vessels which were to approach Fernandina by the inland passage (Cumberland Sound) stood in through St. Andrew's Sound having in tow the Wabash's armed howitzer boats and our infantry. Sunday was spent reconnoitering Cumberland Island and sounding the channel.

Sunday morning I went alongside the Ottawa,[1] one of the lightest and fastest gunboats which was to tow my howitzer boat through with all the light draft vessels under command of Capts. Drayton[2] & Rodgers while the rest went round outside. After the most vexatious delays, caused by getting aground, intricate navigation &c. the Ottawa alone got through and stood for Fort Clinch, which was discovered to be evacuated. We have been told so much by some negroes before reaching it but did not think such a thing possible.

Sending a boat to hoist the American flag we stood up for the town uncovering a heavy masked battery which we expected to open on us, but soon found that too deserted, while several white handkerchiefs were waved from some houses nearby; but as we passed a little further we were fired upon from where a train was standing on the Florida RR, ready to start. We fired a shot or two at the train killing two soldiers and hurried on for a steamer that we supposed to contain the

---

which forms the border between Georgia and Florida. It was the first antebellum U.S. fort in the Confederacy recaptured by Union forces. Fernandina and St. Mary's were the two principal towns in the region.

1. Another of the 90-day gunboats, the USS *Ottawa* carried four guns and, like the *Seneca*, fought through the whole war, assisting in the capture of three blockade runners while on blockade duty.

2. Percival Drayton (1812–65) had the rank of commander at this time; he was promoted to captain in July 1862. He was a native of South Carolina who had entered the navy in 1827 as a midshipman. In 1861 his brother Thomas went with the Confederacy, but Percival remained with the Union. At the battle of Port Royal Sound Percival commanded one of the Union warships while Thomas commanded the Confederate forces. Here, quite literally, was a brothers' war.

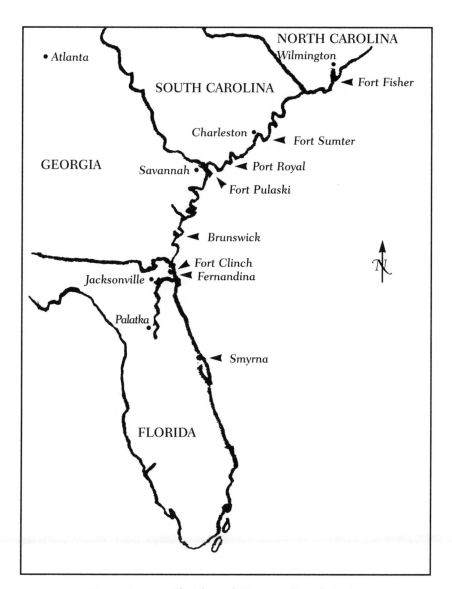

Operations in Florida and Georgia, March 1862

garrison of the fort and which was making a desperate attempt to escape up the Amelia River. We fired a shot to bring her to but she paid no attention, and having every reason to think her to contain troops, fired directly at her several times, but the Ottawa's gunner made such remarkably poor shots that she was not touched. Not daring to go any further with the gunboat, Capt Rodgers jumped into my boat and we started to carry her by boarding, expecting, as Capt Rodgers said "to have some brisk work."

Fortunately for us she got aground and about dark we came near her. I was in the bow of the boat directing the helmsman, and being lame, I told two of my men to throw me on board of the steamer as soon as they could, which I think they must have done at about a cable's length for I went flying through the air and came down on the deck with a smash that almost knocked me senseless. I jumped up and what do you suppose I confronted?—the terrible Mississippi regiment of which such awful tales are told, and who would have annihilated us if they had only waited?—No a crowd of *women and children* who were weeping and crying and making a most awful row. One lady with a child in her arms said to me—"Oh Sir, don't hurt my dear husband." My dear madam, said I, if you will just keep your dear husband from hurting *me* he was never safer in his life. As our men clambered up the sides of the steamer with their boarding cutlasses between their teeth and saw the *enemy* before them they stood the most perfect picture of foolish astonishment while some burst out laughing and jumped down into the boat again. Can you imagine anything more perfectly ludicrous. At a word from the captain all the men went back into the boats and a gentleman in uniform came forward and he was an officer of the Confederate army and he surrendered the boat.

Capt Rodgers told me to find the captain of the steamer and have the engine stopped which I did, and then went into the cabin where the crying was going on furiously and where Capt Rodgers was trying to answer everybody that nobody would be hurt, and in which he succeeded admirably, he has such a kind quiet way about him. . . . There were several very pretty girls aboard, and I, of course, devoted myself to reassuring them, while the Capt. attended to the married ladies and babies. In a few minutes they were all quiet and I overheard one lady say to another "why they *are* gentlemen, aren't they? They will not hurt us." . . .

We finally got the steamer afloat and brought her down abreast the town and came to anchor about ten o'clock. I then received orders to go to the bridge where the Florida RR crosses to the mainland and guard it with my boat till daylight and then to come down to the town while the Ottawa (the only vessel yet in) went up to St Marys. I had twenty men in my boat whom I stationed as videttes on the mainland after securing the drawbridge on the Fernandina side. . . .

We were not disturbed during the night, and at daylight I saw everything secured and started for the town. When about half a mile below I saw three negroes walking on the track towards the bridge and soon after they reached it a fire sprang up under that part of the bridge on the mainland, and at the same time about fifty armed rebels came out from under the embankment and tried to fire the main part of the bridge. We pulled in for them as fast as we could and shelled them with the rifled howitzer with such effect that they all ran back into the woods as fast as they could carrying some of their comrades with them. The bridge was but little injured and one of the gunboats coming up I went down to the town which was occupied by our sailors and marines, who went out on the tracks and brought in two engines and three cars.

Our men behaved splendidly and excepting the case of one who got drunk and went into an unoccupied house and took some bedding (for which he was immediately put in irons) molested neither people nor property. There were nearly twenty families remaining and they all spoke in the highest terms of the conduct of our men. . . . Tuesday the troops took possession and I am sorry to say have pillaged most of the houses.

It is the surprise of everyone that the rebels evacuated the place as they did. Fort Clinch is in a good state of defense, the bastions complete and case-mated, besides which they had fine heavy batteries defending the approaches to the town. . . . We captured nine guns part of them rifled and all of the best and heaviest caliber.

Roswell to Flora

USS *Wabash*
Port Royal
April 4, 1862

. . . They did behave nobly on board the Cumberland;[1] it makes my heart thrill whenever I think of those brave men. Heaven grant that

1. The *Cumberland* was the first ship sunk by the CSS *Virginia* (popularly called

our Navy may always show the same spirit in defense of right and liberty. Oh! how tame this occupying abandoned places, and taking deserted batteries, with just a sight of the retreating enemy seems beside such glorious work as that of the Cumberland and Admiral Foote.[1] I would gladly exchange into a gunboat in the Mississippi or in the Gulf. When I come North I shall, if possible, unless we attack Charleston, which will probably be done soon. I hope so. . . .

But I must tell you something of our expedition up the St. Johns. After taking Jacksonville and the batteries in the river we went up to Pilatka in one of the gunboats, and found the place almost deserted— and those who remained seemed quite surprised that we did not burn & destroy.[2] As soon as they found that "nobody was hurt" they sent out word and some of the refugees came back. We then returned to Jacksonville and got the captured steamer Darlington, and went up after the yacht "America" and the steamer St Mary's, the former of which we found in Dun's Creek about 150 miles above and the latter in Howe Creek still further up among the cypress swamps.[3] After a week of hard work with the scanty means we had we raised the famed

---

the *Merrimac*) at Hampton Roads on March 8, 1862. She went down fighting, continuing to fire her broadside guns against the Confederate ironclad until the last moment; unfortunately, they had little effect. This action and the epic fight between the *Virginia* and the USS *Monitor* next day revolutionized naval warfare.

1. Flag Officer Andrew H. Foote (1806–63) commanded the Union river flotilla that captured Fort Henry on the Tennessee River on February 6, 1862, and helped Ulysses S. Grant's army troops capture Fort Donelson on the Cumberland River February 16. Foote's promotion to rear admiral was confirmed by the Senate in July 1862.

2. The foremost port city in Florida, Jacksonville fell to the Union navy on March 12. Pilatka is 50 miles upriver (south on the St. John's) from Jacksonville.

3. Of the three Confederate ships mentioned here, the *America* is the most famous. Built in 1851 as a racing yacht, she had scored a surprise victory over a large fleet of British yachts in a 53-mile race around the Isle of Wight in that year, winning the 100-guinea cup offered by the Royal Yacht Squadron, which thereafter became the "America's Cup" to be competed for in the premier event of yacht racing. The *America* ran the blockade from England to the Confederacy in 1861 and was evidently sunk in the St. John's River to prevent her capture. The navy raised and refitted her as a three-gun warship which actually captured a blockade runner in October 1862. After the war she competed again in races; in 1921 a citizens' group presented her to the U.S. Naval Academy, where she remained proudly on display until broken up in 1946. The *Darlington* was a sidewheel steamboat (built in 1849) that the Union navy converted to a two-gun gunboat for river work; she was later transferred to the War Department for use as an army transport. No record can be found of the *St. Mary's*.

America and brought her down to get provisions and go back for the steamer, but found orders for our howitzer boats to proceed down the coast to assist in the attack on Smyrna. You have no doubt heard of the occupation of that place, and of the unfortunate affair that succeeded, and in which our men were shot like sheep by concealed marksmen. Our men were very much off their guard and the howitzer boat far astern of the others.[1]

While we were raising the America we had information of two companies of rebels who were watching to catch us off our guard, but they had not spirit enough to attack us openly; although we were in a narrow creek where they would have had a great advantage and where we were cut off from all support. At Brunswick they also fired into a small boat & killed or disabled most of the crew.[2]

Florida is now completely ours, and if properly managed, I have no doubt could be brought back into the Union in a short time. The Union feeling however is every where much exagerated though we found some true people. Strange to say the ladies are the most bitter against our Government, though perhaps the men would be as much so. I happened to be able to render some ladies at Jacksonville a service and had several invitations to visit them. But did not go to see any of them. At Pilatka however we were not so fortunate, for a lady gave us "a piece of her mind" as we passed along the street. . . .

Roswell to Flora

> USS *Wabash*
> Port Royal
> April 13, 1862

. . . To-day we have glorious news from the West—the surrender of Island No. 10 and the battle of Corinth.[3] You cannot tell how much

1. Smyrna was a coastal town 60 miles south of St. Augustine. On March 22 a howitzer boat reconnoitering Mosquito Inlet was attacked by guerrillas; two Union officers and three sailors were killed.

2. This incident had occurred on March 9, when three naval vessels landed at Brunswick on St. Simon's Island, Georgia, 70 miles south of Savannah, and took possession of the island.

3. The capture of the fortified Island No. 10 (the tenth island down the Mississippi River from its confluence with the Ohio River at Cairo, Illinois) on April 7, 1862, by

we felt cheered by such news. . . . But how sad it is to think of the killed and wounded, and of the gloom that will overspread so many once happy homes. *Our* dead have fallen gloriously and as soldiers would wish to die, but we can only sigh over the fate of those others, our *countrymen* who have suffered themselves to be so fatally deceived. Our men have returned from the batteries before Pulaski,[1] where their fine gunnery was the admiration of all. One of them dismounted three of the rebel guns in succession. . . .

Roswell to Flora

> USS *Wabash*
> Off Charleston
> May 13, 1862

. . . Soon after I commenced this letter the "Officer of the Deck" bellowing through his trumpet—"Steamer Ahoy!!"—"What Steamer is that?"—"Steamer Planter from Charleston!"—and you may imagine our surprise when we learned that fifteen negroes had run her out of Charleston harbor, past all the forts and reached our fleet outside.

She is an armed steamer having six guns on board and was lying at the wharf between two other steamers nobody being on board except the negroes, when they backed out and steamed down the bay with the rebel flag flying; as they passed Fort Sumpter they saluted the flag on the fort by dipping their colors and as soon as they were clear of the guns they ran up a white flag. . . . [2]

---

a combined army–navy task force, opened the Mississippi to Union shipping almost to Memphis, which itself fell to the Union river navy on June 6. What Lamson calls the battle of Corinth was the battle of Shiloh, April 6–7, a bloody and hard-bought Union victory.

1. Fort Pulaski, guarding the mouth of the Savannah River 10 miles below the city, fell to a devastating bombardment of land-based Union artillery on April 11, thereby virtually closing off Savannah to blockade runners.

2. This letter and that of May 18 one describe a famous exploit, the escape of the CSS *Planter* (built in 1860) from Charleston under the command of its slave pilot Robert Smalls. The Union navy converted this sidewheel steamer into a two-gun gunboat for work in shallow waters. Smalls served as a pilot for the navy during the rest of the war. Lamson had an uncanny knack for being where the action was.

There is a great deal of excitement here occasioned by Gen. Hunter's order freeing the slaves. We are most anxious to know if he had authority from Washington for doing so. . . . [1]

**Roswell to Benjamin Stark,
U.S. Senator from Oregon***

USS *Wabash*
Port Royal
May 13, 1862

Knowing your interest in Oregonians I take the liberty of thus addressing you to ask a favor, which your influence will readily obtain, and for which I shall be very grateful.

I have been on board this ship ever since I left the Naval Academy, and have seen a great deal of service on the coast, but now there seems to be but little that the Navy can do excepting blockade duty, and I am anxious for more active service. Oregon has but few men in the field and those few should do the more on that account.

Will you, Sir, have the kindness to procure my transfer to one of our Mississippi Gun-boats, or to one of our new iron clad vessels. . . .

Being from the West myself I feel a great sympathy with Western men, and when I read of their gallantry on the banks of the Mississippi I cannot resist my desire to be with them in this great struggle.

I had the honor of firing the first shot at the bombardment of Hatteras and at the battle of Port Royal for *Oregon*.

I learn that Capt Blake is going to apply to have me ordered to the Academy as assistant instructor in Naval Gunnery and I am anxious to avoid such orders till the war is over.

1. Major-General David Hunter (1802–86), an antislavery man, had succeeded Thomas W. Sherman as Union commander of the "Department of the South," theoretically consisting of the states of South Carolina, Georgia, and Florida (but in fact the Union army controlled only the offshore islands and a few coastal enclaves). On May 9 Hunter issued an order freeing all the slaves in this department by martial law. He had not consulted the president before doing so, and Lincoln rescinded the order. Eight months later, of course, Lincoln issued a similar edict—the Emancipation Proclamation—covering all of the Confederacy.

*Stark Papers, Oregon Historical Society, Portland.

Roswell to Flora

> Steamer *Planter*
> Port Royal
> May 18, 1862

. . . You will no doubt hear before you receive this of the negroes running this Steamer out of Charleston harbor. . . . The boat was the best one they had, and was used by General Ripley[1] and staff for visiting the different forts and batteries and for transporting guns and munitions, and they (the negroes) timed their passing of the Fort so that it should be light enough to distinguish the boat plainly but not light enough to tell a white man from a black one. . . . The Steamer has two guns mounted, a long thirty two pounder forward on a pivot and a six inch howitzer aft, and had on board four very heavy guns which were being taken to Fort Ripley, a new fort on the "middle Ground" between Fort Johnson and Castle Pinckney.[2] . . . The magazine is well filled with ammunition. She is a fine boat, in excellent order, and as she was built for running in these inland waters will be invaluable.

The enterprise was planned by Robert Small[s], the black pilot, who proposed it to the others some time ago. . . . Nine men, five women and three children came in her. When the Steamer reached this place the Commodore sent me on board . . . to take command of her, and the next day sent me to Beaufort to find good quarters for the families. . . . They are altogether better fixed than they ever were in their lives before, and it would do you good to see how happy they seem at being free. When they ran up the white flag and were out of range of Sumpter, Robert Small[s] said "We're all free niggers now." . . . Robert has his wife and three children and he says it was the cruel treatment his wife received that made him first determine to make the attempt to escape. They all express their firm determination not to be taken alive after leaving the wharf, and if fired into

1. Brigadier-General Roswell Sabine Ripley (1823–87), commander of the Confederate Department of South Carolina.

2. Part of the complex of forts in Charleston Bay that made Charleston the most heavily defended port city in the Confederacy.

to sink rather than stop the vessel well knowing what their fate would be if taken. They say the slaves are treated with the greatest cruelty in Charleston now. . . .

I do not know how long I shall continue in command of the boat for she is not a man of war and it would be contrary to naval etiquette to put a regular officer in her.

**Roswell to Benjamin Stark,
U.S. Senator from Oregon***

> USS *Wabash*
> Port Royal
> June 6, 1862

Your kind favor of the 21st ult. is at hand. . . . I am very glad you did not procure my transfer to the Mississippi Flotilla under the circumstances, for nothing would induce me to leave the Wabash except the prospect of immediate active service, and the conviction that this class of vessels can do but little more during this war.

I fully appreciate the advantages of my position on board so fine a ship and of serving under such officers, and have endeavored to improve them, but this ship draws so much water that I see no prospect of our being able to do much more.

Will you Sir, procure my transfer to the Monitor, or to one of the other iron clad vessels, as soon as a vacancy occurs. . . . I do not ask this, Sir, from any spirit of discontentment as I fear you think: for I could not be more delightfully situated than at present, but I am anxious for more active service than this ship can be engaged in, and am willing to make any sacrifice of comfort to obtain it.

Our *fleet* will no doubt be actively engaged very soon, but this *ship* draws too much water to be in the fight, while we learn that some of the iron clads are to be sent to Commodore Du Pont.

I thank you, Sir, for your kind words of commendation, and it shall be my constant endeavor to do my duty to my country, and Oregon at all times. . . .

*Stark Papers, Oregon Historical Society, Portland.

Roswell to Flora

> U.S. Gunboat *E. B. Hale*[1]
> Port Royal
> July 5, 1862

This afternoon Captain Rodgers told me that the Flag Officer had found it necessary to detach the Lieutenant commanding this vessel, and that I would be ordered to the temporary command of her. You cannot imagine my disappointment when I saw my hopes of seeing my friends thus dashed to the ground;[2] but if it is necessary, as the Flag Officer says it is, I am willing to lose even that much anticipated pleasure to be of service. I came on board immediately and have been fitting for sea as fast as possible. I shall probably sail for Stono and James Island on Monday or Tuesday. The Commodore and Captain Rodgers said a number of flattering things to me which however did nothing to reconcile me to the idea of not seeing you all, and the only thing that does is the conviction that just now I am needed here and can do more for the good cause than by going home. . . .

The Hale carries five guns and is one of our most effective vessels in the rivers and inland waters. . . .

Here I am sitting alone in my little cabin with the moon shining in through the drawn curtains as it used to do into the dear old music room at Shelburne Falls. I almost wish I had *no* friends and that I could become as hard and stern as some of the old Northern Vikings loving *only* the sea and martial glory. . . . I have not told you anything about what a trial it is to leave the Wabash to which I am so much attached.

1. A five-gun shallow-drafted screw gunboat built in 1861.
2. Lamson had been counting on a furlough after more than a year of continuous service.

Roswell to Flora

USS *Pawnee*
Stono River, S.C.
July 19, 1862

. . . After bringing the "Hale" up the Coast I reported on board this ship for duty as "Sailing Master," and in addition to the duties of my own department have a gun division, and to releave the other officers, keep a regular watch—so you see I have not much time to spare. We are lying near the battle ground on James Island[1] the lower part of which we are still holding in hopes that another attempt will be made to take Charleston. We will be glad to see blue water again for it is intensely hot and the flies and mosquitoes are intolerable—besides typhoid fever has made its appearance. . . .

Now for this ship and my new shipmates and messmates—The Pawnee is the finest ship in the Squadron except the Wabash, and as she carries a very heavy armament and draws but little water, is the most efficient ship on the coast. Our Commander Captain Drayton is a South Carolinian and a brother of General Drayton of the C.S.A.—an excellent officer, a very pleasant gentleman, and as true a patriot as ever drew a sword for the "Stars and Stripes." When I received my orders Commodore Du Pont said he had sent me to the best ship he had and to the best Captain. Our "First Lieut" and "Executive Officer" is a sailor of the old school, a little rough, but an officer who knows his duty and does it, and tries to make us all comfortable. The happiness and comfort of a man of war depend more on the "First Lieutenant" than even on the Captain, for he has charge of the discipline of the Ship, most of the internal arrangements, boats, &c. He stands between the Captain and the ships company and it is he with whom you come immediately in contact in carrying on the routine and duty of the Ship. The other officers are quite young men and very pleasant fellows, and altogether I have never seen a happier ship, or one more anxious to go into Charleston. I go on shore occasionally to take observations for regulating my

1. The battle of Secessionville on June 16, a Union defeat that ended the army's attempt to attack Charleston via the back door of coastal islands.

chronometers, but the enemy's pickets are so near that it is not safe for small parties to go far. . . .

Roswell to Katie

USS *Pawnee*
Stono Inlet, SC
Sept. 3, 1862

. . . Many thanks for the paper containing an account of your Sunday School Anniversary which interested me very much and brought vividly to my remembrance the two pleasant Sundays spent in Mt. Vernon two years ago. . . .

Last Sat. I passed my *final* examination before a board ordered by the Admiral. I was seven hours before the board and was glad enough to get through with it. Our class have been preparing for it for three months and are being examined in the Squadrons where they are serving.

You have no doubt seen the recent legislation for the Navy—I think one of the best things they did was to abolish the "grog" fore and *aft*. You know it has been customary to give the sailors whiskey before breakfast and before dinner. Last Sun. the "Grog Tub" was brought up for the last time, and it was amusing to see the wistful looks some of the old salts gave their long tried friend, as they came up as their names were called and took their last "tot." Some of them think it rather hard that Uncle Sam should cut away their main stay after supplying them so long, and really rendering it almost a necessity, but the better class of the men heartily approve it. With the "Grog Tub" we lose the curse of half the punishment on board ship—such is the opinion of the best officers I have seen and my own observation fully agrees with it.

I like this ship very much, and find a very pleasant mess of officers on board. The Admiral said I might come back to the Wabash if I wished but on many accounts I prefer this vessel—she carries a heavy battery, is of light draft, and if *any* wooden vessels attempt to go into Charleston will be one of them. We are the flag ship of this division. Capt. Drayton went to Port Royal yesterday by order of the Admiral to confer about *something*; we hope some movement is to be made for it is getting intolerable lying here *looking* at the rebels and at *Charleston* too, while our soldiers are *fighting* them around Richmond.

Lately I have been reading Gasparin's late work "America before Europe"—he is the only foreign author I have seen who shows a real earnest sympathy for us, and a conscientious regard for the *Right* in this great struggle.[1] His book is very interesting. He devotes a chapter to the difficulties of the blockade, and one would almost think he had been here so well does he appreciate them. This entire coast is but a net work of islands, and innumerable inlets connecting at intervals with the ocean by channels of considerable depth. You can form a good idea of it from the fact that small steamers can go from Charleston to the St. Johns without once going to sea. In these passages lay numbers of small craft, some owned by Southerners, some by *Northerners*, and many by English, ready to take advantage of a dark night, or of a storm that should drive our cruisers off the coast. Admiral Du Pont has taken possession of all the principal of these passes and inlets, and thus established an "Inner Blockade" which is more effectual than the "Outer," though the duty is far less pleasant on account of the *heat*, and the miasma from the swamps.

I am now reading Tasso's Jerusalem Delivered when I have time to spare.[2] The Wabashes wrote me that they did not have a very pleasant time while at Phila, as they could not leave the ship much. Capt. Rodgers wrote me the other day that our class were to be promoted to be lieutenants as soon as the reports of our examinations reached the department. Forrest my roommate you remember wrote me a long letter the other day as he was leaving Port Royal his vessel having been ordered North for repairs he said if he got leave he might pass through Mt. Vernon and if so would try to call on my friends there.

You must judge my letters very leniently if you can "find *no* fault" with them for we have so little news that I fear they must be stupid; however I am glad they had no other fault.

---

1. Comte Agenor Ettenne Gasparin (1810–71), a liberal French aristocrat who wrote *L'Amerique devant L'Europe, principes et interets* (Paris, 1861), which was translated by Mary Booth and published in English as *America Before Europe: Principles and Interests* (New York, 1862).

2. Torquato Tasso (1544–95), an Italian poet whose masterpiece was published in English in 1857 as *Jerusalem Delivered*.

Roswell to Flora

> USS *Pawnee*
> St. Simons, Ga.
> Sept. 19, 1862

. . . Your kind letters of Aug 31 and Sept 2 came an hour ago, and I had just set myself down to read them when the Captain sent for me and gave me my promotion to the rank of Lieutenant in the Navy. I have just received the congratulations of my messmates. I do wish I could be somewhere where I could do something more for our Country than we seem to be likely to have an opportunity of doing here, and where I could do something more to merit my promotion. This half inaction is almost intolerable to me; my only consolation is that I am obeying orders, and doing my duty to the best of my ability in the place where the Government assigns me.

Thank you for your kind interest in our sick. You cannot *tell* how any expression of kindness towards them goes to my heart. There are no stouter arms, more willing hands, or braver truer hearts in the Service of our Country in its dark hour than are to be found in the forecastles of our men of war. But while I am thankful for your kind offer I am glad to tell you that our sick are very well provided for and have everything they need. There is a perfectness of organization in every department of the Navy that they do not have in the Army. I have often heard this admitted and admired by Army officers themselves. . . .

You know that Preston, Forrest and myself were rivals for the head of our class during our entire course at the Naval Academy. Preston passed one, I passed two and Forrest three. At the last examination I hear that I passed higher than Preston, probably because I have seen more service. I also passed one for each of the first two years at the Academy. Some of the Wabashes told me they saw my report, and that the Board gave me but one mark less than a "4" which is the highest. . . .

We have papers on the 12th inst. The news is rather discouraging but I have the firmest confidence in our success finally—the right must triumph.[1]

---

1. The discouraging news concerned the Union defeat at the second battle of Bull Run August 29–30 and Lee's subsequent invasion of Maryland plus the initial stages

Roswell to Katie

USS *Pawnee*
St. Simons, Ga.
Sept. 22, 1862

I have not yet received an answer to my last, but avail myself of your request to write whenever the "spirit moved" as an excuse for this letter, which I warn you in advance will be devoid of interest; we have so little news on this coast. Last week we went up to the mainland and shelled out a detachment of rebels to prevent their erecting a battery, and then returned to the dull wearying blockade which grows more irksome with every mail we receive from the North. Three days ago I received my promotion to be a lieutenant in the Navy from the 1st of July, four years from the day I reported for my first examination, at the Naval Academy. This is a much more interesting place than Stono was, as we can occasionally go on shore, and there is one very pretty road through the plantation of the somewhat noted rebel T. Butler King.[1]

. . . When we were at Port Royal the Admiral promised me a short leave as soon as he could make the arrangement, our Capt. Rodgers said he would remind him of it; so I think I shall get it. A man-of-war is allowed but a certain number of "watch officers" which makes it more difficult to get leave; as one of these officers must *always* be on duty. . . .

What do you think of the war now? I remember you said in one of your letters you "did not think they would hurt us very much;" but do you not admire the admirable management and generalship of their leaders? But I have no doubt of the final success of the *Union* cause any more than I have of the final triumph of true principles. It looks rather stormy now, and now is the time to prove our mettle the op-

---

of the dual invasions of Kentucky by the Confederate armies of Generals Edmund Kirby Smith and Braxton Bragg. The news of Antietam (Sept. 17) had not yet reached Lamson.

1. Thomas Butler King (1800–1864), a wealthy planter and slaveholder on St. Simon's Island, Georgia, who served as a Confederate diplomat. Four of his sons fought in the Confederate army.

portunity may not last long. I do wish the Navy could do *more* for the cause we all hold so dear. I do believe we are willing to make any sacrifice for our *flag* and *country*, and are ready to prove that the spirit of the American Sailor still animates it. . . .

Roswell to Flora

> USS *Pawnee*
> Off Fort Mifflin
> Delaware River
> Nov. 9, 1862

. . . We received orders at Wassaw on the 1st inst to go to Port Royal, and there we received orders to proceed to Philadelphia to refit the ship. We sailed from Port Royal on the evening of the 3d and had fine weather till we reached Hatteras, off which we experienced one of the most terrific gales I have ever been through—much more severe than the one a year ago in the same latitude. The Pawnee behaved splendidly, lying-to under a three reefed spanker and mizzen storm stay sail, and steaming slowly off shore. On the night of the 7th we stood in for the land and made the lighthouses at the Capes of the Delaware last night after dark. We had just taken their bearings and were running in when a storm of snow and sleet came up so thick as to completely shut out the lights and leave us with nothing to run by except the leadline. We struck the channel and succeeded in getting in to a good anchorage. Today we came up the Bay and this evening sent our powder ashore to the magazine preparatory to going up to the Navy Yard tomorrow morning. This ship is the last of the original fleet to return home. At the Capes were the wrecks of several ships lost during the gale, which was a most severe one here.

The Admiral told me before we left that he had written to the Secretary of the Navy asking him to give myself and two other officers on board a leave of absence, as we had been on continual service longer than any other officers of the fleet. I really need a little rest, the doctor says, for I have been quite sick of most of the time since I wrote you last—the effect of the malaria of the swamps where we have been lying and my eyes have troubled me a good deal, but are getting better now. I did duty as watch officer and master both till the doctor forbade my being called when I was asleep and when I waked I found myself on the sick list. I am better now and hope in a few days to be allright again.

We do not yet know what will be done with the ship—whether she will be put out of commission and the officers detached and ordered to other vessels, or whether we will get leave while the repairs are being made and all join her again. If I can get on board a ship that suits me I will not ask for leave if I am well enough to go. . . . You know I am enlisted for the War—if that permits I shall visit my friends.

Katie to Roswell

Mt. Vernon, Ohio
Nov. 14, 1862

Do you know it has been nearly six weeks since I wrote to you? I was writing last Sunday evening and I said I would wait till next Sunday and then if I had no letter I would write again. But on Wednesday afternoon I went in Mothers room and she gave me a letter from sister Mary. I read it and was commenting on it when she asked me if I didn't want another. I rather thought I did and she gave me yours. Mine must have been a long time on the way. I am so sorry you are sick. I think you ought to come out here and recruit. . . .

Change and rest at least will do you good. Mother had a letter from father on Wednesday.[1] He had just returned from McClellan's headquarters. He was sent with the order relieving him of the command. He said it was the hardest duty he ever had to perform. I do feel so sorry for McClellan and I think the President will find out that he has done him injustice in removing him. I wonder who will be the next General found fault with. It takes them all the time to try the officers and there is none left for fighting. But it makes me heart-sick to read or talk of the war, everything looks so dark. Still you know it is always

1. Kate's father was Brigadier-General Catharinus Putnam Buckingham (1808–88), on special duty with the War Department. His most notable exploit during the war was to carry Lincoln's order to McClellan's camp in Virginia on November 7 just before midnight removing McClellan from command of the Army of the Potomac and appointing Ambrose E. Burnside in his place.

darkest just before day, and there may be brighter times in store for us. . . .

Mr Reese is as much in favor as ever, he is not a very talented preacher, but a faithful pastor. I think you will like him. He has a pretty sister here visiting perhaps she might be the "best fish" but alas, she is already caught, so I can't promise you anything in that quarter. But she is a very pleasant girl! . . .

There was great rejoicing among the small fry when I told them that perhaps Cousin Roswell would make them a visit. Jack says "Good! It will be first rate to have him come here."

O N E   O F   T H E   M O S T

G A L L A N T   O F F I C E R S   I N

T H E   N A V Y

J A N U A R Y – M A Y   1 8 6 3

I N NOVEMBER 1862 Lamson finally received his coveted furlough. He spent Christmas with Kate Buckingham's family in
Mount Vernon, Ohio. During the preceding year Lamson's correspondence with his cousin Flora had been more frequent than with
Kate. But an affection for his younger cousin (Kate was nineteen, Flora
twenty-two) had evidently been growing in his heart. Cupid struck
powerfully during the holidays. Kate and Roswell confessed their love
to each other and announced their engagement. It would turn out to
be a long one. A decided shift in Roswell's correspondence thereafter
occurred, as his letters to Kate became full and frequent and those to
Flora fade to infrequency.

After his furlough Lamson reported for a new assignment as assistant
to Commodore Charles H. Davis at the Bureau of Navigation in Washington. Although Lamson was frustrated by the lack of action during
this tour, it was far from a dead-end assignment. On the contrary, the
navy seems to have reserved such postings for its most promising young
officers in order to give them a variety of experiences important to their

future careers. Lamson's activities during the previous eighteen months on the bays, inlets, rivers, and inland waterway passages along the South Atlantic coast also made his knowledge valuable to the Bureau of Navigation.

———•◆•———

Roswell to Kate

> Bureau of Navigation
> Navy Department,
> Washington
> Jan. 14, 1863

. . . I am engaged from half past nine to four p.m. Monday I took possession of my room at Mrs. Andrews. . . . Yesterday morning I was much surprised to see my old classmate and shipmate Preston (Com-dre DuPont's aid) who came from the Wabash with some despatches from the rebel government to Slidell[1] and others in Europe. Their agent attempted to run out of Charleston in a schooner and was captured. Preston told me all about my old shipmates; we dined to-gether, and had quite a visit. He left this morning to return.

As soon as the iron clads can be collected at Port Royal an attack will be made on Charleston. Gen. Hunter is to cooperate with about 12000 men part of whom *are embarking now*. Unless the weather proves very bad the attack will be made *within* thirty days. This is from head quarters, and I give it to you sub rosa.

You have no doubt heard of the sad affair at Galveston. Lieut Zim-merman[2] was my classmate and a brave fellow.

When I hear of such things I feel almost as though I *ought not* to

1. John Slidell (1793–1871), Confederate envoy to France. Along with James Mason, he had been taken from the British mail steamer *Trent* by Captain Charles Wilkes of the U.S. Navy in November 1861, provoking an international incident between the United States and Britain that threatened to lead to war. The Lincoln administration had defused the crisis by yielding up Mason and Slidell, who proceeded to London and Paris where they spent the rest of the war futilely seeking British and French diplomatic recognition of the Confederacy.

2. Lieutenant Charles William Zimmerman, killed on New Year's Day, 1863, in a surprise attack by Confederate troops and gunboats that recaptured Galveston, Texas, from Union occupying troops and their supporting ships.

be here, but they think I am useful here I suppose. . . . I am willing—anxious to be wherever I *can* do most for the "stars and stripes."

Since our repulse from Vicksburg[1] our prospects for the campaign *look* rather dark, but when the navy get at Charleston, I hope and *believe* we shall hear more cheering news. Preston says the Admiral expresses his determination to succeed or sink every ship in the attempt.

I forgot to take the measure of your finger—but will see you again I *hope*. I don't think I need urge you to write. Direct to this Bureau. . . . Now—my darling Kate—the most I can say to *you* is to repeat the "old story" ego te amo[2]—old but always new, & I hope I shall repeat it many times, unless you get tired of hearing it. Write me if you are lonely. Heaven bless you, my darling is the prayer of Roswell.

Roswell to Kate

Washington
Jan. 25, 1863

Your sweet loving letter of the 14th inst came last Wednesday to make my heart glad and happy. I was getting very impatient to hear from you, and I cannot tell you what pleasure your kind loving words have given me—as I read over your letter I *see* you not away in Mt. Vernon, but *here* close by my side, your head resting on my shoulder, and again I look into your sweet face and into those eyes that tell me I am loved. It is only when I try to gather the sweet vision up close to my heart that I realize that I am here, you there, and the uncertainties of the future before us. . . .

I hope I am every day growing more devoted to my God, to my Country, and to you. What more *could* I want, what more could I have to inspire me with courage, and to fill me with happiness? Your *presence* only is wanting. A soldier without a lady-love is like a ship without a compass; but with the blest assurance that *one* true and gentle heart beats warmly and constantly for him, *prays* for him, and will receive

1. On December 29, 1862, Union troops commanded by Major-General William Tecumseh Sherman attacked Confederate defenses at Chickasaw Bluffs a few miles north of Vicksburg and were driven back with heavy casualties.
2. Latin for "I love you."

him on his return *whatever* may have been his fortune, so he but comes with an unsullied honor, he no longer *drifts* over the ocean of life and duty, but steers his course by a compass ever pointing to a star that shines to cheer his heart, to inspire his energies, and to reward his efforts.

You, my dearest Kate, are such a star to *me*. . . .

Yesterday I intended to go to the Presidents reception but went to the Navy Yard on business, and did not get back in time. I shall go next Sat. and will give you an account of it. Mr. Lincoln looks completely worn out—almost haggard, and seems very much depressed. Mrs. L. seems to bear the cares of state more lightly judging from her appearance. . . .

My eyes are getting much better—It would quite cure them to *look* at *you*.

Roswell to Kate

Washington
Feb. 25, 1863

. . . When your letter came we had just had an audience of savan[t]s in the Commodore's room among whom were Profs. Agassiz and Pierce of Harvard, Prof. Bache of the Coast-Survey.[1] Agassiz is a heavy looking man, with a broad but extremely pleasant face, and of course a delightful man to listen to, as a man of his knowledge always must be.

On Sat. I attended the Presidents reception for the first time since I came here. There were a great many people of *all* sorts present, and all seemed to enjoy it very much.

1. These three men were among the most eminent scientists in the United States. Jean Louis Rodolphe Agassiz (1807–73) was born in Switzerland. He came to the United States in 1846 to give a series of lectures on natural history (geology) and was persuaded by Alexander Dallas Bache (1806–67) to remain as chair of the Department of Natural History in the Lawrence Scientific School at Harvard. Bache was superintendent of the U.S. Coastal Survey, a former professor of natural philosophy and chemistry at the University of Pennsylvania, and the first president of the National Academy of Science. Benjamin Pierce (1809–80), an astronomer and geographer, was president of the American Institute for the Advancement of Science, and in 1867 succeeded Bache as superintendent of the Coastal Survey.

You have heard so much of Mr. & Mrs. Lincoln that you are almost as well acquainted with them as though you had seen them. When I was presented to Mrs. Lincoln she remarked that "The streets of Washington were very muddy" the truth of which there was no gainsaying as I never saw anything equal them in all my travels, but with her characteristic kindness she added she "hoped they would dry up."

Mr. Lincoln spoke very highly of the Navy and with much regret of the death of Capt. Woodhull [Commander Maxwell Woodhull] who was killed at Balto. the day previous while a salute was being fired in honor of Gen Butler.

Those who know Mrs. Lincoln best all speak of her as a good kind hearted lady.

The promotion of those of my class who passed their examination last summer has been confirmed by the Senate—our commissions to date from the 1st of August 1862. My eyes are improving and do not trouble me except when I read or write by gas light; so you must have no uneasiness about me, dearest, but take good care of yourself, and I shall await with less impatience the time when I shall take care of you. God help us both to do our *duty* and to be resigned to his will. So much happiness is quite worth working and waiting for.

Last Friday evening we went to Speaker Grow's[1] reception which was the greatest *jam* I have seen here yet. Among the many celebrities was Clarke Mills the sculptor.[2] After a look through the rooms at a few persons one comes to see these receptions are stupid enough, for you are obliged to listen to such strings of fashionable nonsense as leaves you in doubt whether you have been among rational creatures or not. . . .

You need not be surprised at any time to hear of my receiving orders for sea, for pleasant as I find Washington, I would rather be on active service, particularly if I can go to Admiral DuPont though I am willing to go any where.

1. Galusha A. Grow (1822–1907), congressman from Pennsylvania and Speaker of the House.

2. Clarke Mills (1810–83), who developed new techniques of sculpture in bronze. His equestrian statue of Andrew Jackson in Lafayette Square across from the White House was the largest bronze sculpture ever done to that time. He also cast the bronze of "Liberty" for the new Capitol dome which was being erected during the Civil War.

———•◦•———

ON FEBRUARY 28, 1863, Assistant Secretary of the Navy Gustavus V. Fox wrote to Acting Rear Admiral Samuel Phillips Lee (1812–97, a cousin of Robert E. Lee), commander of the North Atlantic Blockading Squadron, which was responsible for maintaining the blockade along the Virginia and North Carolina coast: "Your second Lieutenant is to be detached, and we send you young Lamson in his place. Lamson was expected to go on other duty, but in anticipation of your movements upon the enemy I thought you might wish [him] upon your staff, at least for this fight, a young man that Du Pont and Rodgers consider one of the very best in the service. Davis has had him in the Bureau for a month and speaks in highest terms of him."*

———•◦•———

Roswell to Katie

> Bureau of Navigation
> Washington, DC
> March 7, 1863

I am preparing to leave Washington on Monday for the Minnesota at Hampton Roads, and am quite busy, but must snatch a few minutes to thank you for your dear letter of the 3rd and to tell you again the "old story" that I love you with all my heart.

Washington has been very pleasant—I have received a great deal of kindness and made many agreeable acquaintances, but I shall leave it without any regret, except that I cannot go to Charleston, and that I cannot see *your dear face* before I go to sea. . . .

You are the star I sail by, and you shine to guide me both by day and night for unlike the Astronomical bodies there is no light that can obscure *you* to my sight; no clouds that can cover your dear image, or the remembrances of those *happy days.*

---

*Official Records of the Union and Confederate Navies in the War of the Rebellion, ser. I, vol. 8, pp. 577–78; hereinafter *O.R. Navies.*

Roswell to Katie

USS *Louisiana*[1]
On the Chesapeake Bay
March 9, 1863

I sent you a letter, this morning, from Washington and now I must write you a few lines to tell you my heart is not going further from you; *it* remains in your dear keeping though the distance between us is lengthening with every revolution of the engine. . . .

You are struck by the number of sentries and officers on duty in the depot at Washington, I suppose to stop deserters, but you cannot turn around without having one at your elbow. We passed some very picturesque and comfortable looking camps just out of the City, but the entire ground is cut up by waggons and horses till it is a mass of the deepest and thickest mud I ever saw.

The "Annapolis Junction!!" . . . As I looked through the trees down the road leading to the dear, dull, slow, sleepy old city—proud of its ancient houses built of imported bricks, and of the descendents of "old families" that inhabit them, my mind went back through their untold struggles and trials; victories and defeats from which I hope I have learned a lesson of *patience* and *perseverance* that will aid me in doing my duty through all the years of my life. I shall always have a great affection for Annapolis; though it has nothing but what I have enumerated except the hotel where Washington stopped and which Annapolitans think an excellent one on that account alone without reference to the discomforts of its table and rooms, a painting of Washington resigning his commission in the room where it occured, and certain traditions of ancient grandeur.

But pardon me for leading you so far from the track. At Balto. I took a carriage and reached the boat just in time, stuck my orders in the face of a "soger" who was going to charge bayonets to keep me from coming on board, and found all the rooms taken except a "family room" which I secured, and a part of which I gave up to a wounded rebel Captain and his escort who is taking him to Fortress

1. The USS *Louisiana* was a schooner-rigged screw steamship built in 1860. The navy purchased her in 1861 and converted her to a three-gun warship. Lamson would encounter the *Louisiana* again on a momentous occasion in December 1864.

Monroe. The Captain is from North Carolina and was wounded and taken prisoner in one of the skirmishes after the rebels crossed into My Maryland.[1] He is a jolly fellow and announced his creed to be "Enemies *on duty*, we'll *fight*; friends, *off duty*, we'll *drink*" to which I heartily acceded adding "water" which so disgusted him that he ordered two glasses of whisky to drive away the unpleasant idea of drinking water. . . .

This has been such a beautiful day that I have quite forgiven Washington the unpleasant weather during most of my stay. . . .

Roswell to Katie

> USS *Minnesota*
> Hampton Roads, Va.
> March 10, 1863

. . . We reached Fortress Monroe this morning about eleven o'clock, and I went on board a small steamer, tender to the flag ship and was soon on board. I reported to the Admiral [Samuel Phillips Lee] who is a very gentlemanly, pleasant old fellow who introduced me to the Captain N[apoleon] B[onaparte] Harrison who directed me to report to the Executive officer Lieut-Commander [Edward C.] Grafton. I am the third officer in rank, counting the Captain; my room is the second on the starboard side; the Executive officer has the first. . . .

Asst. Sec. Fox had written to Admiral Lee to appoint me his Flag Lieutenant, but the ship is so short of officers that he could not do it now. He said he would write to Washington this afternoon for more officers and would place me on his staff if possible to get them.

He showed me a letter Admiral [Charles H.] Davis had written him, more complimentary than I deserved.

I should like the appointment very well—will write you when I learn anything more about it.

This ship is just like the Wabash, carries fifty guns and a crew of between seven and eight hundred men. On the spar deck (upper) she has a two-hundred p'd'r rifled pivot forward, an eleven inch pivot aft, and eighteen nine inch guns in broadside. I have command of the entire gun-deck where there are twenty-six nine inch guns, and four

1. In the campaign that culminated in the battle of Antietam.

one hundred p'd'r rifles—thirty in all with three hundred men at one discharge of her ordnance she throws over five thousand (5,138 lbs) pounds of cold iron.

She is a splendid ship, but I can see by glancing around the decks that she is not in that perfect state of discipline and preparation that we had on board the Wabash.

Of course I cannot tell you much of my messmates yet, but to *lump* them they are a good hearted set, but a little old and crusty. I'll give you a more particular description when I know them better. This afternoon I took the deck from four to six and I felt a thrill of pride as I looked along her decks peopled with true American sailors, that could not be damped by even the cold No'th-East rain storm that was howling through the rigging. (The pride I mean, not the sailors, for some of them, like myself, were decidedly damped outside.)

We are lying directly off Newport News, about seven miles from Hampton Roads proper—toward Norfolk. The Galena and Sangamon, iron clads, are just above us in the mouth of the James River to look out for the "Merrimac No. 2."[1] All the shores of the bay are dotted with camps, and at various points earthworks can be seen crowned with heavy guns. I expect I shall be a little lonesome for a few days, but I shall think of *you* the more. . . .

Roswell to Katie

USS *Minnesota*
Hampton Roads
March 11, 1863

I will write you a few lines this evening before I go on watch at "Eight-bells" (eight o'clock).

Last night at twelve the quartermaster came down with his "Twelve

---

1. The USS *Galena* was one of three experimental ironclads authorized and built in 1861. She was constructed on traditional lines and sheathed with 3 ¼" of iron armor on her sides, armed with six guns in broadsides and on bow and stern. The USS *Sangamon* was built in 1862 on the *Monitor* model, with low freeboard, iron plating on the deck as well as sides, and two large guns in a revolving turret. "Merrimac no. 2" was the CSS *Virginia II*, which the Confederates were building in Richmond to replace the famous *Virginia* which fought the *Monitor* on March 9, 1862, and was subsequently scuttled by the Confederates when they abandoned Norfolk.

O'Clock, Sir." Very well, quartermaster, how is the weather on deck? The old fellow looked at his tarpaulins and Sou'wester as though their dripping condition was answer enough, and replied "A little thick, Sir," as he lighted my candle and went out.

I soon relieved the officer of the deck, and did find it a *little* thick, dark, blowing and raining hard; but *"Katie* is in a snug berth," and it was not much the storm troubled me. As soon as I was assured that everything about the Ship was secure, I sent the "watch" except the sentries and lookouts, down on the gun deck where they could keep dry till ordered up.

This morning I rose a little after eight, and as is usual with the officer of the mid-watch breakfasted a little later than the others. My boy "Augustus" had kept my breakfast hot, and having assured me I was to have a nice one set before me with a dignity well calculated to impress me with the luxuriousness of Minnesota fare a plate of beefsteak, another of boiled veal, one of mutton chops one of sausages, one of stewed tripe, all served in the nicest style, and two plates of bread, but *no vegetables;* I could not help laughing at such a *characteristic* breakfast, and I have no doubt if there had been any other varieties of meat in the market we should have had them. You can form a pretty good idea of "living" on board a man-of-war or any where else I expect where woman does not rule over the cuisine.

This afternoon I drilled my men at the great-guns—they drill tolerably well, but must drill a great deal better—must come up nearer to Wabash style in quite a number of particulars: if men do not do just right it is the fault of the *officers;* men can always be controlled and influenced if the proper means are employed to do it.

I have three volunteer officers who seem well disposed to do the best they can, and I have no doubt I shall get along with them nicely, but they do not seem to know how to infuse any *spirit* into the men.

The Ericsson[1] came in this morning from Port Royal; four of our ironclads attacked Fort McAllister without doing it any damage.[2] It

---

1. The *Ericsson* was a steamer chartered by the navy in 1862 and armed with three guns, but apparently never commissioned as a naval ship; her name does not appear on the naval register. She was named after John Ericsson (1803–89), the Swedish-born inventor of the original *Monitor* ironclad.

2. An earthwork fort built by the Confederates on the Ogeechee River as part of the defenses of Savannah. On January 27 and February 1 the USS *Montauk,* a *Monitor*-class ironclad, and several smaller wooden ships attacked Fort McAllister without doing it much damage. (Lamson was mistaken in stating that four ironclads attacked

does not defend Savannah as much as the papers make people think, but was built originally to keep us from cutting out the Nashville.[1] It is at the mouth of the Ogeechee River which runs into Ossabaw Sound. We expect the Keokuk and Catskill,[2] iron clads, every day. The Keokuk will remain here.

Roswell to Kate

USS *Minnesota*
Off Newport News
March 14, 1863

. . . At 9½ a.m. we had an inspection of the crew at quarters as usual, and then I drilled the men with broad-swords. I am the only lieut. on board and I have *all* the drills to superintend and most all of it to do besides keeping watch. There are only three watch officers besides myself, and the Captain said as soon as he could get another, I should be excused from watch and act only as the ordnance officer of the ship, which would give me quite enough to do; but I am not afraid of a little work, and am *willing* to *do* all I can. We have almost a regiment of men on board, besides the ship to take care of, and only three regular officers *including the* Captain and Executive officer. The Admiral told me day before yesterday that he had written to the Department for two more lieutenants and expected them soon, and should assign me to duty on his staff as soon as they arrived. I like the com-

---

the fort). This was a sort of dress rehearsal for the planned attack on the forts defending Charleston by several ironclads. After the first attack on Fort McAllister, Rear Admiral Du Pont wrote to a friend: "I asked myself this morning while quietly dressing, if one ironclad cannot take eight guns—how are five to take 147 guns in Charleston harbor?"

1. The CSS *Nashville* was a sidewheel passenger steamer built in 1853 and seized by the Confederates at Charleston, where she happened to be when war broke out in 1861. They fitted her out as a cruiser to prey on Union merchant ships, and sold her as a blockade runner in 1862 named *Thomas L. Wragg*. She was subsequently reconverted to a privateer named *Rattlesnake*, though she continued to be known popularly as the *Nashville*. All these changes of name seemed to bring bad luck; the ironclad USS *Montauk* destroyed her by gunfire on the Ogeechee River on February 28, 1863.

2. The USS *Catskill* and USS *Keokuk* were ironclads completed in 1862; the *Catskill* had a single revolving turret, the *Keokuk* two stationary turrets.

mand of the splendid gun-deck batteries very much and shall be loth to give it up even for the staff of an Admiral. . . .

Troops are being transported from Newport News to Norfolk all the time, and from there to Suffolk for what purpose is not known. We manned our rigging to-day and gave the transports three cheers as they passed—the troops returned it, their bands playing The Star Spangled Banner. Some of Gen. Wil[l]cox's officers invited me to come ashore and take a ride about the camps and out in the country which I shall do the first opportunity I have.[1] . . .

Roswell to Kate

USS *Minnesota*
March 19, 1863

. . . The Admiral received a reply from Washington that another lieut. could not be sent him now; so he directed that I should be relieved from watch, and take charge of the ordnance and Gunnery of the ship, the Master's Dept. (Instruments and Navigation) and do such duty on his staff as he could not intrust to the Ensign who acts as his aid.

This arrangement gives me quite enough to do during the day, but I am not disturbed at night unless something unusual occurs. I am almost sorry, for I used to think of *you* during the night watches, and I never was tired or sleepy, I never knew till recently how much I used to think about you before I had any reason to suppose you cared any thing for me.

The North Atlantic Squadron blockades the coast from the mouth of the Piankatank River (Chesapeake Bay) to the coast of South Carolina. The flag ship generally remains at the rendezvous of the fleet, but goes to any part of the coast where active operations are going on or where the presence of the Admiral may be needed. This is not where

---

1. When Major-General Ambrose E. Burnside was removed as commander of the Army of the Potomac in January 1863 he reverted to command of IX Corps, which the War Department then transferred out of the army. They came first to Newport News and some of them went across the James to Suffolk, Virginia, but most were transferred to Kentucky and some went eventually to Mississippi to participate in Grant's campaign against Vicksburg. Brigadier-General Orlando Bolivar Willcox (1823–1907) commanded a division in IX Corps.

I would *wish* to be, but where I am *ordered* to do duty. I would *wish* to be in the fleet to attack Charleston. . . .

Roswell to Kate

USS *Minnesota*
March 21, 1863

. . . The 9th Army Corps which has been encamped at Newport News has been ordered to Balto. to go west to reinforce Rosecrans.[1]

The news from Port Hudson is very bad if true—I will not believe it till we have it from better authority than rebel papers.[2]

I congratulate you on the stand your Ohio legislature[3] has taken, as expressed in their resolutions—we *can* fight as long as traitors can, and make as many sacrifices; and we *can* restore the Union if all will only show that devotion to her cause which is their most solemn *duty*. Such sentiments, coming from the third state in the Union in population, are quite refreshing after the action of the New Jersey Assembly.[4]

The Keokuk started to sea last Monday, but on the way out the pilot ran her foul of a buoy and the chain wound round her propeller which obliged her to return. We have had men at work under water, in submarine armor, and hope to get it clear this evening. . . .

1. Major-General William Starke Rosecrans (1819–98), commander of the Army of the Cumberland operating against the Confederate Army of Tennessee between Nashville and Chattanooga. None of the IX Corps directly reinforced Rosecrans; most of it reinforced Grant's campaign against Vicksburg, and when that bastion fell, part of the IX Corps joined the campaign against Knoxville in tangent with Rosecrans's campaign against Chattanooga.

2. Port Hudson was a Confederate fortification on the Mississippi River about twenty-five miles north of Baton Rouge. David Glasgow Farragut's fleet of seven ships attacked the works on March 14, 1863, attempting to pass upriver to join the campaign against Vicksburg, but only two of the ships made it. Several others were badly damaged and the USS *Mississippi*, a ten-gun sidewheel steamboat, was sunk. Port Hudson finally fell to a Union army siege on July 9, 1863, five days after Vicksburg surrendered.

3. Patriotic resolutions passed by the Ohio legislature supporting the Union war effort, in defiance of "Copperhead" efforts to brand the war a failure and to demand an armistice.

4. A series of resolutions passed by the Democratic majority in the New Jersey legislature denouncing the Emancipation Proclamation and calling for an end to the war by negotiations.

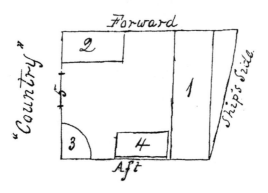

Roswell to Kate

USS *Minnesota*
Hampton Roads
March 23, 1863

. . . Well, dear Katie, here I am in my little room writing to you, and as usual wishing I could look into your dear eyes; "loving eyes they are to me." I have not given you a description of my room yet, have I? The Wardroom, you know is where all officers below the Captain of the ship, and above midshipmen, mess. The State rooms are on each side, and the space between (called the "Country") is the dining and sitting room, and quite a large nice room it is on board such a ship as this. The "Line officers" have the rooms on the starboard side, in the order of their rank, the senior having the forward room; on the port side are the Chief Engineer, Surgeons, Paymaster, Marine Officers & Chaplain; all called "Idlers" (except the Engineer) because they keep no watch, and have but little to do generally. My room is the third; Lieut-Comdr Grafton, our Executive officer has the first; and Lieut Comdr Queen the second. I will give you the deck plan of my "Castle."

The berth (1) extends the whole length of the room; underneath it are two tiers of drawers, and over it against the ship's side are shelves for books &c., fitted into the ships timbers. (2) is the bureau, the top drawer of which is fitted up very nicely as a writing desk, with seven small drawers for stationery and four pigeon holes for papers; the front turns down for the desk. (3) is the wash-stand which can be shut up close when at sea; (4) the chronometer chest, which, being the navigation, I keep in my room; and the top of which serves as a (small) sofa. (5) is the door opening into the "Country" which has as few *rural* charms as you can well imagine. The door and most of that side are made of open work, for ventilation, with curtains that can be drawn at pleasure. I have one window (dead light) through the ship's side, which I can keep open in fair weather, and with smooth sea. Two of the ship's enormous oaken knees and one beam, project into the upper part of the room, and around them are places for stowing charts and other articles, and there is a sword rack against the after bulkhead. There is no room lost, you see, and not much to lose. An arm chair completes the furniture, my servant Augustus has charge of everything except my writing desk, and keeps things, as neat as possible, and in nice order. Don't you envy me a *little*? I am sure you *do* though you will *say*, no doubt, that you would rather drift about in a large room ashore. You have never cruised in a Midshipmen's steerage or you would appreciate the comfort of even a *small* room. One of the drawers of my desk is devoted to *your* letters, and I always carry one of your photographs in my pocket. . . .

Tuesday Evening
March 24, 1863

My letter was suddenly interrupted last evening by the appearance of the "orderly" with "The Admiral wishes to see you, Sir"—a message he brings me about twenty times a day. The Admiral gave me orders to go down to the Roads this morning at six o'clock, with Commander Totten, of the Brandywine,[1] to hold a survey on the Bark "Edisto" and U.S.S. Wyandotte[2] to ascertain the amount of damage received by each vessel in a collision that occurred between them, and to ascertain who was to blame for the accident. We surveyed the two vessels and examined their officers; and then went on board the Brandywine. I wrote the report of the Survey while the Capt. smoked, and his clerk made two copies while we dined, and tied them up in red tape. Capt. Totten has been over forty years in the service, is the author of "Totten's Naval Text Book," and a sailor of the old stamp—bluff and hearty, kind

1. Benjamin J. Totten (1806–77), who commanded the 44-gun sailing frigate USS *Brandywine,* which had been launched in 1825.

2. The *Edisto* was a merchant ship and the USS *Wyandotte* a screw gunboat (built in 1853) carrying seven guns.

hearted and pompous, and fond of his pipe and his "grog" (when ashore for you know we have *none* now, on board ship). He is a very pleasant old gentleman, and I like him very much. . . .

Every where you see officers and soldiers in all sorts of uniforms, contrabands and waggon trains—quite a different state of affairs from the time when "Old Point Comfort" was such a favorite Summer resort and fair ladies and gallant gentlemen wandered over the peaceful battlements of the Fortress. . . .

Roswell to Kate

USS *Minnesota*
Hampton Roads
March 29, 1863

. . . Everything is going on as usual you see I have become so accustomed to change that I am always at home, and it seems as though I had been on board a long time. I drill once and generally twice a day, and the rest of the time am employed on staff duty. Yesterday and day before I was on surveys of ships. The Executive Officer often asks me wether I belong to the ship or the staff, but I have not been able to find out yet, but *do* whatever is *to be done*. Yesterday the Massachusetts[1] came in from Port Royal, and I met a couple of old shipmates on board. In the recent attack on Fort McAllister our ironclads were very roughly handled; the Montauk had to be hauled up on the beach for repairs and the Passaic had her deck badly smashed in. The papers you remember had extravagant accounts of the "crucial test." It is not publicly known that they were damaged. This will delay the attack on Charleston for some weeks.[2] . . .

1. A screw steamer built in 1860, acquired by the Navy in 1861, and converted to a five-gun warship.
2. The USS *Montauk* and USS *Passaic* were single-turreted ironclads that were part of the fleet being assembled to attack Fort Sumter and Charleston. This attack on Fort McAllister on March 3 was the third such effort as a trial run for the big effort against Charleston. The outcome deepened the reservations in Rear Admiral Du Pont's mind about the wisdom of attacking Charleston's forts, but pressure from the Navy Department and public opinion forced him to go ahead, with unhappy results for the fleet on April 7, 1863 (including the sinking of the ironclad *Keokuk*), a failure that led to Du Pont's removal from command.

This afternoon Dr. Jones and my self went on shore at Newport News, and rode out a little ways into the country on some horses kindly furnished us by Col. Hawkins (of Hawkins' Zouaves).[1] We visited the soldiers burying ground and among the graves saw those of some of the Cumberland sailors. "Killed on board the Cumberland March 8, 1862." Never did men fight better or show more heroic devotion to the flag. I hope their example will be emulated throughout the Navy.

Roswell to Katie

> USS *Minnesota*
> Hampton Roads
> April 2, 1863

. . . A Flag-Lieut. is the Admiral's aid, signal officer for the fleet, and has charge of certain departments of supply. It is a confidential appointment. I am doing most of the duties, and the Admiral says he will appoint me Flag Lieut. as soon as he can get another Lieut. for the ship. . . .

Do not fear my having too much *to do*; I like to do all I can, and certainly no one should complain of too much *duty* in such times as these. I only regret that I cannot accomplish *more*; for there is much to be done to bring this ship up to my ideas of drill and discipline. Our Executive officer, Lieut-Com'd'r Grafton is a very *pleasant* man, but has not energy and force enough to control *well* so many men, and the discipline and effectiveness of a ship depend on the Ex. Officer. He is quite an accomplished Officer, but one of those men who cannot *rise to meet* difficulties, and who have but little steadiness and not much industry. Sometimes when things do not go exactly right he says in the most resigned manner—"Oh! well, I cannot help it"—when a little energy and firmness is all that is needed to enforce the *best* discipline.

I do not mean that there is anything *very* slack or irregular on board, but in every particular the ship is *several* degrees below the Wabash. The ship is not so clean, the men are not so neat, nor so orderly, nor so well drilled. There is not that *high* state of effectiveness that there

1. Rush Christopher Hawkins (1831–1920), colonel of the famous 9th New York, a "Zouave" regiment known for its good fighting.

ought to be on board a man-of-war and which can only be attained by making every man know *all* his duty and *do* it. I had not been on the Gun Deck five minutes till I saw that the men were disposed to see *how far* they could go, in committing little irregularities; talking at their quarters, and other small breaches of discipline, some of which I understood, had been allowed. In a week, the Captain said there had been more improvement in the Gun deck than "in a year before," and all the division officers said the men did much better, handled the guns quicker, and *took more interest in the drills.* You can do *anything* with Sailors if you manage them right.

I do get more than "a little out of patience" sometimes, but I always *try* to control myself, and I *very rarely* speak angrily to a man, *never* in terms of reproach or derision; and there is *nothing* that makes me so *much* out of patience as to hear an officer *abuse* a man. I do not *allow* one of my officers to do it.

I have punished but one man, who in less time than I can write it found himself in double irons for four days, on bread and water. As I told you the men were disposed to see how far they could go, and this man failing to profit quick enough by a very kind admonition I gave him was put in charge of the Master-at-arms, and confined in irons.

The effect was instantanious throughout the deck, and I have had but little trouble since. We have a great many men in the Navy now, from the merchant service whose manners need mending; an old man-of-war's man is generally a gentleman in his orderly manners and behavior. I wish you *could* see my "kingdom"; you would see as fine a battery as there is afloat any where, and one which I *hope* will do something for our country and its good cause, more than once again.

This evening we have been having some music in the Wardroom, and very good music too. Our lieut. of Marines plays the violin quite well, and one of the sailors plays exquisitely; so we sent for him and the two played some beautiful pieces. The Major of Marines, to the astonishment of all, sang *part* of a song; stopping, he said, only because we laughed at him so much. Capt. Queen distinguished himself in like manner, and the rest of us whistled. At "Eight bells" we piped belay, some sat down by the wardroom table to read and some went to their rooms to write, and the major talked politics as usual, though no one paid any attention unless to laugh at some of his droll remarks. . . .

Roswell to Kate

USS *Minnesota*
Off Newport News
April 9, 1863

. . . The crew has never been organized into infantry companies, or for landing, and I have had it all to do, besides the drilling; it is nearly completed now; and we shall soon be able to land a battalion of four companies (three hundred men) and a field battery of four howitzers with one hundred men. The men are making fine progress, and the Captain has complimented me several times on improvement in the drills. I have got the volunteer officers to take more interest in them and give them lessons in tactics &c. Our Executive Officer is not at all the man for such a ship as this; I hear that he will be relieved soon, and for the good of the ship I hope he will be, though he has treated me with the greatest kindness and has expressed himself very much pleased with what I have done. It requires no small amount of steady patience and industry, with a good knowledge of human nature, and a high professional knowledge to organize a man-of-war such as this, and keep her up to the high standard of discipline an American ship should attain to.

I was called before six o'clock this morning and I have been busy ever since, except at lunch and was called away from dinner twice. All the flag of truce boats going up or down have to report to me, have their orders &c examined before they can pass. To-day there have been three going up with prisoners, and two coming down with our released soldiers.[1] One of them brought a copy of the Richmond Dispatch of to-day. In it are several reports from Charleston which say the attack was commenced on the afternoon of the 7th inst. and continued from three to five. All our ironclads were inside the bar, but the Keokuk had been *sunk* and the Ironsides disabled. The attack was discontinued. In

---

1. In 1862 the Union and Confederate armed forces had signed a cartel for the exchange of prisoners of war. One of the principal points of exchange was City Point on the James River near Petersburg, so boats carrying Union and Confederate prisoners for exchange were constantly going up and down the James River.

Fort Sumpter one man was killed and several wounded, and in Moultrie one gun was dismounted. Beauregard's official dispatch says "the Keokuk is certainly sunk off Morris Island," but he generally has little regard for the truth that no dependence is to be placed in any thing he reports.[1]

I *hope* it is not true but if it is that *Forrest* is safe. I do not believe the news as reported but I cannot help feeling anxious and *sad*. We shall no doubt hear certainly in a few days.[2] . . .

I have told you something of our Mess arrangements, from which you may not have a very high opinion of our *housekeeping*, but I hope you will suspend your judgment till you hear how *I* succeed for I have been unanimously elected to preside over the Mess. I was very unwilling to undertake it, as well because I have had no experience except in the Midshipmen's Mess, as because I am almost the youngest member of the Mess, and have already as much as I can well attend to. Capt Queen, Dr. Wood, urged it so strongly that I finally consented and am housekeeping in earnest. I have a Steward and Assistant Steward, two Cooks and nine Servants, and reign *supreme* in everything relating to them, the Wardroom and the Mess.

I'll write you all about how I get along, the dishes I order &c. What an invaluable messmate I'll make will I not? . . .

---◆---

SOON AFTER HE wrote the preceding letter, Lamson's career took a sudden turn. He was given command of a small flotilla of gunboats to assist troops of the Union army in operations along the Nansemond

1. The reports this time were mainly true. The *Keokuk* sank the day after the attack on April 7 from the pounding she took. The USS *New Ironsides*, an experimental ironclad much larger than the *Monitor*, built in 1862 to traditional design with 20 guns in broadside, was hit more than 50 times in the attack on Fort Sumter and suffered much damage, but did not sink. General Pierre Gustave Toutant Beauregard (1818–93) commanded the Confederate defenses of Charleston. He was flamboyant and prone to exaggeration, as Lamson suggests, but this time his jubilant report of a punishing repulse of the Union fleet was justified.

2. Lieutenant Morreau Forrest, Lamson's roommate at the Naval Academy, was an officer on the *Keokuk*; he was not injured in the battle.

River, a stream that flows into the James from the south about twenty miles upriver from Norfolk. The principal town on the Nansemond was Suffolk, and these operations became known as the Suffolk campaign. It began when Confederate authorities, alarmed by reports of the transfer of IX Corps to Newport News, expected a Union movement up the south bank of the James toward Petersburg. Lee detached Lieutenant-General James Longstreet (1821–1904) with two crack divisions from the Army of Northern Virginia to counter this anticipated thrust. When most of the IX Corps went to Kentucky instead, Longstreet converted his defensive operations into an offensive probe against Suffolk. Union troops in this area were generally second-class units under second-class commanders, specifically Brigadier-General John J. Peck (1821–78). With his own two divisions plus one other, Longstreet had about 20,000 men (not 35,000 as Lamson mentions in the next letter); Union forces were reinforced to nearly 25,000 men during April, aided by the navy in the manner described by Lamson's letters. Longstreet failed to capture Suffolk; Peck failed to prevent Longstreet's troops from gathering much-needed food and forage in the area that were forwarded to Lee's army along the Rappahannock. Events culminating in the battle of Chancellorsville caused Lee to recall Longstreet and his two divisions, which ended the Suffolk campaign in early May.

————•◦•————

Roswell to Kate

> USS *Mount Washington*[1]
> Nansemond River, off
> Suffolk
> April 12, 1863

. . . I have not time now to tell you how I came here, but I am here in command of our gunboats to assist Gen. Peck who is attacked by a large rebel force estimated at thirty-five thousand men, who are attacking him in front, and attempting to cross this way and get in his

1. A sidewheel steamboat built in 1846 as the *Mount Vernon*. The navy bought her and changed her name in 1861 and mounted a 32-pound smoothbore cannon on the bow. Her shallow draft made her ideal for river operations.

rear and cut off his communication with Norfolk, which would be fatal to him as no supplies have been kept here but brought from Norfolk as needed. Gen. Peck desired the Admiral to send as many gun boats as he could into the river to prevent the rebels from crossing, or building batteries upon it, and to defend one side of the town, and he sent me up this morning to command them. I have four here now and expect some more to-morrow. Our troops number [15,000] and are most strongly entrenched the only danger is that the rebels may get *between them and Norfolk*; Gen Peck has information that Gen. Hill is marching from the southward for this purpose.[1]

This morning the rebels appeared in strong force on the Somerton and White Marsh Roads, drove in our pickets and captured twenty of our cavalry. Our drum beat the long roll, and our forces were ready to receive them, but by three they had disappeared except their skirmishers, and Gen Peck is of opinion that they are trying to get in his rear. All the artillery has been withdrawn from this side of the town and sent to the front. The Gen said he depended on the gunboats to defend this side and keep the river open—which is more than ought to be assigned to us, but he seems to think "gun boats" can do any thing even in a narrow stream where it is more difficult to maneuver than to fight them. I was out to the point of our lines this morning and saw the last of our pickets driven in by the rebels. It was quite an exciting scene, the drums beating the long roll, the Infantry falling in or marching to the different works, and the artillery and cavalry hurrying to their positions. Gen. Peck was injured yesterday by his horse falling and was in a carriage driving from point to point, with aids and guard galloping after. I arranged with him the positions the gun boats were to occupy, and then returned on board made the signal to clear for action and beat to quarters. Orderlies from time to time have reported what was going on but there has only been some skirmishing. . . .

9 o'clock. I have just been down to the lowest gun boat to give the captain some orders for the night—I could write to you *all* night, dear, but I must get a little sleep for I have had none for almost forty-eight hours, and have been at work all the time.

---

1. Major-General Daniel Harvey Hill (1821–99), commander of Confederate troops in North Carolina. The report of his approach toward Suffolk was unfounded.

Roswell to Kate

> USS *Mount Washington*
> Nansemond River
> Six miles below Suffolk
> 11:30 p.m., April 13, 1863

I must write you a few lines this evening to let you know that I am safe and well. This fore noon I rec'd several dispatches from the Gen. saying the enemy were coming in on the road I was to guard, and I sent one of the gun boats down the river to reconnoitre. The rebels did not appear till about three o'clock when I opened fire upon them from this and the other boats. They had disappeared in some woods when Maj. Gen. Key[e]s, Commanding this Department, sent to ask if I could take himself and staff down the river.[1] The rebels had extended their line from the road and had posted a large number of riflemen in a point of woods below. As we came opposite this point they opened a very sharp fire upon us which we returned with as much good will from our guns with canister and shrapnel. The rebels were in the bushes and behind logs and trees, while we were much more exposed on the decks; at some places they were only a few yards distant, and the balls sung and whistled and struck like hail stones. I counted the marks of eight that struck within three feet of where I was standing, and one just passed my side, striking within a few inches. Several of the men say they saw them aim at me a number of times; probably they saw my uniform. The men behaved *splendidly*, and worked the guns during the hottest of the fire. Gen. Key[e]s complimented them most highly. There is nothing like an *American Sailor* for true grit, at least I think so: I would stake my life on their faithfulness. The Gen. being a passenger and having nothing to do went to a safe place, where he could see but not be exposed. Our loss is two killed and three wounded, the latter not seriously.

I immediately started up again, but one of my boats was unfortunate enough to get aground, and it got so dark that the pilots could not see the channel. This river is very narrow and crooked, and the greatest care is necessary to get a vessel through it at all. I shall go up at day-

---

1. Major-General Erasmus Darwin Keyes (1810–95).

light in the morning, when we may have another chance at the rebels. The fight lasted for about half an hour, and was as hot a fire as I have ever been under. The rebels must have lost quite a number as several were seen to fall and roll down the bank.

My own opinion has been that this attack is but a feint to prevent us from sending reinforcements to North Carolina where our troops are hard pressed.[1] The enemy has a large force, and will attack without doubt if they have a good opportunity or if they can cross this river. To-day was a good day for them as a slight rain last night [settled] the dust, and so aided to conceal their movements.

What horrid work this is, it makes me heart sick to think of the condition our once happy country is in.

Good night, *dear* Katie, I think of you always, and you help me to do my duty. When there is most danger you are nearest to me.

Roswell to Kate

> USS *Mt. Washington*
> Nansemond River
> 8:00 p.m. April 14, 1863

I am well and safe, have been fighting rebel batteries from 6½ this morning till 6 this evening. The rebels fired into my engines and exploded one of my boilers.

The Mt. Washington is a wreck of splinters. I shall have her towed down with the wounded, and I shall remain on board the "Stepping Stones."[2]

---

1. A reference to fighting between Confederates and the Union forces based in New Berne, North Carolina. Lamson was wrong on both counts. The Confederate attack on Suffolk was not a feint, and by the time he wrote these words the Northerners at New Berne were more than holding their own and had gone on the offensive.

2. USS *Stepping Stones*, a six-gun sidewheel steamer built in 1861. The action that Lamson describes had occurred when the two gunboats *Mount Washington* and *Stepping Stones* tried to run past a newly constructed Confederate earthwork on the Nansemond that appeared to contain nothing but riflemen. The gunboats shelled the works briefly and then started to steam past them, whereupon the Confederates wheeled seven artillery pieces out of the woods and opened fire at a range of 400 yards. After taking a shot through the boiler the *Mount Washington* drifted downriver and ran aground, giving enemy artillery a stationary target. The *Stepping Stones* finally towed

Do not be alarmed for me dear Katie for the worst is over. I would not write this but fear you will hear in some other way. I may not be able to send letters every day but will do so as often as possible.

You have helped me to do my duty to-day.

Lieutenant Roswell H. Lamson's report to Rear-Admiral Samuel P. Lee, Commanding North Atlantic Blockading Squadron, dated "Off Wood Yard, Nansemond River, Va., April 19, 1863, 8 a.m."*

Sir: The expedition I proposed for last night comprised two columns, one to land up the river and attempt to get in rear of the battery by the route proposed for the expedition of the night of the 16th instant. When they had thoroughly alarmed the enemy in his rear, I was to run this vessel, with 500 men on board, right under the upper end of the batteries and land them, with four of my howitzers, worked by my own men, who were to have assistance in dragging them up the bank. The landing place can not be touched by a single one of their guns and it is only a few yards into the works. General Peck sent for me to ride up to Suffolk yesterday morning to arrange the affair, and the entire direction of it was given to me. The Eighth Regiment Connecticut Volunteers, under Colonel Ward, were to go up the river in the *Coeur de Lion,* Captain Brown,[1] and parts of the Thirteenth Indiana Volunteers and Eighty-ninth New York, under Colonels Dobbs and England, were to be embarked on this vessel. I arranged a system of signals with Lieutenant Cushing,[2] so that I could draw his fire and

---

her out of range, after a fierce duel between the Confederate guns and another Union gunboat that came to Lamson's aid had left five Union sailors killed and fourteen wounded. Confederate casualties are unknown. This affair prompted Lamson's plan to capture the principal Confederate fortification on the river, Fort Huger, described in the following letters.

O.R. Navies, ser. I, vol. 8, pp. 740–41.

1. USS *Coeur de Lion,* a sidewheel steamer built in 1853 as a lighthouse tender and acquired by the navy in 1861. Commanded by Acting Master Charles H. Brown, she carried three guns.

2. Lieutenant William Barker Cushing (1842–75), commanding the seven-gun sidewheel gunboat USS *Commodore Barney.* Cushing had been one year ahead of Lamson at the Naval Academy and rivaled Lamson as one of the best and most aggressive young officers in the Union navy. He and Lamson became good friends as a result of their cooperation in the Suffolk campaign.

direct it to any point I desired; my other gunboats were to cover the landing in front and take a position in the bend above, where they could pour in an effective fire.

The plan was perfectly feasible and only required promptness and determination to succeed without much loss. My vessels were all ready and at the wharf for the troops; the commanders had received their instructions, and the guns ready for landing at the proper time, but the troops did not arrive till almost two hours after. I embarked the 200 on the *Coeur de Lion*, but it was so late before the others were ready that we could not have reached the battery before broad daylight. I told General Getty[1] that I thought it was too late, but I would proceed if he desired. He said he would say nothing about it; that the expedition was mine. I thought it would not be prudent to attack in broad daylight, and so sent the men ashore to wait till to-night.

I have examined the position thoroughly; it is the key to the river, and unless it is taken our boats must run down in the night. They are not putting in any more artillery, but from the bend above I can get an enfilading fire and have forced them to abandon one of their earth-works and move farther down. I have had officers climb the highest trees commanding a view of it, and have been to every point where the battery can be seen to advantage. If I had 200 sailors I am confident it would not have annoyed us so long. I shall make the attempt to-night unless the army fails the third time, and shall guide the column myself.

Since I came here I have not ceased to urge upon General Getty the high importance of taking and occupying this point, for if we once get the enemy out of his pits, 100 men and a couple of boats can keep him out. The general has approved everything I have said, but for some reason his officers have failed to do their part; ours has been done exactly as I told them I would do.

We have fought the rebels every day since last Sunday, except to-day, with a heavy loss compared to our force, and the army have lain on their bank or in their earthworks without a man hurt, and have utterly failed to render me the assistance and support they ought to have given. . . .

If we take the battery all is secure. I am most anxious to do so, as

---

1. Brigadier-General George Washington Getty (1819–1901), commanding a division in VII Corps at this time.

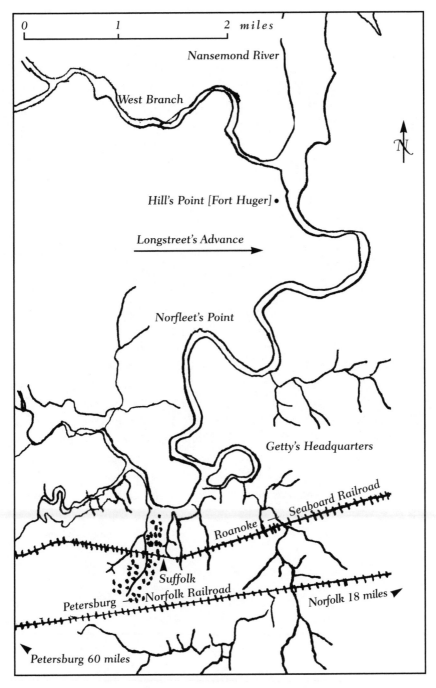

Operations on the Nansemond River, April 1863

well on account of the advantage of the position as a great desire to send you one of the guns that was used against the *Mount Washington*. . . .

———•———

AT DUSK ON April 19 four gunboats commanded by Lamson carrying two infantry regiments (8th Connecticut and 89th New York) did carry out the surprise attack on the Confederate earthwork named Fort Huger, capturing 161 prisoners (Lamson's count) and five artillery pieces. It was a brilliant action for which Lamson earned great praise from the top army as well as navy commanders.

Acting Rear-Admiral Samuel Phillips Lee, April 25, 1863: "I would respectfully draw the attention of the [Navy] Department to the conduct of Lieutenant Lamson in planning and, with the important co-operation of the troops under Brigadier-General Getty, effecting the capture of a battery of five guns and about 130 men on Hill's Point, which commanded the communications between the upper and lower Nansemond, and which had severely harassed (and in one instance entirely disabled) the little vessels of our flotilla."*

Major-General John A. Dix, commanding the Department of Virginia, to Major-General Henry Wager Halleck, General in Chief of the Union armies, May 23, 1863: "My thanks are due to Admiral Lee, who co-operated by means of his gunboats in preventing the enemy from crossing the Nansemond, and to Lieutenants Cushing, Lamson, and [Acting Master T. A.] Harris [commanding the *Stepping Stones* in Lamson's little flotilla], who displayed great coolness, gallantry, and good judgment in the management of their vessels. Lieutenant Lamson deserves particular mention as having suggested the capture of the battery on the river and having aided Gen. Getty in carrying the plan into execution."**

———•———

*O.R. Navies, ser. I, vol. 8, p. 775.
**War of the Rebellion: Official Records of the Union and Confederate Armies, ser. I, vol. 18, p. 270.

Roswell to Kate

Suffolk, Va.
April 24, 1863

... Yesterday evening I came up to confer with Gen. Peck and finding that Gen. Corcoran[1] was going out to attack the enemy I volunteered on his staff and have just come out of the 8th fight I have had with the rebels since the 12th Inst. Our loss to-day was about forty killed and wounded. This is the first time I have seen our soldiers in action; the men behaved very well, but Corcoran is *very* little of a general. You have no doubt seen accounts of our capturing the rebel battery last Sunday evening. I planned the whole affair gave every order that was given, and landed with the storming party with four of my howitzers manned by my sailors. Gen. Getty did not give an order during the whole affair, but sat in the cabin of the Stepping Stones till we had the battery. It is well known here who did it, and I have been complimented for the affair more than I should like to tell you, but the reporters here are all under the control of the army, and so nothing is said about it. After our success Gen. Getty came up to me, took me by both hands, and said in the presence of his officers and mine, "Mr Lamson the whole credit of this success is due to you, who planned and executed it," repeating it several times. The Sword of one of the Commanders of the enemy's force was sent to the Admiral by Gen Getty and he refused to keep it saying that I was entitled to it. I have never seen men so devoid of Common justice, and of all generosity as these army Generals. When you know the circumstances you will not wonder that I speak so strongly. *Everything* that has been done (till to-day) has been done by the Navy gunboats under Lieut Cushing and myself. Friday the army had a little fight but accomplished *nothing* and the enemy this evening occupy again the ground they were on this morning. Gen Peck told his generals this evening that I had done more fighting than any other man since the attack on Suffolk and yet in the dispatches it is the *army* who have done everything. It is so well known here that he cannot speak otherwise. We have lost *one seventh* of our men in the gun boat fleet killed and wounded and one boat completely

1. Brigadier-General Michael Corcoran (1827-63), commanding a brigade in VII Corps. Later that year he died accidentally when a horse fell on him.

shot to pieces. Our sailors have done some of the most desperate fighting of this or any other war. I have the ball that struck me on the 14th Inst. and will have it set for you to wear on your watch chain. My arm is almost well again. I have not had time to write to you what I was doing: having been as busy as I could be day and night. For ten days I did not have two hours sleep during the twenty four, I will send you copies of my reports, &c, as soon as possible. When the danger is over here I shall return to the Minnesota.

I think of you all the time dearest Katie, and it makes me braver and truer to my duty. You have supported me many times in most trying circumstances. I *do love you*, sweet Katie, and your love and approbation is worth more to me than *all* else. I think of you when the balls whistle around, and I am never so weary that I do not wish I could get to *you*. You are the pole star to which I ever look, and if I can *serve my country* and win your approbation, I shall count all toil and danger, and vexations, as of small moment. . . .

What a dreadful war this is—Countrymen against each other; and brother against brother. I *only* wish I could do more towards ending it. We *must* crush the rebels, the old flag *must* again wave over our whole country. I shall try to do my duty God helping me and Katie loving me.

I am staying at Gen Peck's Head Quarters tonight; he read me his dispatch in which he compliments me in a manner that I cannot repeat I will send you a copy of his official report.[1] . . .

Roswell to Kate

USS *Stepping Stones*
Nansemond River
April 30, 1863

I am very weary this evening, but I *must* write you a few lines to thank you for your dear letter of the 19th Inst. . . . Your letter was written on the day we captured the rebel battery at Hill's Point; and perhaps you were writing to me while we were storming the works; I

---

1. Peck's report, and a subsequent longer one on the whole campaign, states that Lamson "played a brilliant part" in the operation and describes him as "one of the most gallant officers in the U.S. navy" (*O.R. Armies*, ser. I, vol. 18, pp. 276, 281).

thought of you, and wished you could see our flags planted on the parapet. . . .

On the morning of the 14th April, I started to return to Suffolk, and on the way up engaged a rebel battery at Norfleet's Point which blew up my boilers, and I drifted ashore under their fire; this vessel towed me off, but in crossing the bar off the West Branch the Mount Washington grounded, and the rebels immediately opened upon me with ten pieces of artillery, and two or three-hundred sharpshooters. This was at 11 a.m., and I fought them till 6 p.m. We have since captured the officer who put their guns in position and he says four of his pieces were permanently disabled and that their loss was quite heavy. I wish you could have seen the Mount Washington after the action. Her boilers, cylinders, and steam drums pierced and ten shells went through the smoke pipe, and the rest of the machinery much damaged. Her pilot house riddled, wheelropes shot away, and her decks and bulwarks completely splintered, everyone who has seen her says there has not been another vessel so shot to pieces during the war. The flag-staff was shot away, and when the flag fell into the water, the rebs cheered exultingly; but they did not enjoy it long before we had the dear old stars and stripes waving over us again, with every one more determined than ever to fight them to the last timber of the vessel. Master's Mate Birtwistle, and Seaman Theilbery went with me on the upper deck, and helped me haul up the flag staff by the ensign halliards, raise it, and lash it to the stump that was still standing. It was only through the kind providence of God that we were not all killed or wounded; I saw a number of escapes that seemed almost miraculous. After the action was over, the sailors gathered around me on the deck, took hold of my hands and arms, threw their arms around me, and I saw tears starting from eyes that had looked the rebel battery in the face unflinchingly.

That evening I sent the Mt Washington with the killed and wounded on board down to the flag ship, in tow of a transport that had come up and came on board this vessel. I had eaten nothing during the twenty four hours, and was hungry and weary enough; the first action commenced before breakfast, and there was no time to cook afterwards. About the middle of the afternoon one of the men brought me a plate of bread and meat, but knowing that he had had nothing to eat, and that most of the men had not I distributed it amongst them.

Gen. Longstreet's plan appeared to be to cross this river, and get between Gen. Peck at Suffolk and Norfolk, from which place he gets his supplies. I think Longstreets force is greatly overestimated by Gens. Peck and Dix, who are very much alarmed, and continually talk of the enemy's "massing in front." The only *fighting* has been done on the Nansemond, and the enemy has *never* showed himself in *any* strong force, at any other point. The army have been digging like gophers, and have a line of entrenchments of sixteen or eighteen miles in extent with redoubts and batteries at all assailable points. The army lie behind their works and *imagine* they are surrounded by an overwhelming force. Gen Corcoran's sally is the only offensive movement they have made, and that amounted to nothing. I never saw such childish actions as I have witnessed here. Four times, the army have failed to cooperate with me in movements that had been *agreed* upon, and without any reason for their failure. I no longer wonder that we are not successful in crushing out the rebellion. I told Gen. Getty yesterday that I was tired of being disappointed of *promised* cooperation. I have not failed in a single instance to do just as I told them I would do.

This morning Gen. Getty sent a request that I would come to his head quarters to arrange a movement against the enemy. We went to Gen. Peck and arranged for a "reconnaissance in force." Gen. Getty will command the force, and I hope something will be accomplished. I could tell you of some army movements that are so absurd you would hardly believe any "General" would order, but which have been ordered by "Generals" who figure most conspicuously in the papers.

May 1, Evening

. . . We are having beautiful moonlight nights now, and if you will come and spend a couple of hours you shall have a row by moonlight in a "gig" manned by blue-jackets. My "fleet" look very pretty anchored in "line ahead," and I *know* what they can do, and what they *will* do for the "Stars and Stripes." I have only to *wish* anything done, and it is accomplished. I have had the pleasure of handing their promotions to two of my officers for "gallant conduct in the face of the enemy" during the fight on the 14th. . . . I have received most flattering letters from the Secretary of the Navy, from Admiral Lee, Senator Grimes, and others.[1]

1. Admiral Lee's official letter to Lamson, dated April 29, 1863, praised his "courage, skill, and energy" and concluded: "The naval forces have well sustained themselves in the trying circumstances in which they have been placed, and borne themselves in a manner deserving commendation. It gives me pleasure to inform you of the approval

Roswell to Kate

USS *Teaser*[1]
Nansemond River
May 3, 1863

I have just a moment to write you dearest before the dispatch boat goes down to the Admiral. This morning Gen Getty advanced against the enemy with three columns one of which crossed here and has been driven back by the enemy, and we have been protecting their rear. The Commander of the column is on board and says his men behaved "shamefully." We sent a boat howitzer and sixteen sailors ashore to support, and they did more fighting than a whole regiment of soldiers. We have been listening all the afternoon to Gen Getty's artillery, but wether he is advancing or is driven back we cannot tell though we think he is successful. This is the second Sunday we have spent in this way. . . . I have seen a number of Rebel prisoners to-day, rough looking fellows, but good fighters; they were in the battery that fought the Mt. Washington and say they thought they would capture her without failing when she got aground.

Dear Katie I do love you most dearly, and my heart is always with you. My Country and my Katie are the objects of my devotion next to our Heavenly Father.

---

by the Department of your gallant conduct, and I desire you to have this letter read on the quarterdeck of each of the vessels which have born [a] part in the naval operations referred to" (*O.R. Navies*, ser. I, vol. 8, p. 782). It is not clear which letter from Secretary of the Navy Gideon Welles Lamson refers to here. He did receive such a letter dated May 4; it is reprinted in note 1 to Lamson's letter of May 8. James W. Grimes (1816–72) was a senator from Iowa who had known Lamson's family when they lived in Iowa. He was an influential Republican and a member of the Senate Naval Affairs Committee.

1. Ex-CSS *Teaser*, a shallow-draft screw gunboat captured by Union forces on the James River after she was disabled in action on July 4, 1862, and armed with one 32-pounder rifled gun.

Kate to Roswell

Mt. Vernon, Ohio
May 7, 1863

Your dear good letter of April 30th came yesterday. I was very glad
to hear from you again of your safety and of your *love*. It always makes
me so glad when you tell me that, not that I can doubt it but—I like
to hear it again. You have indeed been in great danger and I am afraid
you still are, but how faithfully God is taking care of you. I do thank
Him for it, and pray that he will watch over you all the time.

. . . It must have been very pleasant to be able to give promotions
to your officers. I think some one ought to give you one too, I am sure
none can deserve it more, and I shall think the Government is very
unjust and ungrateful if they do not promote you.

This is a rainy dreary day out doors, but we are hearing so much
good news that it is bright enough within and we do not notice the
weather. Our news from the Rappahannock if it only proves true is
very encouraging.[1] If he succeeds in conquering Lee (and it will be a
disgrace to the country if he does not) it does seem as though the
rebels could not hold out much longer. The news that delights us most
though just now is that of the arrest of Vallandigham.[2] He was to be
tried in Cincinnati today, and when convicted (as he certainly will be)
he will be sent beyond the lines, Mr. Harper, our Copperhead neighbor
went last night to Cin. to plead in his favor. I hope they will keep him

1. A reference to initial optimistic reports of the battle of Chancellorsville, in which
Union commander Joseph Hooker got around the flank of Lee's forces at Fredericksburg, but then yielded the initiative and lost the battle to Lee. Later references in this
letter to subsequent reports about Chancellorsville show how fragmentary and contra-
dictory were the first newspaper dispatches about Civil War battles. But when the
dust finally settled, everyone in the North realized that Chancellorsville had been a
humiliating defeat.

2. Clement L. Vallandigham, leader of the Northern Peace Democrats or "Copperheads," who had been arrested at Dayton, Ohio, by order of General Ambrose Burnside. He was subsequently tried by court-martial and convicted of treason for his
disloyal speeches; as Kate predicted, Lincoln commuted his sentence of imprisonment
to one of banishment to Confederate lines. Vallandigham went to Canada, was nominated *in absentia* as the Democratic candidate for governor of Ohio, but lost the
election in the fall.

too, and if they would only arrest Mr Cox[1] I should be satisfied. But he is to[o] cautious to expose himself to any danger, and is very careful to do or say nothing that can be proved as betraying his sympathy with the South. How *can* men be such traitors to their country! They must have fallen very low to be capable of it. You see *some* "Army Generals" can do something Burnside arrested Vallandigham. . . .

We have just had a dispatch from the foundry. Eb sent it up "We are beaten on the Rappahannock—Hooker is trying to recross the river there will be terrible slaughter"—Oh! what will become of our poor country! and whose fault is it? I surely thought Hooker would have been victorious this time. It has taken the brightness away, we are all a good deal depressed, but there is *hope* left yet. We may be reinforced, and conquer them yet; or there may be different news in the morning. What would we do without hope. But there is no such thing as giving up. Right *must* triumph in the end, but oh, how far off that end seems. These sad tidings make me long so to see you dearest; it would be such a comfort, but now it seems as though the time must be indefinitely prolonged before you can come again. I know you are doing your duty, and nobly—I would not for the world have you leave it for me, but I shall be *so* glad when it is so that you can come. What terrible sins our country must have committed that they should be punished so terribly.

Mother says I must give you her love and tell you she is so nearly distracted by the news that she cannot say any more. Mother always gets discouraged so easily. She says she hardly cares whether she lives or dies now—but I do not want to die yet; brighter times must come some time. . . .

Friday morning

Eb has just come up and brought us better news, contradicting entirely the statements of yesterday, except that of Hooker's crossing the river which they say was done on account of the rising of the river as a matter of prudence. We have of course had nothing official yet; as the telegraph lines between him and Washington are supposed to be cut, to prevent his movements being prematurely made known—but anything is better than the word that came yesterday. Perhaps I am telling you only what you knew before. But my thoughts are so full of what

1. Samuel S. Cox, a Democratic congressman from Ohio whose brand of Copperheadism was less extreme than Vallandigham's.

may now be taking place that I can think of nothing else, except of *you*, where my "thinkings" always begin and end.

I see by the papers that the Nansemond river is cleared of rebel batteries, and the rebel army has gone so I suppose you will soon be back to the Minnesota. I hope then you can rest and recruit a little, for you must be quite worn out. . . .

Roswell to Kate

> USS *Minnesota*
> Off Newport News
> May 8, 1863

. . . As you have no doubt learned from the papers Longstreet has retreated from before Suffolk and may have joined Lee by this time. Our fight last Sunday was with his rear guard, and on Monday morning the rebel forces had all disappeared. I went through their camps and around their lines, and was astonished to find them so strong—much stronger than our works around Suffolk. Their plan evidently was to have an impregnable line in front of Suffolk, and then to throw a heavy force across the Nansemond, cut off Gen. Peck's communications and force him out to fight them on their own ground.

They lost heavily in their attempt to cross the river, and Hooker's advance called them to defend Richmond. If our army would follow them from Suffolk, it would at least keep a large portion of Longstreets army to defend the line of the Blackwater, and deprive Lee of so many reinforcements.

I came down yesterday, and reported for duty on board. I met with a most cordial welcome from the officers all of whom came on deck to receive me, and the Admiral gave me a letter from the Secretary of the Navy, a copy of which I will send you.[1]

---

1. Letter from Secretary of the Navy Gideon Welles to Lamson
   Navy Department, May 4, 1863
   Sir: Your recent important and meritorious services on the upper Nansemond deserve the especial commendation of the Department. The ability displayed in the discharge of the important and responsible duties which devolved on the naval forces during the late demonstration of the enemy reflect great credit upon yourself and the officers and men under your command. Their zeal and courage in the hazardous positions in which they were placed have not failed to receive the approbation of both

The Admiral has assigned me to his staff as Flag Lieut. of the Squadron—what I wanted, you know, when I first joined the ship.

I am resting a little now, but shall be ready for work again tomorrow. . . .

---

the naval and military authorities. General Getty, with whom you were cooperating, has expressed his obligations to you and your command for gallantry and energy displayed, especially in the capture of a rebel battery on the Nansemond and for valuable assistance rendered to him during his operation in repelling the enemy; and your immediate commanding officer, Acting Rear-Admiral Lee, has reported in terms of admiration of your discretion and valor.

The Department congratulates you on your success, and is proud to see in the younger members of the corps such evidence of energy and gallantry, and execution and ability scarcely surpassed by those of more age and experience.

Very respectfully, etc.

Gideon Welles,

Secretary of the Navy

[*O.R. Navies*, ser. I, vol. 8, pp. 789–90]

CHAPTER 5

THE PEOPLE OF OREGON
FEEL PROUD TO CALL
YOU THEIR SON

JUNE–NOVEMBER 1863

A FTER THE SUFFOLK CAMPAIGN Lamson received a brief furlough and paid a short visit to Kate in Mount Vernon, Ohio. When he returned to the flagship *Minnesota* he performed the varied but routine duties of a flag lieutenant for two months, interrupted by a brief naval demonstration up the James River during which Lamson commanded the gunboat USS *Commodore Barney*. On July 30 he received welcome orders to take command of a ship just acquired by the navy, the *James Freeborn*, built in 1862, a sidewheel steamer carrying three guns and rated at a maximum speed of fifteen knots. By 1863 specially designed blockade runners built in Britain and capable of great speeds were outrunning Union blockade ships, forcing the Union navy to put equally fast ships into blockade service. The *Freeborn* was renamed the USS *Nansemond* in honor of Lamson's achievements on that river. In August 1863 he took her to sea in search of blockade runners, and soon added new laurels to his record.

His first duty upon returning from furlough, however, was the unpleasant one assigned to all officers sooner or later—to serve on a court-martial to try offenders against navy rules and regulations. The sessions of the court met in the cabin of the repaired gunboat *Mount Washington*.

———•••———

Roswell to Katie

USS *Mt. Washington*
Hampton Roads
June 4, 1863

I snatch a few minutes while the members of the Court are opening their mail to write you a few lines, if no more. . . .

The Court is still in session, but I hope will get through to-morrow. We have tried four Officers, and two sailors on various charges, and have one more officer to try yet. . . .

The Cabin shows many marks of the fight up the Nansemond, and I cannot look around without bringing to mind the scene in this same cabin on the evening of the 14th April, after the wounded had been brought in.

Yesterday morning the Mess [in the *Minnesota*] unanimously insisted that I should be caterer of the Mess again. I refused as long as I could but finally consented to go to house-keeping again, or "hotel keeping" I tell them. We have a very large Mess, mostly volunteer officers, and all hands disposed to groan a good deal wether there is occasion or not. Lately, things have gone even worse than usual, and it was amusing as well as annoying to see what a dissatisfied growling unreasonable, and *uncomfortable* state the Mess had got into.

I was extremely unwilling to take the catership again. (I had it a few days before going up the Nansemond) but the Executive Officer, Mr. Parker, the Fleet Surgeon and others urged it so strongly, that I finally consented to be escorted to the head of the table.

If I *do succeed* in controlling their turbulence, and reconciling their diverse tastes, and stopping the growling and swearing at servants, I shall write myself a recommendation to you. They tell me there is a great change already, and I think there is, but there must be a greater one.

Men are all selfish and unreasonable to a greater or less degree but there is always a way to control them.

Roswell to Flora

> USS *Minnesota*
> Hampton Roads
> June 14, 1863

. . . I am glad to hear that Aunt is so comfortable and Uncle so confident that the war will end with the fall of Vicksburg. That will be a great blow to the "confeds" and I think will "break the backbone" but it will not end the war, I fear. The Rebels fight with an earnestness and a determination that are shown by but few of our people and there will be no peace as long as they can keep a man in the field under arms.

I returned from Washington day before yesterday. At no time have our country's prospects looked so bright to me as now—you know I said at the first the war would last five (5) years. I do not think now that it will be much shorter, if any but I have never had a doubt but the *right* will triumph. I do wish I could do more for our country's cause to end this horrible war—I declare, Flora, when I look back and think that we have been at war two years and think how little I have done compared with what is to be done I feel almost discouraged—why do we not strike quickly, decisively and continuously? We certainly have had means enough, men enough and motif enough, and yet we have gained no decisive advantage. Admiral Foote is going to relieve Admiral Du Pont to make another attempt on Charleston.[1] . . .

Roswell to Kate

> Fortress Monroe
> June 18, 1863

. . . I have been here three days, making arrangements with Gen. Dix to ship some contrabands for the Navy upon the order of the

---

1. Foote was assigned to command the fleet at Charleston because of the Navy Department's dissatisfaction with Du Pont's lack of success. Foote died on June 26, 1863, on his way to Charleston, and Rear Admiral John A. Dahlgren (1809–70) took command of the fleet at Charleston. He fared little better than Du Pont.

Secretary. He wants one-hundred for the Naval Battery at the Navy Yard at Portsmouth, N.H. and the same number for the "Roanoke," which will arrive in about ten days.

It seems strange to send negroes to garrison a fort in "Yankeedom," but I have no doubt if properly drilled they will make very good sailors. We have always had some on board every vessel in the Navy, and they make valuable men for certain kinds of duty. I think we will have no difficulty in getting as many as we want here; we ship them as "Landsmen," at twelve dollars per month, and rations; half of their pay can be paid to their families here, every month. It is the best prospect the negroes have ever had offered them. Gen. Dix has them brought in, and I ship them and send them on board the Receiving Ship, Brandywine. Mr. [Thomas H.] Looker, the paymaster of the Brandywine lives in one of the casemates, and I have taken up my Quarters with him; and have found him, a real *good Christian man*, a character not *very* often found on these coasts. His wife was here with him till recently and he has his "castle" quite nicely fitted up. A number of officers wives are living in the casemates, and in the quarters inside the Fortress, and there are several young ladies also. . . .

Roswell to Kate

USS *Minnesota*
Newport News
June 28, 1863

. . . The Roanoke is expected to arrive the first of this week when this ship will go to sea to visit the different stations of the fleet. The Admiral will take a small steamer and go through the Sounds of North Carolina. I will probably accompany him.

Capt. Crosby is absent now, so I have the duties of Fleet Captain to attend to, which keeps me busy all the time.

That is the reason I have not written you before this week, though I have been unreasonable enough to expect letters from you; it seems *so* long since your last one. I suppose you are all in a state of excitement in regard to the Penn "Raid."[1] I fear it will be more serious than at first supposed. If it only wakens our people up a little and puts a little

---

1. Lee's invasion of Pennsylvania that culminated in the battle of Gettysburg.

more spirit and feeling into them in regard to the war, it will be a great benefit to us. . . .

Roswell to Flora

USS *Brandywine*
Hampton Roads
June 30, 1863

. . . I was ordered to report to Commander Glasson this morning as a member of a Naval Court of Inquiry into the causes of the loss of the U.S.S. "Sumter."[1] Yesterday I went to the Navy Yard at Portsmouth (Va.) to hurry off some vessels to go up the Potomac to Washington. I was in hopes to go somewhere where I could see some active service during the "Crisis," but see no chance now the Naval Brigade is given up.[2] One week of Nansemond service would be worth five years of this sort of life. When I think of what is going on I feel almost stifled by this sort of work and get so impatient that I can scarcely compose myself to do anything.

The Tacony's cruise is over and ended with a brilliant dash, did it not? Read, or "Savey," as we used to call him at the Naval Academy was not considered very brilliant, but was one of those wiry, energetic fellows who would attempt anything but study. He and I were always good friends till he turned "secesh."[3]

What do you think of Gen. Hooker's removal—I have not been so

1. Commander John J. Glasson was captain of the USS *Brandywine*. The USS *Sumter* was a five-gun screw steamship built in 1853 and used by the navy as part of the blockade fleet. She sank after a collision with the army transport ship *General Meigs* off Smith Island, North Carolina, on June 24, 1863.

2. Because of the emergency created by Lee's invasion of Pennsylvania, some officers proposed to form a brigade of marines and sailors to reinforce the army.

3. The *Tacony* was a sailing bark built in 1856 and captured by the commerce CSS *Clarence* at sea on June 12, 1863. Finding the *Tacony* a better ship than the raider *Clarence*, which was a converted merchant vessel previously captured by the famed CSS *Florida*, Confederate Lieutenant Charles W. Read burned the *Clarence* and transferred his crew and a single 12-pounder cannon to the Tacony. Read then proceeded to capture 15 fishing boats and merchant vessels off the New England coast from June 12 to 24 before the Union navy finally ran him down and captured him on June 27. A native of Mississippi, Read had graduated from the Naval Academy in 1860.

much pleased for a long time. Gen Meade[1] has a hard task before him—just assuming command in the face of the rebel army under such a *general* as Lee—and such a critical position. The *Right* must triumph at last. Our soldiers are undoubtedly brave and let us hope that they will be better led this time and drive out the invaders. . . .

Kate to Roswell

Mount Vernon, Ohio
July 3, 1863

. . . We are watching anxiously the movement of Dix on Richmond[2] as well as that of Meade and Lee. It is such a satisfaction to know that our armies are doing *something* at last and not lying idle as they have done for so long. If one *only* knew how much of the "papers" news they might believe it would be still more satisfactory. We shall be very cautious in crediting another report of the capture of Richmond, having been deceived so many times already. What do you think of the change of commanders in the Army of the Potomac? Every one seems to be loud in their condemnation of Hooker, poor man. I pity him—We hear rumors of McClellan's having Halleck's place in the Cabinet—and Banks that of Stanton, though of course you know all about that.[3]

The people of Ohio at last are aroused by the Pennsylvania Raid.

---

1. Major-General George Gordon Meade (1815–72), appointed commander of the Army of the Potomac on June 28, 1863, on the eve of what turned out to be the battle of Gettysburg.

2. Major-General John A. Dix (1798–1879), commander of the Department of Virginia with headquarters at Fortress Monroe, sent three columns of troops totaling 16,000 men toward Richmond during the last week of June to threaten the Confederate capital and prevent any reinforcements being sent to Lee in Pennsylvania. After some skirmishing, which convinced Dix's surbordinates that Richmond's defenses were strong, they withdrew during the first week of July without accomplishing anything of importance.

3. Such rumors circulated frequently during the war, particularly at times of crisis. Halleck was not a member of the Cabinet, but general-in-chief of the army; Edwin M. Stanton was the very capable though acerbic secretary of war; Major-General Nathaniel P. Banks was the not-so-capable commander of the Army of the Gulf, which was at that moment besieging Port Hudson. The rumors were unfounded.

Even in this little town of Mt Vernon the stores are all closed at three o'clock for drilling. We have had several very enthusiastic meetings. I don't believe the rebels would stay very long on this side of the Ohio river—at least not in Ohio. . . .

Monday morning, July 6

I was interrupted just here and have not had time since to finish your letter. I expect you are getting very impatient by this time for a letter. Yesterday was Communion Sunday. I thought of you many times and wondered where you were and what you were doing—and wishing you could go with me. I had a small class in Sunday school the day was so warm that I suppose some of them could not come. After school was over just as we were starting for home—Mr White brought us the glad tidings of Lee's defeat. Of course we do not feel certain how much to believe of it—but you know you cannot help hoping it may prove true. It *ought* to be at any rate. Ned and I walked down to the foundry after church expecting to find Mr White there and get some more news but found he had not been there at all. So we had our walk for nothing, but we shall hear something more definite today. We had it rumored on Saturday that Vicksburg had surrendered, but that has happened so many times before that it needs confirmation.[1] If we could only know the truth at once of whatever happens it would be a satisfaction, but suspense is hard to bear.

Ned has just come up and says the good news is confirmed so now we can begin to believe it a little.—Now for Richmond, Charleston and Vicksburg!

I *hope* I am patriotic—but I think I rejoice in victory quite as much because it brings nearer the time when you can come again and when sometime we may be together always. I do get very lonely sometimes, dear, and my head aches for its dear nesting place—of course I shall be glad for our country when "this cruel war is over." Do you not think things seem to be coming to a crisis? . . .

---

1. This time the rumor was correct; Vicksburg had indeed surrendered to General Grant on Saturday, July 4.

Roswell to Flora

USS *Minnesota*
Newport News
July 5, 1863

. . . Admiral Foote's death is indeed a loss to the country and especially to the Navy. He was a Christian hero and I doubt not has received his reward in that happy home where there are no storms and where there is no war. You no doubt saw the touching order of the Secretary of the Navy announcing his death. On the day after it[s] receipt we fired thirteen minute guns in his honor.

Yesterday was the "Glorious Fourth," and as usual we dressed the ship and fired a national salute (21 guns) at noon. A picnic was arranged for the officers at Newport News which they enjoyed very much. I was busy till two o'clock and had just got ready to join them when a rebel flag-of-truce came down the James River and I had to go to find out what they wanted. Alexander H. Stevens, Vice-President of the C.S.A. was on board with Judge Ould, his Secretary, and wanted permission to go to Washington with important communications from Mr. Davis to Mr. Lincoln. The Admiral sent me to Fortress Monroe to telegraph to Washington for instructions, I received a telegram to await dispatches, which I did and came up this morning and informed Mr. Stevens that he could not go to Washington. Mr. Stevens came on the C.S. Steamer "Torpedo" commanded by Capt Hunter Davidson who was an officer of our Navy and was an instructor at the Naval Academy while I was there.[1]

My health is not quite so good as it was, but I do not mind it much. I send you a view of "Fort Lamson" one of the largest works erected

1. Alexander H. Stephens (not Stevens), 1812–83, was indeed vice president of the Confederacy. He was on a confidential mission to Washington, ostensibly to discuss prisoner-of-war exchanges, but perhaps to carry secret overtures for peace from the Confederate government. Stephens's mission was timed to coincide with Lee's expected success in Pennsylvania, which Southern leaders confidently expected would persuade Lincoln to give up trying to win the war and negotiate a peace. Instead, Union forces won at Gettysburg, Lee retreated to Virginia, and Lincoln refused to allow Stephens through Union lines. Hunter Davidson (1816–1913) commanded the CSS *Torpedo*, a converted tugboat carrying two guns and responsible for the placement

to defend Suffolk. It mounts ten guns the photograph is from a sketch sent me by Gen. Getty.

Roswell to Kate

> USS *Commodore Barney*[1]
> Off Sand Point, James River
> July 11, 1863

. . . The Admiral was ordered by the Department to make a demonstration up the James River, wether it will be only a demonstration or an attack on the rebel forts along the river from Fort Powhatan to Fort Darling[2] will depend on the orders we receive from Washington. I *fear* it will only be the former. We have nine vessels up here, including two iron clads, the "Sangamon" and "Lehigh";[3] the others are Gun Boats. I was afraid I should not come up as the Admiral told me yesterday he wished me to remain to get some vessels to sea, but the Commodore Barney's Captain being on leave, he gave me command of her for the "demonstration" or whatever it is to be. Gen. Dix after marching up the hill, marched down again, and I see by the papers accomplished all the objects of his campaign. If we had his army here now to cooperate we could do something, but gun boats alone cannot take and *hold* the forts. . . .

The Commodore Barney carries five nine inch shell guns, one one-hundred pounder rifle, and a howitzer with a crew of one-hundred

---

of "torpedoes" (mines) in the James River below Richmond to prevent Union ships from coming upriver.

1. USS *Commodore Barney*, a sidewheel ferryboat built in 1859, acquired by the navy in 1861 and armed with seven guns. In August 1863 she was damaged by one of the "torpedoes" planted by Hunter Davidson's CSS *Torpedo*.

2. A series of Confederate forts on the narrow part of the James River below Richmond. Fort Darling at Drewry's Bluff seven miles south of Richmond had stopped the navy's attack on May 15, 1862, seriously damaging the USS *Galena* on that occasion. See map, p. 161.

3. Like the *Sangamon*, the USS *Lehigh* was a single-turreted Monitor-class ironclad completed in 1863.

men. The cabin is very comfortable, but would be *so* much pleasanter if you would *only* come and sit on the sofa and talk to me. . . .

Is not the news from Vicksburg cheering? and our reports from Meade's army are favorable to us though his successes have not yet been so decisive as we could wish. Before you read this, however, I hope Lee's army will be *destroyed*. We ought to do it; we must have *more* than *three* men to his *one*, in Maryland, and he is getting short of ammunition.

The attack on Charleston has commenced again; this time it will be an attack by the army and navy both, and Fort Sumpter is to be breached by regular approaches from Morris Island. Dahlgren has relieved Du Pont—Capt West of the supply steamer gave me an account of Du Pont Rodgers and Corbin taking leave of the "Wabash." It must have been quite affecting, every one was so much attached to them. There is scarcely an officer on board of her now who was on board when she went into commission or at the Battle of Port Royal. I cannot bear to think of my being a *stranger* on board of her.

You ask me if the Navy is not a little "prejudiced" against the army and I must say candidly that I think it is. You may have heard me say before that sailors are the vainest people in the world—they are proud of the sea, proud of their ships and their *sweet-hearts*, proud of what sailors have done, and they look down with a sort of complaisance upon "lubbers" and "sogers." Now I leave it to you and others to justify this pride or not, but it exists, and there is not a *sailor* in the service that does not feel it. . . .

Roswell to Flora

USS *Commodore Barney*
Off Fort Powhatan, James
River
July 13, 1863

Your letter of the 9th Inst. reached me this evening just as I returned from an expedition on shore to take possession of the rebel fort that so much has been said about. A few days since, the Navy Department ordered a demonstration up the James River to ascertain the strength of the enemy's forts and to prevent them from sending any more forces north. . . .

The Admiral sent for me this evening to arrange an expedition to destroy the forts to-morrow morning. The rebels have a strong force at Petersburg which they could bring down in a short time, so we may have some fighting unless they are willing to see their really fine and formidable fortifications destroyed without an effort to prevent it. Capt. Crosby and myself will land at six o'clock in the morning with as many armed boat's crews as can be spared from the vessels. Do not have any fears about my health—I have been fried and roasted a great many times and now I am getting boiled in this hot steaming river and then I think I will have myself put up in cans like "roast beef" and then I will be allright. . . .

I have never had but one opinion of the war—a long, hard fight and victory to us at last—our prospects look bright now.

Roswell to Kate

USS *Commodore Barney*
Off City Point, James River
July 16, 1863

. . . Day before yesterday we spent destroying the fortifications at Fort Powhatan. All the men that could be spared from the vessels were landed, one detachment under Capt. Crosby, and one under myself, and we effectually destroyed the magazine, tore up and burned the platforms, destroyed the reveting, and the parapets as much as possible, filled up the embrasures, and generally demolished the works so that they cannot be mounted with heavy artillery without an immense amount of labor. I was at work from four a.m. till after sundown.

Yesterday morning the fleet moved up to this point, and I came up in the afternoon after posting a picket in the fort to give notice of any attempt to repair the works. The Gun Boat "Shockokon"[1] remained to guard the point. This (City Point) is the place where all exchanges of prisoners are made between us and the rebels. We send their men to this point in steamers and take our own down. From here there is a railroad to Petersburg and Richmond. The Commodore Barney is lying above the fleet as the "guard ship," and in the order of steaming, going

---

1. USS *Shokokon*, a large sidewheel steamer built in 1862, acquired by the navy in 1863 and fitted out with five guns.

up, the Admiral has given me the post of honor—the advance. We will go up and make an examination of the fortifications about Fort Darling, and we may exchange a few compliments with them by way of trying their calibre, but I do not anticipate any fighting unless their vessels come down. It was Fort Darling, you remember that cut the ironclad Galena to pieces. Capt. John Rodgers commanded her.[1] He said he "was ordered by the Department to test her, and he tested her," and so completely that she came out of action looking like a sieve, and with not much crew left. The Admiral's orders (from Washington) are *not* to attack; so you need not have *any* anxiety about the Barney. We have got much further up the river than we expected to get already. Don't be sad about the news from New York—the rioters will soon be quelled, and the draft *once made* I do not think the war can last *very* much longer.[2]

There are some beautiful residences along the banks, in some of which the families still remain. Yesterday we passed McClellan's camping ground at Harrison's Landing; near it still stands the house in which Gen. Harrison was born, and just below is President Tyler's plantation.[3]

Roswell to Flora

> USS *Commodore Barney*
> Off City Point
> July 18, 1863

I wrote you a few days since as we were going up the river—after destroying Fort Powhatan we went up nearly to Fort Darling where the Lehigh (one of the monitors) unfortunately broke some of her machinery, and we were obliged to come back—indeed we should not have gone much farther anyhow as all had been accomplished that the

---

1. Captain John Rodgers (1812–82), who commanded the *Galena* during the attack on Fort Darling at Drewry's Bluff on May 15, 1862. Not to be confused with Commander C. R. Perry Rodgers.

2. A reference to the draft riots in New York City; after four days of mob violence against the draft (July 13–16), the rioters were indeed quelled by the police and troops, at the cost of more than 100 lives, most of them rioters.

3. William Henry Harrison (1773–1841), a prominent general in the wars against Indian leader Tecumseh and in the War of 1812, elected president in 1840 but died after one month in office, succeeded by his Vice President John Tyler (1790–1862).

Department designed, and we had got much nearer Richmond than they expected we would get. We met only sharpshooters on the banks who did not annoy us much as we threw pickets ashore at night to keep them from firing upon us from the trees and banks. This vessel was the guardship in advance, and I had charge of all the pickets. I put an officer (volunteer) in charge of one picket with orders to keep himself and his men under cover and to fire on anyone approaching him—hearing a party of rebels approaching, he stepped out in full view of them and politely inquired what port they were from and where they were bound. They replied by knocking him down with a shot through the shoulder. Two rebels then walked up to him and one of them, half turning him over with his foot, remarked, "Another Yankee done for," and they walked off. As soon as they were gone he jumped up, not very badly hurt and went on board his vessel, a wiser and I hope a more obedient man. He deserved (almost) to have had the bullet through his head.

We came down here to-day and are now at anchor off this point where a flag-of-truce boat to take down some of our exchanged soldiers who have been prisoners [is also anchored]. Don't you admire Gen. Lee—in the face of such superior numbers to get his army, artillery and baggage over the swollen Potomac with such trifling loss.[1] I said all the time he would do it. The news from the west is cheering and I have no more doubt now than ever of our final success.

But enough of the news—I sat down to write because I was lonesome—a selfish motive, I admit, but I have not a single person to talk to. There are more than a hundred brave fellows on board who would jump to do my slightest wish or bidding—yet I am isolated as though I were in the middle of Sahara. In the day time I find plenty to do and I like to walk about the decks watching the amusements of the sailors—their sewing, embroidery, dominoes &c &c and to see that they are well cared for and everything is ship-shape, but in the evening I should like to see my friends for a few minutes, at least. I have a standing invitation to take tea on board the Flagship whenever duty will permit, and Admiral Lee is a very pleasant gentleman and a very kind man—he has been exceedingly kind to me. He is a hard worker himself and makes his officers work too, I can assure you; I only wish we had a more active field for our exertions. . . .

1. Much to Lincoln's distress, Meade allowed Lee's army to escape across the Potomac to Virginia on July 13–14 with only minimal additional damage after Gettysburg.

Roswell to Kate

USS *Minnesota*
Off Newport News
July 23, 1863

. . . I wrote you twice while up the James River, when near Fort Darling the Lehigh disabled her machinery, and as she had already burst her 15 inch gun the Admiral determined to return without going farther up; which would have been of no use as he had express orders not to attack it.

The whole expedition was without much object, and was sent only at the solicitation of the War Department which had some fears for Gen. Dix, though he was well on his way back to Fortress Monroe. Last Sunday morning three of our vessels got aground near City Point; and we were at work all day getting them off. . . .

We arrived here Monday evening, and I returned on board and resumed my usual duties.

The ship is "under sailing orders," all ready for sea, and we will probably sail on Saturday for the southward, to visit the blockading fleet. The Admiral will take a small steamer and go through the Sound of North Carolina, where we have quite a flotilla. I shall probably accompany him. The Str Philadelphia[1] has been fitted up for the Admiral and his staff, and she will join us off the coast.

The Minnesota will cruise along the coast for a month or so, and then return; we will return in the Philadelphia, after having inspected all the ships of the fleet. Such is the program, now; to be changed according to circumstances, of which I will keep you informed.

It is rather warm for going further south, but I think it will be rather a pleasant trip, especially in the Sound where I have never been. . . .

I *do wish* I was at Charleston, and if it were possible I would be there; it seems to me I have done so little for our country though I have tried to do my duty. . . .

---

1. USS *Philadelphia*, a sidewheel steamer built in 1859 for passenger service on the Chesapeake Bay, acquired by the navy in 1861 and armed with two guns.

Roswell to Kate

Washington, D.C.
Aug. 1, 1863

You expect I am at sea, no doubt, Dear Katie, and I expected I should be, but just before the ship sailed, last Thursday, I received orders to come here to complete the arrangements for the purchase of a very fine fast steamer of three-hundred and fifty tons for the Navy. Admiral Lee has wished to get her for some time as she is faster than anything we had.

He paid me the compliment of saying he would rather have me command her than any other officer in the Fleet, and requested the Department to order me to her which they did this morning, and issued orders to the Navy Yard at Norfolk to afford me every facility for fitting her for sea at once; so I hope to be at sea soon and in my own vessel.

Several Lieut. Commanders and Commanders [one and two grades higher than Lamson's rank of lieutenant] wanted the Command of her but she was given to me without my asking or saying a word about it. . . .

Roswell to Flora

Baltimore
Aug. 9, 1863

I wrote you a note from Washington telling you that the Navy Department had bought the steamer. The morning after I drove out to Silver Springs and breakfasted with Mrs. Lee[1] and left in the evening for Fortress Monroe. I took the steamer to the Norfolk Navy Yard but finding it would take several weeks to fit her for sea there, I brought her up here telegraphing to the Department my reasons for so doing. They gave me permission to put such an armament on board as I think

1. Elizabeth Blair Lee, the wife of Samuel Phillips Lee and sister of Montgomery Blair, postmaster-general in Lincoln's cabinet, and of Major-General Francis P. Blair, Jr., a division commander under William T. Sherman.

best and to fit her out to suit myself. As many men as can work are employed upon her day and night and I hope to get to sea by the last of this week. The Dept and Admiral Lee are very anxious to get her off and I am making every effort to complete her equipment. She is a fine vessel and the fastest now in the Navy. Commodore Dornin[1] showed me a letter yesterday from the Department naming her the "Nansemond" as a compliment to me. I need not say I am very much pleased with the name. I have had about a hundred applications from officers to go in her including most of those who were in the Nansemond Flotilla. She will carry three guns, two of them long range rifles. . . .

Roswell to Flora

USS *Nansemond*
Hampton Roads Aug. 20, 1863

I left Balto yesterday evening, having been detained a little longer than I expected because they had not men enough on board the Receiving Ship for my crew. I have never worked harder in my life than I did in Balto. and they said my ship progressed faster, and was equipped more rapidly than any other vessel that has been there. Everybody at the Ship Yards said they would be glad when I got away. I will not attempt to give you an idea of the trouble and vexation and labor of fitting a vessel for a cruise in a hurry. And as I had every thing placed at my own command I felt more anxious to lose no time—I went to Washington one day last week to see about my officers, and they gave me those I asked for, and I did not even make a suggestion about the vessel that they did not accede to, and I had permission to take officers from any vessel I wished.

My vessel is in splendid order, and nicely fitted out considering the time, for I could not stop to have many little things done as I wished.

I wish you could see what a nice cabin I have—light and airy—two rooms—one with a berth, wash-stand, and a chest of drawers—and the other contains a dining table, side-board, secretary and a sofa—

1. Thomas A. Dornin, superintendent of the Baltimore Navy Yard.

Brussels carpets on the decks, and tweed hangings for window and berth.

I wish you could see my outfit—I am sure you would approve my taste in the selection of my crockery, and I have a double distilling back action patent coffee pot that will make a cup of hot coffee in a few minutes at any hour of the night, in the hardest gale that ever blew off Hatteras.

Charles Adams ("a fellow citizen and a brother")[1] is my steward and cook, and James waits on the table and takes care of my room. Both of them are excellent servants, and Charles is a very fine cook. He has been at sea a good deal, and for some time waited on Admiral Du Pont. I am allowed three servants, but two are quite enough. The Wardroom is very comfortably fitted up and the officers have a nice room on the upper deck to sit and smoke in. I have an excellent lot of officers; Mr Porter,[2] my Executive officer, was on board the Minnesota, and is a fine officer and a pleasant gentleman. I am thinking of inviting him to mess with me—it is so stupid sitting down to dinner alone. . . .

I am laying in the stream and shall sail at early daylight to-morrow morning. . . .

There happen to be no pilots here now, and I cannot wait for one, so I must be my own pilot. I am going off Wilmington, N.C. first. When I reached here this evening a number of officers from the Fortress came on board to congratulate me on having so fine a command and on the compliment paid me in her name. Of course it was very gratifying, but I am thinking of what the Nansemond will accomplish for Our Country—I *hope* she will be of some service.

Roswell to Kate

> USS *Nansemond*
> Beaufort Harbor, N.C.
> Aug. 28, 1863

We sailed from Hampton Roads a week ago this morning standing out in the teeth of a North Easter which blew a very heavy gale till

---

1. An abolitionist phrase to describe a black man.
2. Ensign Benjamin H. Porter, who would be killed almost at Lamson's side during the assault on Fort Fisher January 15, 1865.

we had passed "Hatteras." Some of the old coasters advised me not to go out, but I knew the Admiral was anxious for me to get out, and if we could not stand a gale with a port under our lee we should not stand much chance off this stormy coast. The "Nansemond" behaved to the *admiration of every one*; and proved herself as good a sea boat as any I have ever been in—all the old salts are delighted with her. Lookout Light House was the first land I made, sighting it just as I expected to, as it was clear enough that morning for an observation of the Sun. I hove to most of Sat. night as I did not wish to approach the fleet in the dark, and early Sunday morning found them standing in to engage a battery the rebs had brought up on the beach to keep us away from an English blockade runner that had been driven ashore, while they got out part of the cargo. We had quite sharp practice for an hour, when the rebs fell back and we landed in our boats through the surf and after much labor brought off two pieces of artillery they had been forced to leave. I also sent a boat to the wreck of the steamer and brought off sixty pairs of blankets, and several bales of heavy woolen goods. I gave each man on board a pair of blankets and intend to sell the remainder and buy them water proof suits for the Winter. We had one man wounded on board the James Adger.[1]

I went on board the Minnesota reported to Admiral Lee and took dinner and tea with him. He expressed himself perfectly satisfied with everything I had done, and said I had fitted her out in a remarkably short time. From Sunday till yesterday morning I was cruising off New Inlet, which is the only approach to Wilmington now used, but saw nothing. At night I would run in close to the bar and sometimes so near their forts that we could hear them talking on the ramparts, and during the day lie further out. All the officers of the fleet express the greatest admiration of the Nansemond, and indeed she is in every respect one of the *very* finest vessels I have ever seen of her size, (400 tons, nearly) and there is no other vessel in the Navy that at all equals her in speed. She is as beautiful, and as graceful in her motions as a lady, (almost) and I am as proud of her as possible. I could not get a full crew in Balto., but those I did get were excellent men, (picked) so I asked the Admiral for an order to fill up her crew from those men on board the Minnesota who were with me on the Mt. Washington.

---

1. USS *James Adger*, a big sidewheel steamer built in 1852 for trans-Atlantic service, purchased by the navy in 1861, and armed with nine guns. She participated in the capture or destruction of no fewer than 10 blockade runners.

When I went to get them at least half the crew came and asked me to take them; I could hardly walk across the deck the men came around me so fast to ask to go with me. I have fifty men, as true blue jackets as ever walked a deck, and ten officers. Mr. Porter, my Executive Officer was for a long time on board the Minnesota, and is an excellent officer, and a very pleasant gentleman; he is devoted to the vessel, and relieves me of a great deal of care. Mr. Hunter Mr. Waring and Mr. Henderson, the "Watch officers" are all good officers and try to do everything according to the customs of the service, but I have not quite the confidence in them that I have in Mr. Porter.

I have not had my boots or clothes off to go to sleep since leaving Hampton Roads—when off Wilmington I am on deck most of the night, and when it is stormy I never take off my storm clothes so that I can go on deck at once. People generally know nothing about our "Blockade" except that vessels run past and get in to Southern ports quite frequently. They do not know the difficulties of stopping vessels during dark nights, and of the greater difficulties of finding and seeing them. There are no men in the employ of the government that endure more hardship and exposure and severe labor than those on board our blockaders, and who get so little credit for it. Some nights I do not get an hours sleep; I have been twice under the fire of the Wilmington batteries [Fort Fisher, at the mouth of the Cape Fear River fifteen miles south of Wilmington] and while trying to watch the bar have been a half dozen times within a biscuit's toss of the breakers. I am confident nothing has passed me, and if I am fortunate enough to sight one of the runners I am fast enough to catch anything on this coast.

Yesterday morning a heavy storm came up from the North & East and as I was in need of coal the Admiral said I had better bear off for this port. We left our station about nine a.m. and experienced one of the most terrific gales I have ever seen off this coast. The force of the wind was so great that it was impossible to stand on the deck without clinging to something, and the sea frequently broke higher than the top of the wheel house—sometimes at least twenty-four feet high. The Nansemond steamed it nobly, and elicited the admiration of every one. One very heavy sea stove in our galley and put out the fire and also my breakfast which was waiting for me—but I had a plate of cold pork and beans from dinner the day before. Towards evening I hauled in for the land, and smooth sea told me I was under the lee of Cape Lookout. Towards morning my soundings and rec[k]oning making me off old Topsail Inlet. I let go an anchor and at daylight found myself just where I wanted to be, and ran in before a pilot could come out to me though I hoisted a signal for one.

So far I cannot complain of a want of excitement since I came out for we have heard the whistle of a storm or a shot almost ever since we sailed.

I am coaling as fast as possible and shall leave for New Inlet Bar to-morrow morning. This is a dull looking place though I have not yet been ashore enough to tell you much about it. I am anxious to get to sea again, as the tide will soon serve the blockade runners, about day light and then they will probably try to get in. . . .

Roswell to Kate

USS *Nansemond*
Beaufort, N.C.
Sept. 14, 1863

The supply steamer Newberne[1] joined us off Wilmington about a week ago and brought me a *letter from you* dated the 24th Aug. which is the last I have received I cannot tell you how much pleasure it gave me to hear from you after being without a letter for so long but I am getting impatient again, though I know it is unreasonable for I have not written to you since we were here before two weeks since. But I have not written to any one not even my mother, I have had so little opportunity for writing or sending letters after they were written. I'm on deck most all night— *all* the time when cruising close in to the bar and the forts, and in the day time I sleep a little and have a great many things to attend to about the ship. I sailed the day after writing you, and till last evening have been off New Inlet. We had pretty good weather during the time to make up for the two weeks of steady storms we had at first. The Nansemond has already the reputation of going in much nearer the forts and the bar than any other vessel; indeed we go so much further in shore that we scarcely ever see any of the other vessels during the night. Last Monday night I met a large Confederate steamer right *on the bar*, and within six or seven hundred yards of "Fort Fisher" and the "Mound Fort," and ran him

1. Although used as a supply ship, this fast screw steamer USS *New Berne*, built in 1862 and capable of 13 knots, was armed with six guns and was also used as a blockader, helping to destroy two blockade runners.

ashore. I had anchored with a kedge and hawser just on the edge of the bar, and on one side of the channel, having a man stationed with an axe to cut the hawser in case I should not have time to weigh the anchor, when we saw the rebel coming out. I kept still and gave him a good chance to run by or fight, for he carried five guns, but as soon as he saw us he turned round quickly and started back, and we lost sight of him in the darkness. At daylight we discovered him high and dry on the outer edge of the bar with the surf breaking all around him. From the descriptions we have I think it was the Robert E. Lee,[1] one of a line of fine, large fast steamers owned by the Confederate Government armed and flying their flag. These are the vessels that take the cotton over on which the rebels raise their European loan. Of course we could not approach him during the day as some two forts and batteries were covering him with their guns, but we could have destroyed him at night, and I requested permission from Capt Case,[2] the Senior officer present to go in at night with my vessel and some boats and set fire to him. He said he thought the plan would succeed but as there were only four vessels off the place at that time he did not like to take the responsibility of risking one of them. Capt. Case is an officer of high reputation and large experience, and it may seem presumptuous in me to criticize his judgment *but I shall always think that vessel ought to have been, and could have been destroyed*, and without any more risk to ourselves than must be taken in any offensive operations against an enemy.

Capt. Case was expecting to come here for coal which would have left me the senior commander, and I told him that if the steamer was still on the bar I should go in immediately—he laughed but could not be prevailed upon to let us make the attempt. After working three days and two nights the rebs got her cargo of cotton out, and succeeded in getting her off.

I left New Inlet Bar last evening at nine o'clock and came in at daylight this morning for coal and supplies. We shall be in about every two weeks.

---

1. The *Robert E. Lee*, built in 1860 as an Irish Sea ferry named *Giraffe*, was one of the most successful blockade runners, making 22 trips until captured by the USS *James Adger* and another ship off Bermuda on November 9, 1863. She was renamed the USS *Fort Donelson* and put to work as a blockader, capturing one runner.

2. Captain A. Ludlow Case (1813–93), commander of the blockade fleet off New Inlet at the mouth of the Cape Fear River.

All is going on nicely on board, and we are getting things a little more into man-of-war shape, it takes about three months to get a ship in *good* order.

Blockading is weary work but it is exciting; to run along the edge of a reef, and fight out a North-easter is more to my liking than lying at anchor till the ship grounded on the beef bones thrown overboard. The old blockade runner who was to be my pilot ran away just before I came down so they know all about my vessel, and they never lose a chance to give us a shot; so far they have fired over us. . . .

I often think how much better it would have been for you to have loved some one differently situated from myself, and who was better situated to take care of you as you deserve. If I could only be with you all the time to care for you and watch over your comfort and happiness, I should be quite satisfied and feel more as though I deserved some of your love. . . .

Sept. 15

I shall sail this evening and run off to the southward in hopes of falling in with some of the blockade runners at day light. . . .

Father (Jeremiah) to Roswell

Willamina, Ore.
Sept. 20, 1863

Yours of Aug. 9th dated at Baltimore is just received. I need not say that it affords us great pleasure to hear of your good success. The people of Oregon feel proud to call you their son. How thankful we ought to be that you can be of service to our country now in her time of need. I have just returned from the state agricultural fair held at Salem. It was a splendid affair for Oregon. All of our family and Henrys attended. How much we wished that you could have been there. There was a large exibetion of the products of Oregon. It lasted four days, and it was estimated that not less than ten thousand people were there. Gov. Gibbs[1] delivered the anual address. The day time

1. Addison Crandall Gibbs (1825–86), elected governor in 1862 on a coalition ticket of Republicans and War Democrats.

was spent in exibiting the products of Oregon and discussing the agricultural interests of Oregon, the evenings in discussing the affairs of our nation. Speeches were made by Gov. Gibbs, Gen. Alvord US Army, Judge Williams and many others, all took position that the government must and shall be preserved.[1] Mr. Perne made an abolition speech which was considered as tending to disunion. Know doubt there were coperheads or rebels present but they dare not say a word. The Statesmen (Bushes paper) does not sustain the government as it should, and to say the least is a good deal tinctured with coperheadism. . . .

The union party of Oregon are determined that at the next election, the only issue shall be, shall the government be sustained in putting down this gigantic rebellion or shall it not, while the rebel party desire to draw in some other side issue such as what shall be done with the negroes? or something about the unconstitutional acts of the government, there by drawing the attention of the people from the real issue before them. As for me I intend to support no man or sett of men that do not go for supporting unconditionally all the efforts that the government is making to put down the rebellion and save our government from dissolution. Gov. Gibbs and all of our leading men spoke of you and approved of your course and said that if they could be of servise to you in anny way they would be happy in doing so.

Nothing worthy of notice has taken place at home since I last wrote. The same rotine of farming looking after sheep cattle and other stock still goes on. I rented the dairy to a last years emigrant, he proved to be a lazy trifling rebel he made his living and I lost the entire use of the cows this season. Farming in Oregon has become a dull and unprofitable business, but as most all that I have is invested in it and no sale for land I shall have to do the best I can. If I could get an appointment from government I should like it perhaps you can aid me in getting it.

Henry is making a living and that is about all. Dorinda is at home but will return to school. Edward has been helping on the farm during the summer, but will go to school soon. . . .

---

1. Brigadier-General Benjamin Alvord (1813–84) commanded the District of Oregon during the war, where he had little to do except to keep an eye on Indians and "Copperheads." Judge Williams has not been identified.

Roswell to Kate

> USS *Nansemond*
> Off New Inlet Bar
> Sept. 30, 1863

I have just left the deck in charge of the officer of the deck and pilot, and came in to sit down a few minutes, which I will spend writing to you as we will have an opportunity to send letters the last of this week. I am running in close to the bar and the forts, as it is quite dark, and the moon has not yet risen—as soon as she rises I shall run out a little, and anchor for the night as nothing will try to come out after moon rise. . . .

Last Sunday I was assisting one of our vessels that had got disabled, and while we were busy at work I thought—"Katie is going to church now"—"what *would* we do without those true hearts to pray for us, and watch for us, and love us"—"*What would we do without them.*" . . .

Separation is *indeed hard* to bear, and I fear more so for you than for me, because I have so many things to occupy my attention and so much of excitements; *not* because I *love* you less, or *wish for you less.* Your duties are more quiet though quite as arduous. . . .

Roswell to Flora

> USS *Nansemond*
> At sea
> 3:30 a.m. Oct. 4, 1863

You may wonder at my writing at this hour, but I am running up the coast towards Cape Lookout and have been on deck to give the officer-of-the-deck some instructions and it is such a beautiful moonlight night that I cannot sleep. The Nansemond is going along easily and gracefully eleven knots an hour—a pleasant breeze and a light sea from the Westward. I wish you could see how beautifully she moves through the bright moon-lit waters. It is almost a year since I was at Shelburne Falls.

Since I wrote you last I have been blockading off Wilmington N.C.

I think I told you about driving a vessel ashore that was trying to come out. While I was at Beaufort (N.C.) coaling the last time the "Connecticut" cruised off to the Eastward and fell in with the "Juno" which she captured, and on her way back she chased and drove ashore the "Phantom."[1] There are eleven vessels now blockading off New Inlet, N.C. Capt. Sands[2] is Senior officer. As I left my station off the bar this evening the "Daylight"[3] took me for a blockade-runner and without giving the proper signals opened fire; as it was quite dark, the moon not having yet risen, his shots did not come very near and I was looking out for the blockade-runner when whiz came a shell over the stern of the Nansemond I gave him the private signal and soon after saw a vessel firing at him I beat to quarters and ran down to have a hand in the muss and found that the "Iron Age"[4] had mistaken the "Daylight" for a blockade-runner and had opened fire on him. I ran within hail of the "Daylight" whose captain apologised for shooting at me, sometimes it is so dark and cloudy that it is difficult to make out the signals, but a shot or two occasionally makes people keep on the *qui vive*. The rebels took me for a blockade-runner the other night and showed me their signals which I answered at a venture and ran in so close that we could see the men making the signals. As soon as we make Cape Lookout I shall haul in for Old Topsail Inlet and go into Beaufort for coal and repairs to the boiler.

I have been intending to give you a better idea of the blockade and the difficulties attending it, but have not had time. I am sure that no men work harder and get less credit for it than those in the blockading fleets. The Nansemond is getting in better order every day and all on board are contented and has happy as can be. They are building me a nice "Gig" (Captains boat) in Baltimore which is to be fitted out in the nicest style—I have a splendid "Gig's crew"—They were with me up the Nansemond River and the Coxswain wears a medal for bravery there of which he is proud enough. . . .

1. USS *Connecticut*, a large sidewheel steamer built in 1861 and carrying 12 guns. She participated in the capture or destruction of nine other blockade runners in addition to the *Juno* and *Phantom*.

2. Captain Benjamin F. Sands (1811–83).

3. USS *Daylight*, a screw steamer built in 1860 and acquired by the navy in 1861 for blockade duty, and armed with eight guns. She participated in the capture or destruction of 12 blockade runners.

4. USS *Iron Age*, a nine-gun screw steamer built in 1862; she helped destroy or capture three blockade runners, including the *Robert E. Lee*.

Roswell to Flora

> USS *Nansemond*
> At sea
> Oct. 12, 1863

... I sailed from Beaufort (N.C.) on Sat. evening and ran to the southward and eastward nearly across the Gulf Stream, but without falling in with anything. Last night, however, to the north of New Inlet I had the satisfaction of capturing and destroying one of the largest Confederate steamers, the "Douro."[1] She had on board 550 bales of cotton, 279 bales of tobacco, 20 tierces ditto, and a quantity of turpentine and rosin; all belonging to the Confederate government. I captured part of her officers and crew. The captain finding he could not escape from me, ran the ship on the beach and escaped to the shore with part of his crew. I cleared away my boats and boarded the "Douro" before the rest could escape. She went on the beach at a high speed, and there being a heavy surf and a falling tide, I found, after two hours effort, and after parting all my hawsers that I could not get him off; and he was close under a rebel battery. I set the ship on fire, and then lay off and shelled the rebs and the steamer's machinery till she burned completely. She made a magnificent fire the bursting turpentine barrels throwing up beautiful jets of flame. The steamer and cargo were worth nearly 250,000—more than that to the rebels for their European loan depends on the amount of cotton they can get out. If we could have got her off the beach we should have had a handsome lot of prize money—if the land sharks had not got it all as they usually do. The *first* duty of a blockader, however, is to prevent ingress and egress and to damage the enemy—his second duty to make prizes. I am glad the Nansemond has done something for the government and hope she will do much more. The rebels never lose an opportunity to give her a shot and she never loses a chance to give them two in return. The prisoners have given us some most valuable information—I sent them to the senior officer to-day.

---

1. A British-built iron screw steamer, the *Douro* had been captured once before trying to run the blockade out of Wilmington, on March 9, 1863. She was sold by the prize court to a purchaser in Nassau, who returned her to blockade running. As Lamson's description makes clear, she would never go to sea again.

I commenced this letter about the middle of the afternoon, when I was called away; between eight and nine this evening after getting into the position I wished for the night guard, I commenced again when the quartermaster interrupted me with "The Officer of the deck reports a vessel off the port bow, Sir"—went on deck and there was a dark shadow on the water some distance from us, but our best night glasses would only make it out a shadow—only after watching it some time, it did not change or vary as shadows do on water, which assured us that it was a ship. We beat to quarters for action and ran for him and when almost near enough to open fire gave him our private signal which was not answered. We thought we had a blockade-runner but when nearer repeated the signal and our hopes fell as the proper reply flashed over the waters. "Beat the retreat"— "hard-a-starboard."

I recommenced this letter but had not written ten minutes when "The officer-of-the-deck reports smoke ahead, Sir, like that from a blockade-runner" you may think it a nice distinction to tell their vessels from ours by the color of their smoke, but they burn a different kind of coal and sailors learn to distinguish ships by slighter marks than that. I went on deck and there was smoke and a shadow, hardly to be seen—it might be a vessel or it might not—but we must go to quarters to be ready if it should be one—for when we got close he might run by before the guns could be manned, and perhaps disappear in the darkness. So all the officers were called again, and the men sent to their stations for action. After running sometime, beat the retreat again—again disappointed. How many times this will happen between now (eleven o'clock) and morning it is impossible to say—but now you have a specimen of our *quiet pleasant* evenings, for the weather now is delightful. When it is stormy and rainy the exercises are somewhat more varied, but none the less interesting. Last night, however will keep us in good spirits for a long time. I shall go on deck till twelve, and then lie down till called at four, unless something turns up sooner.

October 14

... Yesterday I was on board the ship of the Senior officer here now, Capt. Almy. In forwarding my report of the capture of the Douro he sent the Admiral a letter in which he said he wished to call his particular attention to the "marked vigilance, energy and activity displayed by the Nansemond" and other complimentary things.[1] This morning I passed near the Douro a little after daylight when the rebels opened fire on me from one of their batteries we returned the compliment and they ceased firing. The Douro is a complete wreck, nothing above water now but her smoke-stack and the sea breaks nearly to the top of that. . . .

Roswell to Katie

USS *Nansemond*
Beaufort, N.C.
Oct. 15, 1863

I am very sad to-night, and as I always wish to tell *you* whatever makes me sorrowful or happy, I must give you a short account of the incidents of to-day which commenced so hopefully, continued so exciting and ended so tragically.

For several days we have been stationed a little to the northward of the fleet off New Inlet as picket boat. This morning we made a strange sail to the S. & E., and I signalled her to the flag ship, and gave chase and soon the "Howquah"[2] left the flag ship and joined in the chase. The stranger showed no spars, made very black smoke and showed every appearance of being a blockade runner, who had got in nearer the fleet than he intended and was trying to get out of sight again. We were soon in fast pursuit, and the chase appeared to be heading so as to be able to reach the shore in case he found he could not elude us.

There was quite a heavy swell from lee-ward and the Nansemond dashed through it most beautifully, tossing the waves from her bows as though she enjoyed the sport and the admiration we all bestowed upon her. None but those who have experienced it can know the excitement of a chase at sea—a sailors pride in his vessel, his desire of

1. Commander John J. Almy (1815–95). Almy's exact words praised *Lamson's* (not the *Nansemond's*) "highly commendable vigilance, skill, and energy" (*O.R. Navies*, ser. I, vol. 9, p. 232).

2. A screw steamer carrying four guns. Despite what Lamson states in the following paragraph about the *Howquah's* speed, it was rated at only ten knots.

coming up with the enemy, the exhilaration of the motion, the dashing of the waves, and the quick skill required to take advantage of every favorable circumstance of wind and wave, all combine to make it as intensely exciting to those deeply interested as any thing can be. We were making fully *fifteen knots an hour*, and in *two hours*, the Howquah (one of the fastest vessels in the blockade) *was just disappearing from sight astern*. We were gaining in the chase, but it was evident that she was an antagonist worthy the Nansemond's effort for she held her way beautifully at great speed—at intervals she threw up a cloud of black smoke as blockade runners do, and changed her direction occasionally, as though trying to throw us off the track; but she was watched by a half-dozen good marine glasses, and every change met with a corresponding one on our part.

Her hull was becoming more distinct above the horizon and we could see that we were gaining when there came up a squall from the S.E. which nearly shut him from our view.

I made some of the men lie down on the lower deck and look along the surface of the water, as in such cases you can see better the nearer the surface, and every eye was strained to keep sight of him lest he should change his course and so escape.

The squall of wind and rain lasted for two hours during which time we only caught occasional glimpses of a dark indistinct object ahead, and at one time lost sight of him altogether for half an hour. At last the clouds cleared away, and we found ourselves much nearer and coming up quite rapidly. The Nansemond was even exceeding our expectations, and every one was loud in praise of the magnificent way she dashed through the water. We marked our position on the chart, and found that the stranger was running directly for the Lookout Shoals, and that unless we changed our course we should be on them in an hour. We concluded he had determined to wreck her rather than allow us to capture her. My sailing Master, Mr Henderson asked me if he should change our course to avoid the shoals but I told him to follow the chase till one or both of us were on the shoals, or till we brought him to. I knew that at that stage of the tide it was *just* possible that we might go over the shoals without striking, and I intended to follow him across in case he did not haul off. Just before reaching the shoals he hauled in for the land to the l'rd; I hauled in to catch him if possible before he beached her—he steered straight for the shoals again, but I was watching for that maneuver, and succeeded in *getting between him* and the shoals. We were going faster than ever, and we had got him hemmed between Cape Lookout and the land to the l'rd. He had shown no colors during the day though ours had been flying all the time. We were coming within range and I had one of our guns trained on him, when he stopped almost and began to blow off steam. We fired a shot across his bows which brought him to *he showed our own flag*. When he stopped I told my Executive Officer Mr Porter to get our boats ready for lowering, arm the crews and go on board himself with an engineer and three firemen to take charge of him.

Mr Strude, 3 Ast. Engineer requested permission to go, and while Mr Porter was attending to some duty forward he got into the port quarter boat with his three firemen. The boat was as usual hanging at the davits from cranes from which our boats hang ready to drop in to the water, and three of the crew were in her ready to lower her when we stopped. Mr Strude and his men had no sooner got in them the additional weight proved too much for the davits, the after one of which though iron snapped short off and the seven persons in the boat were precipitated into the water. Mr Strude and a seaman named Terry were struck by the falling boat and the iron crane and never rose. The others rose to the surface, the alarm was given, the vessel stopped and my gig's crew jumped into their boat lowered it, and picked them up in almost less time than I can write it. We watched a long time hoping the two missing men would come up, but the blue waters had closed over them forever. This sad accident happened just as we fired to bring the stranger to and just before she showed her colors. It was startling to see the change in the faces of all from high exultation and pride in the achievement of our vessel to deep sorrow for those our comrades who had so suddenly lost their lives in the moment when they expected to be rewarded for their exertions during the day.

Mr. Strude was an excellent officer, and had won the esteem of all by his attention to duty, his knowledge of his profession, and his amiable manners. Last Sunday night I sent him on board the Douro, to take charge of her engines while we were trying to get her off, and in my report recommended him to the favorable notice of the Admiral— now I have to report his death. Terry was a good seaman, always willing and obedient. Either of them would have followed me any where, or done anything to serve me. Mr. Strude was unmarried, I understand he has a mother in Linden.

The strange vessel proved to be Admiral Dahlgren's dispatch vessel, a very fast light steamer in charge of a Volunteer Acting Master, bound to Hampton Roads with dispatches.[1] He wished to show his speed and do what he thought was a smart thing by exciting the suspicions of the blockading fleet, when a vessel was sent out to ascertain his character, show how quick he could run away from her; he said he had no idea of finding anything so fast as we were. Of course he cannot be blamed directly for the sad occurrence—no one can be it was one of those accidents that a sailor is always liable to, his life depending so constantly on the strength of a piece of wood, iron or rope; the strength of a boat or ship and the skill with which it is managed. The men who were rescued seemed to think very little of their own danger, though one of them was unable to swim, and took it as a matter not worth mentioning as far as they were concerned.

I shall make a full report of the affair to the Department, and they can take what notice they see fit of his very singular conduct. God grant that this judgment may not be lost upon us, but that we may so live that when our time comes we may not be found unprepared for even so sudden a change. . . .

Roswell to Kate

USS *Nansemond*
Beaufort, NC
Oct. 16, 1863

. . . I think I wrote you that they were building me a nice "Gig" in Balto. (The "Gig" is the Captain's private boat) The Newberne brought it down a few days ago, and I am very much pleased with it. It is a good sea boat, and finished in the nicest and most complete style, through the kindness of Commodore Dornin, who directed it to be built.

Now, dearest, I am going to ask you to do me the favor to make me a silk "pennant" for it, so that whenever I see it fly I shall be reminded that I sail under your colors. All men-of-war boats carry a flag at the stern, and all Commanders of ships carry a small pennant on a staff

---

1. The USS *Oleander*, a sidewheel steamer built in 1863, commanded by Acting Master John Dennis. Lamson's superior officers also complained about Dennis, but there is no indication in the *Official Records* whether he received a reprimand of any kind for this action.

at the bow of the Gig, so that all other boats may know them and get out of their way, and so that when going on board their own or any other vessel their approach may be known, and they may be received with the proper honors. So you see your pennant will be treated with all due respect. I can have plenty made on board, but I want to fly *your* pennant, for you know I fight for *you*.

The sad accident of yesterday has left a dark gloom over the ship—it seems almost like a dream—the exciting chase, and the sad termination—God help us all *to do our duty* and to *be ready*.

We are taking in some coal—It looks pretty thick outside, but I think I shall sail this evening, as I am anxious to return to my station. . . .

Roswell to Kate

USS *Nansemond*
Off New Inlet
Oct. 22, 1863

The Howquah goes for coal, and I have just time to tell you that since my last I have had two chases, and have captured and destroyed the rebel blockade runner "Venus" [one] of their *finest* and *fastest* ships. I captured the captain, officers, and most of the crew. The Venus had one killed and was almost in a sinking condition when they beached her. A large part of her cargo was *lead* for the rebs. We were exposed to a hot fire from the shore, but no one was hurt.

I have had another little affair on hand which I should like to give you in detail for I am sure you would enjoy it as there is some romance and some love mixed with it.

When Capt. Case went home he gave me his Wilmington pilot, Mr. Bowen, who lived near Wilmington and had a wife and one child there. Mr Bowen has been in our service over two years as a pilot during which time he had only heard that his wife had made several attempts to get to him at Beaufort but had been stopped by the rebels and subjected to very harsh treatment. He tried to get Capt Case to make some effort to get them, but he thought it too dangerous. When Mr Bowen came on board I told him I would make the attempt for although he did his duty faithfully I could see it was with a very heavy heart. Since then I have been trying to get the consent of the Senior

officers here to try it, but did not succeed till last Sun. when I told
Capt. Sands that if he did not give me an *order* to the contrary I should
try; he did not give the order, and on Monday and Tuesday nights we
put the plan in execution, and on Wednesday morning had the satisfaction of seeing Mr. B. look happier than ever before. We got his wife
and child, and also a young brother who had just been drafted in to
the rebel army.

Mrs. B. occupies one of the rooms in my cabin, till we go to Beaufort where she will remain, Mr. B will thus be able to see her every
two weeks. While we were watching for Mrs. B. we discovered the
"Venus" trying to run the blockade and destroyed her as I told you. I
wish you could hear what Capt Sands the Senior officer here says of
the "Nansemond," but as you cannot you must excuse my saying that
she has a reputation here that no other vessel on the blockade has for
service.[1]

Roswell to Kate

> USS *Nansemond*
> Off New Inlet
> Nov. 3, 1863

. . . I am glad the Russian officers have been treated with such distinguished courtesy for their nation has always been friendly to us, and
during this rebellion has fulfilled most honorably its obligations to our
government.[2] Americans, however, generally run wild over anything for-

---

1. In his report of the destruction of the *Venus*, a privately owned blockade runner
financed by British interests, Captain Benjamin F. Sands wrote to Admiral Lee: "I can
not say too much in favor of such vessels as the *Nansemond* and *Niphon* [a seven-gun
screw steamer], with their energetic commanding officers, for blockading purposes.
Give us a few such and we will put a stop to this nefarious British trade and make
Wilmington a closed port. . . . I find the *Nansemond* so useful that I am coaling her
from this vessel [USS *Dacotah*, a nine-gun screw steamer] to keep her here during the
next few dark nights" (*O.R. Navies*, ser. I, vol. 9, pp. 248–49, dated Oct. 21, 1863).

2. During the fall and winter of 1863–64, ships from the Atlantic and Pacific fleets
of the Imperial Russian Navy made courtesy calls to the ports of New York and San
Francisco, staying for months. People in the North made much of these visits as a
sign of Russian support for the Union cause—which was true enough—but an equally
important reason was the desire of the Russian navy to avoid being blockaded into

eign, and I presume the Russians will be so overwhelmed that they will be glad when it is over, and we shall have as amusing accounts of "incidents" as those which followed the receptions of the Japanese and the Prince of Wales. We are perfectly careless of the cost, however, and *whole souled* hospitality can never be disparaged.

I have but little doubt but we shall have ample opportunity to test the temper of their metal, and see if they are deserving such regard, for England and France cannot forget the defiance Russia has so recently thrown in their teeth, if they are not forced to resent it at once, and *we* have a few questions to settle with them when the opportunity comes.

I should like exceedingly to see their ships for I have never been on board a Russian man-of-war.

The news from Ohio was indeed cheering but nothing more than we expected from the Buckeye state.[1] If Burnside had let Vallandigham alone he never would have been nominated, I think, but it is all right now.

Last night we expected a vessel out, and ran in quite near the batteries and hove-to—nothing got out except a shot which came over our decks, but without doing any harm.

This morning at daylight I sent a boat ashore and brought off a deserter from the rebel army.

There was quite a heavy surf and the officer in charge of the boat not choosing his time judiciously for going through it, the boat broached-to, and was thrown over and over by the force of the waves— I cleared away another boat to go to their assistance, but the waves tossed them up on the beach, boat and all, and after some exertion they got the boat righted, and watching for "a smooth time" launched her through the surf without much difficulty. There are a number of vessels that will be ready to come out soon, and I am going to take an off shore cruise in hopes of falling in with some of them between here and Bermuda or Nassau. I shall leave after dark to-morrow night, and run to the eastward and southward.

---

icebound Baltic ports by the British navy during a time of tension between Britain and Russia over the latter's suppression of Polish nationalists. The Crimean War, in which Britain and France had fought the Russians, was only seven years in the past.

1. In Ohio's gubernatorial election on October 13, the Peace Democrat Clement L. Vallandigham was buried under a 100,000-vote majority for the Republican candidate John Brough.

We have been having a continuation of North-easters for ten days or more, but to-night is calm and clear, and we have the promise of fine weather.

I should like to have you see the ocean first on such a night as this for when the moon rises it will be beautiful—then I should like you to see the *beautiful blue* of the Gulf Stream,—then I should like to have you look *over* and see the Nansemond in a gale, especially if the water was phosforescent enough to make the waves *show* their teeth. I should prefer you should not see anything of this wearying blockade except the prize money I still hope to send you, for it scarcely seems *honorable* service when there is so much fighting to be done; it does good for the cause, though, for the destruction of a cargo of ammunition and supplies, like that in the Venus, besides weakening the rebels, may be the means of saving the lives of hundreds of our own soldiers. . . .

The wind, the sea and the stars tell me that *"Katie loves me,"* and as I turn to the stars for guidance over the ocean so my heart turns to you for guidance through life. . . .

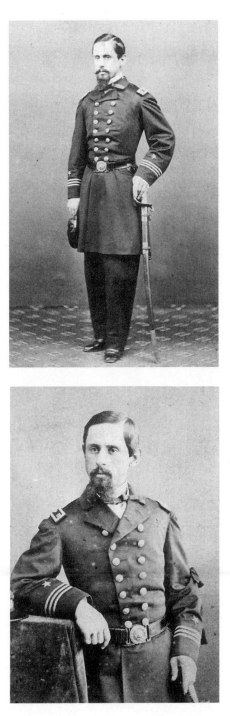

Two photographs of Lieutenant Roswell H. Lamson in full-dress uniform, probably made during his tour of duty in Washington, January 1863. *Courtesy Princeton University Libraries.*

(Above) Catherine Buckingham (Kate), Roswell's fiancée and wife. *Courtesy Princeton University Libraries.*
(Below) Lieutenant Morreau Forrest, Lamson's roommate at the Naval Academy. *Courtesy Princeton University Libraries.*

(*Above*) "Old Tom," a Boatswain's Mate on the USS *Plymouth*, was typical of the sailors in the Union navy for whom Lamson expressed affection. *Courtesy Princeton University Libraries.*

(*Below*) Rear Admiral Samuel Francis Du Pont, commander (then with the rank of Flag Officer) of the Union fleet that captured Port Royal on November 7, 1861. *Courtesy Princeton University Libraries.*

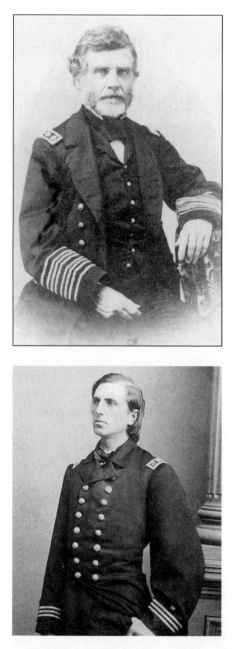

(*Above*) Acting Rear Admiral Samuel Phillips Lee, commander of the North Atlantic Blockading Squadron from July 1862 to October 1864. Lee and Lamson developed a warm professional and personal relationship. *Courtesy Princeton University Libraries.*

(*Below*) Lieutenant William B. Cushing, who began a lifelong friendship with Lamson during their cooperation as gunboat commanders in the Suffolk campaign April–May 1863. *Courtesy Princeton University Libraries.*

(*Above*) USS *Gettysburg*. There is no known photograph of the *Gettysburg* (nor of the *Nansemond*). This illustration is from a postwar painting by Thomas DeSimone, done when the *Gettysburg* was on duty in the Mediterranean. *Courtesy U.S. Naval Historical Center.*
(*Below*) Robert H. Gillette, paymaster on the *Nansemond* and *Gettysburg*, who became a close friend of Lamson's. *Courtesy Princeton University Libraries.*

(*Above*) Rear Admiral David Dixon Porter, who took command of the North Atlantic Blockading Squadron in October 1864 and led the attack on Fort Fisher. *Courtesy Princeton University Libraries.*

(*Below*) Roswell H. Lamson and William B. Cushing, two of the most intrepid officers in the Union navy. The shawl draped over Lamson's right arm is puzzling, since he was wounded in his *left* shoulder in the attack on Fort Fisher. The photograph was probably made before that attack. *Courtesy Princeton University Libraries.*

(*Above*) Lieutenant Samuel W. Preston, Lamson's friendly rival who graduated first in the Naval Academy's class of 1862, just ahead of Lamson, and was killed at Lamson's side in the assault on Fort Fisher, January 15, 1865.
Courtesy Princeton University Libraries.
(*Below*) The USS *Lamson* during her trials in 1909. This "torpedo-boat destroyer" was commissioned in 1910 and performed convoy duty against German submarines in World War I. She was decommissioned in 1919.
Courtesy of U.S. Naval Historical Center.

(*Above*) The second USS *Lamson* in 1927. A destroyer launched in 1920, this vessel never fired a shot in anger and was decommissioned in 1930. *Courtesy of U.S. Naval Historical Center.*

(*Below*) The third USS *Lamson* in 1939. Launched and commissioned in 1936, this *Lamson* was stationed at Pearl Harbor but was away on patrol duty when the Japanese attacked on December 7, 1941. She fought through all of World War II in the Pacific, surviving several kamikaze attacks and earning five battle stars. Her end came when she was intentionally sunk by an atomic bomb in a test at Bikini Atoll on July 2, 1946. *Courtesy of the Mariners Museum, Newport News, Va. (Ted Stone Collection).*

CHAPTER 6

OUR FLAG WAS

THE FIRST

THERE IS A HIATUS OF more than a month in Lamson's personal letters that results in the omission of any description of an event that was to have an important bearing on his future career: the capture on November 5, 1863, of the blockade runner *Margaret and Jessie*. Following this capture, Lamson took the *Nansemond* to Baltimore for needed repairs and obtained a brief leave in order to travel to Irvington, New York, where he saw Kate Buckingham for a few days and no doubt told her all about the exciting chase. The navy decided to convert the captured runner into the USS *Gettysburg*. Built in 1858 as an Isle of Man packet, the iron-hulled *Margaret and Jessie* had been the fastest ship in the world when she came off the ways in Glasgow. Armed with seven guns, the *Gettysburg* became the swiftest vessel in the Union fleet, capable of sixteen knots (about eighteen miles an hour). It did not take the Navy Department long to decide who should command her. In December Lamson received orders to supervise the *Gettysburg*'s conversion and then take her to sea as a blockader.

Because no personal letters describe the capture of the *Margaret and Jessie*, this chapter begins with Lamson's official report of the incident.

———————

Lamson to Rear Admiral S. P. Lee

> USS *Nansemond*
> At Sea
> Lat. 33° 42' N.
> Long. 76° W.
> 8 p.m. November 5, 1863

SIR: I have the honor to submit the following report of the part taken by this vessel in the capture of the rebel steamer *Margaret and Jessie* to-day:

This forenoon, at 10 o'clock, in latitude 34° 05' N., longitude 76° 50' W., we made a dim black smoke to the southward and westward and soon made out from the way it tended that the vessel was running offshore. We stood to intercept her, and discovered a sail (afterwards found to be the army transport *Fulton*) apparently in chase of the blockade runner, and soon after another sail (*U.S.S. Keystone State*) also in pursuit.[1]

By 11:30 we had passed the *Fulton* and were leaving her astern, and at 12 m. opened fire on the chase, our shots falling but little short, and measurements with the sextant assured us that we were gaining on her, when a strong breeze came up from the southwest, bringing quite a heavy sea, which striking under the low guards of the *Nansemond* impeded her progress, and at 1:15 p.m. the *Fulton* passed us and continued a short distance ahead till she brought the chase to by a shot from her bow gun at 3:50 p.m.

As soon as we came up I sent a boat on board with Acting Ensign J. B. Henderson and Acting Third Assistant Engineer E. Aspold to render assistance, and our flag was the first hoisted on the prize.

In a very short time the *Keystone State* came up, and I reported to Commander Donaldson.[2] The prize proved to be the *Margaret and Jessie*, of Charleston, S. C., from Nassau, bound to Wilmington with an assorted cargo, a part of which was thrown overboard during the chase.

---

1. The *Fulton* was a large sidewheel steamer. Its armament is not indicated in the naval records. The USS *Keystone State* was also a large sidewheeler, built in 1853 and acquired by the navy in 1861. She carried 11 guns and was rated at 9.5 knots. The *Fulton* was able to catch the *Margaret and Jessie* in the heavy seas only because the latter was overloaded with cargo, which she began jettisoning too late.

2. Commander Edward Donaldson (–1889).

... She is a sidewheel steamer of 700 tons, and has been a fast and successful blockade runner. [*O.R. Navies*, ser. I, vol. 9, pp. 265–66]

Roswell to Kate

> USS *Nansemond*
> Bound down the
> Chesapeake
> Dec. 11, 1863

Again the Nansemond is dashing through the water, and

> "Again on the deck I stand,
> Of *my own swift gliding craft*."

There is more pleasure in *that* than you may suppose, but I *must* confess to a feeling of *sadness* as I think I am going farther from *you*; and when I think of Irvington and my happy visit there, and then of the storming ocean without *you*, I feel a sort of dread of leaving the one and of encountering the other; as soon as I *see* the ocean I presume I shall feel as usual, and you will help me to encounter *every* danger. . . .

The Nansemond is in much better order than ever before, and much more comfortable, as I had many improvements made that time did not permit having done when we fitted out. . . .

The last evening I was in Balto. I went to hear Hackett play Falstaff, in the Merry Wives of Windsor.[1] He is the only actor I ever cared to see, and I enjoyed the play very much. The other characters were not worth looking at; but it was a treat just to see and hear Hackett. He is supposed to be the best representative of the character that ever lived.

> Cape Henry, Va.
> Dec. 12, 1863

I reported to the Admiral at Newport News early this morning and after getting ordnance stores from the Depot dropped down to the Cape ready to go out at daylight in the morning. I was so busy during

1. James Henry Hackett (1800–1871), a noted Shakespearean actor, most famous for his playing of Falstaff. Lincoln also admired Hackett, but some contemporary critics and historians of drama have been less admiring.

the day that I could not finish your letter, but will try to send it back by a pilot boat.

The Admiral was quite satisfied with the time we made, and was as kind as usual.

I took breakfast in the Minnesota, and had quite a visit with those of my old messmates still there. The Admiral said I should have the Margaret & Jessie if I wished her, and could send one of my officers to see her fitted out.

Have no fears for me, darling, but take good care of yourself, and may Heaven bless you and make you happy always. Remember that I *love you*, and care not for toil or danger in your service and that of *our country*.

Roswell to Kate

USS *Nansemond*
Hampton Roads
Dec. 14, 1863

We passed the Capes of Virginia on Saturday morning at four o'clock, and had fair weather, and a fine run till we approached *Hatteras*, where we got a strong breeze from the S.S.E., which by ten o'clock that night had increased to a very heavy gale—we rounded the cape, and made very good weather till ten minutes before four on Sunday morning when a heavy sea came on board sweeping the port side of the ship from stem to stern; smashing in the bulwarks and engine room bulkheads; eight or ten men were injured, some severely, and the water forced down the engine and fire room hatches till we had nearly five feet of water in the hold, the water coming up nearly to the fires. The concussion was so great that the engine stopped and could not be started for some time. I wore round with the jib and we scudded before it for some time till a wave higher and faster than the rest overtook us and swept the starboard side almost as badly as the port, and sending large volumes of water down into the hold; a wave lifted the stern of the vessel almost immediately after, the water ran forward to the bows which began to settle rapidly when I ordered the bow guns to be launched over board, and in a few minutes four tons of shells were also thrown over. This lightened her so much that she rose, and we succeeded in freeing her from most of the water. We were then standing before the gale, with the wild waves chasing us like so many frenzied fiends, at eight o'clock we rounded the "stormy cape" again, and by the afternoon the gale had abated so that I hauled in to make the land near Cape Henry, but the night was so dark and foggy that we could not see the lights on either cape, and after groping our way with the lead I let go an anchor to wait for daylight. It was a night of some anxiety to me for we could not bring the head to the sea in her disabled condition and we had not coal enough to run more than four hours. Fortunately the night was calm, but this morning was so foggy that we could see nothing till ten o'clock when seeing a squall coming up from the West we got underway to ready when it should drive away the mist. We soon made Smith's Island light house, and soon Cape Henry, and a little after noon were at anchor alongside the flag ship— just in time to escape a nor'wester which is blowing now. The Admiral said he was glad to see us back again, and thought we managed her well to live out such a gale after receiving such serious damage. I thought of *you* darling all the time, but especially on Sunday. I *knew* *you* were praying for me, and you cannot tell what a source of happiness that thought was to me during the entire danger. Never in my life have I seen the hand and power of God so distinctly manifested as during the past two days in delivering us from such imminent danger.

Roswell to Kate

> USS *Nansemond*
> Baltimore
> Dec. 17, 1863

We left Hampton Roads yesterday morning, and arrived here last evening, making an average of over fourteen miles an hour notwithstanding our disabled condition.

This morning I reported to the Commodore, and to-morrow will haul up to the yard for repairs. Commo. Dornin thought we had a very narrow escape, and so we had, though I never doubted but we should weather it out.

I shall go to Washington to-morrow or next day, and then I shall be able to tell you more definitely what I am to do, though I have no doubt but I shall come to New York.

. . . In forwarding my report of our disaster to the Navy Department

Admiral Lee endorsed on it "This report is respectfully forwarded to the Department with a commendation of the efficient conduct of Lieutenant Lamson, and his officers and crew in saving the vessel when in such imminent peril."[1] . . .

It has been rumored among the crew to-day that I am to be detached from the vessel, and since I came on board several of the men have requested to speak with me, and all asked me to take them to the vessel I was ordered to. I was surprised at the earnestness of their entreaties. Some said they would go any where & do anything if I would keep them with me, but they felt as though they could not stay in the ship if I left her. Day before yesterday when I went on board the Minnesota I had not walked from the gangway to the cabin door till a crowd of the sailors were around me, with their caps off asking me to get them with me. One of them said, "you could get two-hundred men, Sir, as soon as you said the word to go any where with you." Some of them handed me their names on slips of paper that I might not forget it. I do not understand it for I am very impatient with them sometimes, and have punished some of them most severely, but I do not think the fine fellows are more attached to me than I am to them.

The Admiral said this afternoon that he wished me to go to New York to fit out the Margaret & Jessie—so I presume I shall be detached within a week and be in New York by Christmas—I long to see you again, my own sweet Katie.

At my request, Admiral Lee has promised the command of the Nansemond to my Executive officer, Mr. Porter and has also promised to promote him if he does well with her. I am very glad for I am *much* attached to the vessel, and I could not endure that a stranger should come on board to command her. . . .

Roswell to Kate

New York
Dec. 31, 1863

I cannot tell you how disappointed I was to hear that I was not to see you here—I had been working hard to get the Nansemond turned

---

1. These were Lee's exact words in an endorsement dated December 15 (*O.R. Navies*, ser. I, vol. 9, p. 350).

over and everything arranged to come on and spend Christmas with you at Irvington, when just as I was ready to leave Balt. Mr Femmer's telegram came, to tell me that you were already on your way home.

Had I known it while I was in Washington I might have got leave long enough to come to Mt Vernon for a few days, but I had received my orders to report here "without delay," and the circumstances under which I was ordered to the "Gettysburg" made me more anxious to get here. When I see you I will give you all the details and tell you how *much* I wished to see you, and the disappointment I felt for *you* and myself. Christmas Eve I spent at Irvington, and the day at Mr Goodnows with Flora.

The Gettysburg has been in the hands of the naval authorities here for over three weeks but nothing had been done to her till I came. I have got quite a force at work on her now and as soon as it is possible I shall try to get leave enough to come to Mt Vernon where my heart is *now*, and where it has been ever since *you* went there. . . .

Roswell to Kate

Hartford, Conn.
Jan. 17, 1864

. . . The Gettysburg required my attention so that I could not leave New York till last Thursday. My Paymaster Mr Gillette (transferred from the Nansemond) met me at New Haven and I am staying at the house of his father Hon. Francis Gillette and visiting here and at Mr Hookers. And now let me tell you something about the people—Mr Hooker is Mrs. Gillette's brother and Mrs. Hooker is, as you may know already, HW Beechers sister.[1] Before coming I received two very fine letters from Mrs Hooker inviting me to visit them and my reception by both families has been kind beyond anything I could have expected. . . . Mr & Mrs Gillette are exceeding pleasant kind people; Mr Hooker

1. Robert H. Gillette had become a close friend of Lamson during their service together on the *Nansemond*. His father had been a U.S. senator from Connecticut for one session in the 1850s, filling a vacancy. Isabella Beecher Hooker was indeed a sister of Henry Ward Beecher as well as of Harriet Beecher Stowe ("Hattie"), author of *Uncle Tom's Cabin*. Isabella was an author in her own right; she was married to the prominent lawyer John Hooker.

is one of the first lawyers in the state, and Mrs. Hooker one of the most interesting, best, & most kind hearted ladies I ever met: she already calls me "one of her boys," and apparently takes as kind an interest in *our* engagement as she does in that of her own daughter. Yesterday I went over to spend the day at Mr. H's the young ladies went to take French lessons leaving Mrs. H. & myself alone for most of the morning. She gave me an account of all the engagements, and I told her of *ours* which seemed to please her very much though she had had an intimation of something of the kind from Hattie Stowe. . . .

They ask so many questions about you all of which I am happy to answer *and I do wish* you could be *here a few days*. I should be *perfectly happy*. I enjoy the comfort and quiet of these New England homes *very much* after having been on board ship so much—and I am getting rest that I needed very much for while I was in New York I was busy on board the Gettysburg during the day, and almost every evening went some where with Cousin Flora, or Mary or Flo and living at a hotel is tiresome in itself especially when my heart was threatening to fly away with my body it wanted so much to be with you. . . .

Last evening all the young folks collected at Mrs Hookers and we had music, inquiry games, and some dancing. . . . This morning I went to church with Mr. Gillette's family, and heard a most excellent and interesting sermon from the Rev. Mr Burton who is called the most able preacher in Connecticut, and is thought by many to be equal if not superior to Henry Ward Beecher.[1] I would rather hear Mr Beecher—he speaks more from his everyday observation of the world and of men and touches springs that few men know to exist. Mr Burton speaks more from books and from his own inward consciousness—he may be the superior in intellect but with my training it is natural I should prefer Mr Beecher. . . .

---

1. Nathaniel Judson Burton (1824–87), pastor at Fourth Congregational Church in Hartford and one of the leading clergymen in New England.

Father (Jeremiah) to Roswell

Willamina, Ore.
Jan. 23, 1864

Your letters giving an account of the destruction of the Duro and Venus have been received. We all rejoice to hear of your safety, and of your usefulness to your country. We should have been twice happy to have heard that you had succeeded in saving the prises, as I see by the New York Herald that your share of the prise money would have been twenty thousand dollars, but as your first object in serving your country is not money I suppose you are satisfied.

In all our public meetings your name is mentioned by the public speakers and applauded by all. The public press also speaks of you often in the highest terms.

All say that when you come home they will give you a public reception. . . .

Our family are all well. Henry is plodding along as usual farming and taking care of his babies. Dorinda has been at home for the last two quarters, but will return to Salem the next quarter. She is quite a favourite at Salem and considering the advantages she has had an accomplished young lady.

Edward has been teaching so hard here in our school district but will go to Salem with his sister   he takes more interest in his studies than formerly and says he intends to prepare himself for a merchant. Do you see any place that would be good for him in your lines of buisness, he wants to go to New York and go into a store as clerk what do you think of it. He is stout and healthey, and has sufficient energy to accomplish any thing that he undertakes.

Buisness in Oregon for the past two years has not been as good as usual, I have not more than made expenses, but the prospect is now better. The mines east of the Cascade mountains are good and the gold begins to come in and the products of the Willamette valley are in demand for the miners.

I have a contract to supply Fort Yamhill with beef on which I shall clear $500.[1] I have just completed a contract with the Indian depart-

1. Fort Yamhill had been established in 1856 to protect Oregon settlers from Indians. It was not far from Jeremiah Lamson's farm near Willamina, Oregon.

ment for to furnish them with work oxen on which in five days I made $550, one half of which I gave Henry.

I think I shall this year make about $1000 on sheep, wool and sheep are both in good demand. But I feel that I am getting to[o] old to attend to much buisness. My great desire in the world is to see my children useful and happy in this world and prepared for the world to come. You have now established a character of your own on which you will stand or fall, it is easy to sustain your present good character, and still it is equally easy to lose it, one misstep may blast your fair repu- tation forever. But I feel that the advise that an anxious father might give would be a mere repitition of what I have formily said so I refrain.

Roswell to Kate

Irvington, N.Y.
Jan. 29, 1864

. . . I came down from Hartford on Monday with Mrs. Hooker, thus making a pleasant ending to a *very* pleasant visit of which I have many things to tell you when I see you.

The train was delayed half an hour so we got supper before going to Brooklyn. Mr Beecher's family had gone out to spend the evening so Mrs H. and myself made ourselves at home till nine o'clock when I went to my hotel (Union Place) and felt home-sick enough. Tuesday I spent on board the Gettysburg where I found evidences of stupidity almost past belief—almost everything going wrong—and I have been at work ever since getting things arranged right, and the work is again progressing finely. She is on the dock now, and a new plate being put in the hull where she had thumped on one of the coral reefs off Nas- sau.

She is larger than was supposed, being over one-thousand tons, and will be a splendid ship when ready for sea, which I fear will not be before the middle of March—there are fifteen-hundred tubes to be put in the boilers, and the work being done at a private ship yard I cannot hurry it as much as I could at a Navy Yard where every thing is under our more immediate control.

Wednesday evening I was invited to Mr Beechers to tea and to spend the evening which passed very pleasantly. There was a "Secesh" lady there from South Carolina whose father owned a large share of the Margaret & Jessie before she was captured; her husband is a Yankee and it was very amusing to hear her remarks about Yankees in *general*, and Yankees in *particular*.

Yesterday morning I went to see the painting of Washington Irving among his literary friends at Sunny Side. Prescott's is, I think, the finest face in the group, which consists of fifteen persons. I was quite disappointed in Longfellow and Holmes especially the former who does not look as though he could produce an Evangeline.[1]

I have an account of the destruction of two blockade runners off Wilmington since I left—I wish I was there in the Gettysburg on the off shore cruising ground, for though I have had quite a pleasant time yet I am disappointed in not seeing you, and so don't care whether I stay ashore another day or not. I came up yesterday, have been persuaded to stay to-day, and shall return to the Gettysburg to-morrow morning, and in the afternoon take Mrs. Hooker to the Matinee at the Academy of Music.

My health has improved very much since I came here—I was not sick, but pretty well tired out when we got back to Balto. And I did not get any rest till I came to New York. I have not felt so well for a year as I do now. . . .

Roswell to Kate

New York
Feb. 28, 1864

I have just returned from Brooklyn where I have spent the day as I usually do Sundays, at Mr Goodnow's house and at Mr. Beecher's

---

1. This painting entitled *Washington Irving and His Literary Friends* was completed and first exhibited in New York City in 1863, to rave reviews. The painting was done by Christian Schussele of Philadelphia, based on a line drawing executed by F. O. C. Darley. It depicts Irving along with 14 other American literary greats including William H. Prescott the historian, Oliver Wendell Holmes the essayist and poet, and Henry W. Longfellow the poet (others included James Fenimore Cooper, Ralph Waldo Emerson, William Cullen Bryant, Nathaniel Hawthorne, and several less well known to history.) The portrait shows all 15 men in Irving's study at his estate "Sunnyside" near Tarrytown, New York. The fifteen were never together there at one time; Darley used photographs of each author to create the composite drawing. Engraved prints made from the painting were an enormous commercial success. The painting now hangs in the National Portrait Gallery at Washington, D.C.

church. Both of the sermons to-day were on the "beauty of holiness," and they were two of the finest discourses I ever listened to; I wished very much that you could hear them, though it might have made you a little vain. I am sure, however, that you would never again wish for beauty other than the *true* sweet beauty that shines in your face and and looks out from your eyes.

Mr. Beecher said the *most beautiful* people in the world were some old people; I have always thought so, but never heard any one say so before—I took an old lady to the Opera not long since,—of sixty years old—but to me she was the most beautiful lady in the room.

I shall look back to Mr Beecher's sermons with more pleasure than to any other events of my stay in New York—his sermons and the Operas I have heard will make music in my heart and ears for a long time. . . .

The Gettysburg is progressing finely, and will be a splendid ship when ready for sea. She will go to the Navy Yard about the 20th prox. and I hope will sail as soon as the 1st of April. I wrote to Admiral Lee yesterday to let him know how she is getting along—he said in his last letter that he was impatient to have me come back. . . .

CHAPTER 7

THE REBS EAT LITTLE

AND FIGHT HARD

MAY–JULY 1864

NOT SURPRISINGLY, it took a month longer to complete the refitting of the *Gettysburg* than Lamson had hoped, so she was not ready for sea until the first week of May. Katie came to visit him in New York, which explains the hiatus in his letters until May 9. As Lamson started south with his ship, Lieutenant-General Ulysses S. Grant, now general in chief of all Union armies, launched an offensive across the Rapidan River with the Army of the Potomac that would bring the contending armies to the James River and Petersburg by the middle of June, and Major-General Benjamin Butler began his campaign up the James River with the Army of the James that would encounter frustration and stalemate in the region between Richmond and Petersburg by the third week of May. Lamson would play an important part in these campaigns, as the following letters describe.

——•◆•——

Roswell to Kate

> USS *Gettysburg*
> Hampton Roads
> May 9, 1864

Arrived safely, this morning being detained trying to get a ship off that we found ashore above Cape Charles, showing English colors and signals of distress.

I did not see you on the bridge above Wall St Ferry but it was so late when we passed (nearly one o'clock) that I could not expect you to wait so long. The ship works finely and we are all well—had a pleasant run.

I have but a moment to write but will write you again to-morrow. . . .

Roswell to Kate

> USS *Gettysburg*
> James River, Carl's Neck
> 25 miles below Richmond
> May 11, 1864

I wrote you a few lines from Hampton Roads, but did not tell you we were coming up here because at that time I did not know exactly what we should do and I feared you might have needless anxiety.

I started up the river without a pilot convoying some supply vessels, but got a man from a vessel I met who knew something of the Channel and with his aid, and the knowledge obtained when up here before I was able to report to the Admiral here last evening.

Gen. Butler is on the right bank of the river with, it is said forty-thousand men [actually 30,000] his line extending in the direction of Petersburg but he has not taken that place yet. We have four monitors here, and a number of other vessels, but what we do must depend on the movements of the army. Last evening on board the Flag Ship the attack of Fort Darling was discussed, but it is doubtful if we can get up on account of obstructions.

We have had two gun boats blown up, one by torpedoes and one by a battery. Last evening the rebs opened with musketry but did no damage I gave my crew a little practice shelling the banks.

We are getting things straightened out and begin to look more like a ship.

My officers are very well disposed to do their duty and anxious to learn, but most of them are very green, which makes more work for me, but I do not mind that.

The banks of the river are very beautiful here and the foliage is luxuriant.

The weather is quite warm—quite a change from the cold April of N.Y.

Of course we are all engrossed by the operations in progress and are watching for "Davids" "Torpedos" and "Devils."[1] I do wish we had a little more sea room so we could get at them to more advantage.

If Lee's army is pressed this way we will have some fighting to hold our position—if not we will advance covering Gen. Butler's right flank—I will write you every opportunity but we do not have regular mails.

As I came up yesterday I reported to several senior officers I found guarding points of the river and every one of them said "The Admiral will be glad to see you with the advance—he knows you of old" or something to that effect. . . .

———•—•———

REAR-ADMIRAL SAMUEL Phillips Lee considered Lamson one of his most valuable officers; on May 12 he assigned him to the command of three gunboats to act as minesweepers (labeled "the torpedo and

---

1. The Confederate navy built several *David* class vessels (named after the original *David* built in Charleston in 1863), small semi-submerged boats carrying an explosive "torpedo" at the end of a spar designed to explode on contact with "Goliath"—a Union warship. Four of these boats plied the James River below Richmond: *Hornet, Scorpion, Squib,* and *Wasp.* The *Squib* attacked the USS *Minnesota* at Hampton Roads on April 7, 1864, but did not do much damage. None of the others managed to attack an enemy ship, but they kept the Union fleet in the James River on edge. "Torpedoes" were mines that the Confederates sowed thickly in the James River; they sank or damaged several Union warships. There was no Confederate ship or class of ships named Devil or Devils; this seems to have been a Union term to describe Confederate gunboats that doubled as minelayers and also carried spar torpedoes.

picket division") to clear the James as far upriver toward Richmond as possible (*O.R. Navies*, ser. I, vol. 10, p. 49).

———•·———

Roswell to Kate

> *U.S. Flag Ship Malvern*[1]
> Carl's Neck, James River
> May 12, 1864

The Gettysburg and I have parted company sooner than I expected and she has gone to sea in charge of my executive officer.

Last evening the Admiral sent for me, and said the Gettysburg was not well suited for the river on account of her length, and the difficulty of turning between the banks, and that despatches from the blockade made it necessary to send a vessel to Wilmington at once, and the "G" must go; but he wished me to remain till this expedition is accomplished—He said he would not detach me from my vessel but would simply keep me here by a *verbal* order, and let my executive take charge till I rejoin her again.

The Admiral had a consultation with Gen. Butler yesterday, and they arranged their movements. The Admiral said he would not separate me from my vessel if I was not willing to remain, but would give me any Command here I wished. Of course I had but one reply and this morning on Admiral Lee's order have taken command of the advanced division of the Fleet consisting of three Gun Boats, a number of armed boats and crews from the different vessels, and a scouting party on each bank.

My Flag Ship is the "Stepping Stones" the same vessel I was on board in the Nansemond River, and from which we landed to storm the Hill's Point Batterys. It seems quite natural to be on board her again, but I left the "G" even for a short time with regret I like her so much.

I am so busy I cannot write more now—am organizing my division, and making the necessary arrangements to clear the way for the Iron Clads and other vessels.

1. A converted blockade runner, the USS *Malvern* was a large iron-hulled sidewheel steamer carrying 12 guns. As the blockade runner *Ella and Annie* (built in 1860) she had been captured off New Inlet, North Carolina on November 9, 1863.

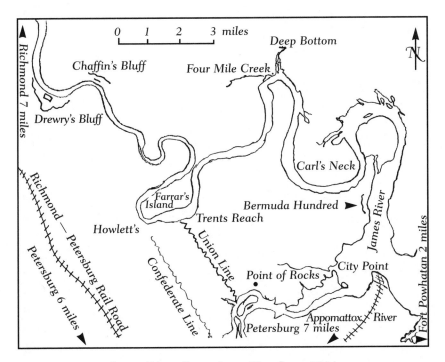

James River Operations, May–June 1864

I think you will hear cheering news from this side of Richmond as well as the other soon. If Lees army is driven back through Richmond we may see something of them here and Grant will undoubtedly be pressing them closely. . . .

Roswell to Kate

> USS *Stepping Stones*
> James River
> 12 miles below Richmond
> May 14, 1864

Yesterday evening I received an order from the Admiral to move up the river with my division, supported by the Com. Morris and Mackinaw.[1] I had some skirmishing with the rebs on the banks, surprised a picket station capturing their arms, but the rebels were too fleet.

1. The USS *Commodore Morris* was a converted sidewheel New York ferryboat ac-

Just below this point I met a "Devil" coming down with a flag of truce flying, brought him to, and went on board. Capt. Hunter Davidson wished to go down to meet a flag of truce boat from Fortress Monroe. I anchored him and sent word to the Admiral below who directed me to tell him that we would hold communication with no such infernal craft, and that if he appeared again we would seize him; so he [went] back up the river in a very bad humor that a Confederate naval officer, and a Confederate man-of-war should be so treated. We advanced very cautiously dragging the river with grapnels & searching the banks for torpedo lines and wires. We secured *nine* torpedos containing from fifty to one-hundred pounds of powder, and towards evening grappled with one containing eighteen-hundred or two-thousand pounds. We got it up to the surface of the water, and will get it out in the morning. It is near where the Commodore Jones[1] was blown up by a similar one. It is quite wonderful the curious inventions they have devised for blowing up our vessels—three have been destroyed already—the Commodore Jones looks as though she *had been ground through a mill*—she was literally torn into *splinters*. Had the precautions been taken that I have adopted I am quite sure she would not have been lost. The monitors moved up this afternoon as far as we have cleared the river. To-day a portion of Gen. Sheridan's[2] Cavalry, of the Army of the Potomac, communicated with our vessels lower down, they came through Mechanicsville and have lost quite heavily. I do not know what the nature of their movement was. Gen. Butler has been having some fighting to-day, but with what result I am unable to say—we have not heard from the Expedition sent to cut the Danville R. R. A Rebel Major came down with a flag of truce, and had scarcely got out of his lines, he said, had not yet hoisted his white flag when one of my sailors ordered him to heave to and brought him in. He said the rebel iron clads would be down in a day or two to finish up our fleet; we invited him to come and witness the fight, and see how his

---

quired in 1862 and armed with six guns; the USS *Mackinaw* was built to navy specifications in 1863 as a sidewheel eight-gun river gunboat.

1. The USS *Commodore Jones* was an eight-gun sidewheel steamer launched in 1863 and sunk by a mine in the James River on May 6, 1864.

2. Major-General Philip H. Sheridan (1831–88), commander of the cavalry corps in the Army of the Potomac, had led a raid behind Confederate lines beginning on May 9, 1864, which had torn up railroads, threatened Richmond, and made contact with Union forces on the Peninsula on May 14. Lamson had met Sheridan when he was stationed at Fort Yamhill in Oregon before the war.

expectations were realized. The iron clads would be *nothing* [compared] to the infernal torpedos that fill the river, and of whose whereabouts we are entirely ignorant. They explode some of them by pulling a trigger, and some by galvanic batteries. So far everything looks favorable for taking Richmond, though we are not so well posted in regard to Grant's movements probably, as you are.

If a brave, determined effort is made, I have no doubt of our success.

The "Torpedo and Picket Division" are some distance in advance to-night, and we are keeping a "bright lookout ahead"—I have been called on deck twice since commencing this, by firing ashore, but a few shrapnel from this vessel made all quiet again. I have now three gun boats, six armed cutters; and forty-five extra officers and men—am to have fifty more to-morrow or next day. . . .

Kate to Roswell

Irvington, N.Y.
May 16, 1864

. . . I thought you would have to go up the river to report to the Admiral and I felt pretty sure that when he once got you there he would want to keep you.

If I remember right the place you have is just the one you wanted and for your sake I am very glad. I know you will do well and I can trust your safety to the care of our Heavenly Father—I know you will do every thing in your power *anywhere*. I shall *always* be proud of *my sailor*. I am glad dear that I *can* give something for my country, and will try to be as brave as many others who too have sent their dearest ones. Truly I should not repine when I remember how many have lost their friends, while you are spared to me. I *will not* think it possible but that you will come back safely.

It seems too bad that you should have to leave the Gettysburg so soon though of course it was better. I hope it may not be very long before you will command her in person again. I suppose if she captures prizes now they will not belong to you or will they? How glad the Admiral must have been to see you back again. . . .

We hardly think or talk of any thing now but the "great campaign" every movement is discussed and maps are studied. Stanton's dispatches are a grand idea giving us something we can rely on. I station myself at the window every morning to watch for the boy with the paper, and one of us reads it aloud to the rest. Mr Fenner comes home once in a while feeling blue because things do not seem to progress as fast as he thinks they ought but we *must not* have such a word as "*fail*" in our dictionary this Spring. We ought to conquer now, if ever, when the country is so completely roused and in earnest but the rebels do hold out desperately. As the "Post" says this evening, it would be better for *every man* in the north to go to Virginia now and crush them completely at any sacrifice, than for the victory to be only half won. For any thing else I *could* not let you go, but I would not be very proud of you if you could stay away now. I like to think that you love me too well to sacrifice any duty for me. And you are dearer to me every day because you are so good and brave and true.

I think the remembrance of the "happy hours" we have spent this spring will help us both to be stronger and more patient for the future, and we can love, think of and pray for each other just as much as though together. . . .

Roswell to Kate

> USS *Stepping Stones*
> 10 miles below Richmond
> May 17, 1864

Since writing to you we have been steadily advancing up the river. The "Torpedo Division" leading, and clearing the river and banks. I raised one torpedo containing two-thousand pounds of powder, and found four others containing about twelve-hundred pounds.

We have had some skirmishing with the rebels along the banks which we had to clear before we could find the wires and lines by which the torpedos are exploded. I came near capturing Capt. Davidson at one of his torpedo stations.

My division have been working very hard for the Admiral is anxious to get up as fast as possible, and they all have to await our movements. I expect a reinforcement of men this evening.

To-day while dragging the river at a point about three miles below Fort Chafin [Chaffin] the rebels opened on us from a line of heavy earthworks distant about two-thousand yards. I had learned that there were some torpedos in that part of the river and was searching for them. We maintained our position till I received orders to drop my vessels out of range.

While this was being done I proceeded up half-a-mile farther with the small boats, but could not find the torpedo lines. I had one man wounded, a piece of shell stuck under the bows of my gig while looking for the lines. We have information that there are torpedos enough in that part of the river to blow the whole fleet out of the water, but I have [no] doubt but we can find them or at least cut the wires.

It is very annoying to have to contend with an enemy of this kind— that lies hid in the bottom of the river—and that you only discover by its terrible effects.

I do wish we could get the river all clear so that we could go into the rebel batteries at Chafin's and Drury's [Drewry's] Bluffs.

Now when Grant is doing such splendid fighting and we are needed as near Richmond as possible it is quite irksome to be obliged to feel our way along as we are compelled to do now.

Yesterday we captured several prisoners and today my advance captured one of the enemy's guns. The country on both sides of the river is quite well cultivated, but all the people have gone to Richmond.

Evening

We have just received information that Gen Butler has been obliged to fall back to his line of entrenchments—from Point of Rocks across to Dutch Gap on the James River. Day before yesterday he captured a line of rifle pits from the rebels, and this morning they retook it, and drove him some distance.[1]

This may necessitate our falling back to protect his right flank.

19th 10 a.m. Some heavy firing yesterday and this morning—am ordered by the Admiral to go down the river and station some Gun Boats and pickets to prevent our communications from being interrupted.

Heaven take care of you Katie, and help us *all* to do our duty now. How much I wish to see you again.

1. The battle of Drewry's Bluff May 12–16, in which a small Confederate army commanded by Pierre G. T. Beauregard stopped Butler's thrust toward Richmond and forced him to entrench a defensive line across the neck of land between the James and Appomattox rivers several miles north of Petersburg.

Roswell to Kate

> USS *Stepping Stones*
> James River
> May 24, 1864

. . . You ask about prizes in case the Gettysburg should take any while I am absent: I am still her commander and would share in her prize the same as though actually on board; I am only detained here by a verbal order from the Admiral. . . .

I have seen the account of Gen. Butler's operations, you spoke of, and am sorry to say it did not represent the exact state of the case.

Gen. Butler advanced from Bermuda Hundred with near forty-thousand men [30,000]: took and partially destroyed the Petersburg R. R., and advanced towards Fort Darling, taking their outer line of rifle-pits. This was done very handsomely by Gen. Gi[l]lmore;[1] the next morning Gen. Beauregard surprised Butler, and after a severe fight drove him out of the rifle pits and back to the position he now holds between Farrar's Island and the James River, and Point of Rocks on the Appomattox. Our loss in this affair was about five-thousand [4200], and the enemy regained the rail-road and turnpike from Petersburg to Richmond, an object of the *utmost* importance to them. Gen. Butler requested the Admiral to drop down to this point to protect his right flank: he has a strong line of entrenchments, and I have heard several of his generals express the opinion that "the rebs would have a hard time taking them." Gen. Beauregard commands in his front with a force estimated at from twenty to twenty-two thousand men.

Last Thursday [May 19] I went to Gen Butler's head quarters with a communication from Admiral Lee, and hearing firing to the front I got a horse and an orderly and rode out to see what was going on; the rebels had just charged one of our lines of rifle-pits and driven our men out and back into our main line of works. The rebels then occupied the pits and commenced entrenching them selves with the greatest industry. By the middle of the afternoon we were ready to attack them in force, and they were ready to receive us. A brigade was

---

1. Major-General Quincy Adams Gillmore (1825–88), commander of X Corps in the Army of the James, one of two corps in that army.

thrown out on the right and several regiments on the left, and after a severe fight we were partially successful in retaking the right of the line of works, but in the center and on the left our troops were driven back with heavy loss, being as badly managed as it would be possible to handle men in action. One regiment advanced to charge the rebels, across an open field; the rebels let it advance about half way when they opened with a battery directly across the center of the flank of the regiment, from another battery directly in front, and gave them a terrible fire of musketry at the same time—in five minutes the regiment was swept away, killed, wounded or taken, except a few who escaped back to our lines, among whom was the Col., wounded in three places.

I rode up to a wounded officer and leaned down to speak to him, when a shot struck the stretcher on which he was lying, and passed between my horses legs; a few minutes afterwards I had my face filled with dirt thrown by a bursting shrapnel.

It was too sad to see our brave fellows cut up so badly, and all to no purpose.

The rebels still hold the rifle pits and occasionally shell Gen Butlers camps from them.

I was talking with Col. Hawley[1] after the fight I referred to and had just turned to leave him, when a rebel shell struck a caisson near by and blew it up. We have shelled the rebels considerably, and stopped their work in a battery they had commenced, and the troops have been slashing the woods in front of Gen. Butler's lines so that we could throw our shells along the front of them in case of attack.

All this does not look like any advance on Richmond, and I greatly fear that the hopes of the country in this direction will be disappointed—of course the Navy can do nothing in a river like this except to *support* and *assist* the army, and we are requested to lie where we are.

Butler is no match for Beauregard, and I have no doubt but most of Beauregard's army has been sent to reinforce Lee, and that he is hemming Butler in with a very few men.

Every movement of Butler shows that he is on the defensive and it will be some time before he makes another advance—the rebels undoubtedly know this and are taking advantage of it. I have no doubt but a determined advance under any competent leader, with the as-

1. Col. Joseph R. Hawley (1826–1905), commanding a brigade in X Corps.

sistance we could render would sweep every thing up to Fort Darling, and even that strong hold could not hold out very long, and the way to Richmond would be clear.

My orders were to clear the river of torpedos, and open the way for the fleet; and I did it thoroughly, up to the guns at Fort Chafin,[1] getting further up the river than anyone has been since the war commenced, except Commodore John Rodgers.

My hopes are in *Grant* and I fear he will have but little help from this side even towards keeping supplies and reinforcements from Lee. In the meantime my division lies ahead of the fleet looking out that torpedo boats and rams do not come down for us, instead of our going up for Richmond.

How nobly the Potomac Army has been doing, and how sure that we are not emulating its splendid example it makes me blush to think of our inactivity.

The "Stepping Stones" is not so pleasant a vessel as she was under Harris. She is commanded by an Acting Master who pays so little attention to neatness in his cabin that I shall shift my flag to the Delaware where I shall be more pleasantly situated. I would have made the change before, but Campbell seemed so anxious to make me comfortable. . . .

Roswell to Kate

> USS *Delaware*
> James River
> May 30, 1864

. . . Important movements are going on here, whether for better or worse remains to be seen.

Most of Gen. Butlers force is being transferred in transports to the White House on the Pamunkey River, leaving a small force here to keep up appearances, and be gobbled up if the rebels choose to take the trouble.

---

1. Fort Chaffin (with two f's) was located on the left bank of the James opposite and about a mile below Fort Darling and eight miles downriver from Richmond. Like Fort Darling, it was on a bluff that provided a clear field of fire for more than a mile down the James.

Gen. Smith[1] goes to the White House and is to march up the Pamunkey and South Anna Rivers to attack Gen Lee's right flank when Grant attempts to drive him from that line.

Many think Lee will fall back at once to Richmond in case Smith would join Grant's left wing. This movement is, of course a secret at present so do not mention it publicly till it is accomplished. About fifteen-thousand men remain here under cover of the fleet—this of course stops our advance up the river for the present, we hope, however that it will not be very long before we shall be moving up in conjunction with Grant and Smith.

Day before yesterday the Admiral directed me to put down a line of obstructions ahead of the iron clads to catch floating torpedos, fire-rafts, torpedo boats, &c. I planted a hawser with buoys, anchored it securely with kedges and had a netting made to hang below it; this forms a good protection for the iron clads, but it tells the rebels we do not intend to advance at present.

Dearest, the rebs have just opened from several batteries in the woods—excuse me till I see about it—

7 p.m.

The rebels opened a pretty sharp artillery fire on Gen Butler's lines—when I got on deck the signal was already flying from the Admiral for the Iron Clad Onondaga[2] and this vessel to "commence action," and in the course of an hour we silenced the rebel fire—Excuse me again, dear but the Admiral has signalled for me to "Repair on board the flag ship" and so it goes day and night.

9 p.m.

Well, dear, you see I am back again at last; my picket line of boats have had their instructions and have gone to their stations. About the time our firing ceased the low dull booming of distant artillery was heard in the direction of the Pamunkey—I listened a few minutes "too far for our vessels"—"too rapid for ships: field artillery" "*Can it be* Grant?" and I almost jumped out of the boat. I have examined the

1. Major-General William F. ("Baldy") Smith (1824–1903), commander of XVIII Corps in the Army of the James, was ordered by Grant to reinforce the Army of the Potomac near Cold Harbor.

2. The USS *Onondaga*, a double-turreted ironclad. After the war she was purchased by the French navy, in which she served until 1903.

map and it *must* be Grant, or Smith marching marching up from White House. God grant it may be the guns of the Potomac Army telling us of a nation saved, and that we may soon be covering Grant's left as well as Butler's right—and then for up the river again.[1]

Oh! why must we be lying here idle when there is so much to be done. The Admiral has talked of sinking some vessels in the channel above us to prevent the rebel vessels from coming down to attack us or the Army, and he asked me this evening what I thought of it—our vessels are certainly as good as theirs, and we will have torpedos attached to all our iron clads and gun boats in a day or two so we shall be able to fight them in any way they like best—we want to bring on the fight by all means, and *we want the river clear of all obstructions so that we can advance.* They have three iron clads quite a number of wooden gun boats, and about a dozen fire vessels at Fort Chafin—their iron clads, the "Virginia" "Richmond" and "Fredericksburg" are very formidable vessels, but if they come down the river I do not think they will go back again. . . .

**Robert H. Gillette (paymaster
on the Gettysburg) to Roswell**

> USS *Gettysburg*
> Off Wilmington
> May 31, 1864

I was very glad to hear from you yesterday through Mr McGloin[2]—I have many times wondered where you were and what you were doing, & more times wondered when you were going to return to us. Certainly there will be a general rejoicing when you appear, for although we are all very comfortable, and things go on very well, yet dozens of times every day we hear the expression "Well—I wish Capt Lamson would get back"—We have now had several very good nights for prizes, and I feel quite certain two or three vessels have run out, & one run in—I am somewhat disappointed at our being detained on the inner block-

---

1. The guns that Lamson heard were an artillery duel between the Army of Northern Virginia and units of the Army of the Potomac arriving at Totopotomoy Creek about fifteen miles north of Lamson's flotilla on the James.

2. Acting-Master William McGloin, who was in command of the *Gettysburg* in Lamson's absence.

ade—[1]I am sure this vessel is much better adapted for outside blockade duty, but I suppose we shall be detained here until you come.
Experience is *everything* on this blockade in my opinion, & that is where
we miss it more than any where else—Caution is very good but I am
constantly reminded of that which I have often heard you say viz—
"nothing risked is nothing gained"—We have been stationed to the
southward of New Inlet but last night were ordered to *our* old station
that is the Nansemond's off Masonboro—We lay most of the night
several miles off—We had a pilot who assured us of what Mr. Sands
& myself knew that it was safe to keep much nearer & that we could
not see vessels running along the beach from where we were lying. We
however kept off on the ground "that it would be impossible for any
vessels to run between us & the shore without our seeing them," at
the same time anyone who ever had experience, would not hesitate to
say that a whole fleet could pass without any of us seeing it, even
though we kept the best kind of a lookout.

I do not know as you would wish me to speak of these things, I did
not intend to when I sat down but upon the second thought I concluded to although I know it is intruding on my part to comment on
that department. I trust that you will take these comments in the same
way that they are given—I do not give them in a complaining way at
all. I presume you hear from us in different ways, & are thus enabled
to judge of what we are doing. I have no doubt but that experience &
time will make our chances better & until we have had that we need
not hope to make any captures—that is on the inner blockade. The
"Fort Jackson" went out last night for a *cruise*. The "Glaucus" came
very near burning up a few nights ago. She was burned to a mere shell.
Capt. Porter is very anxious to go north for repairs, but probably will
not be able to for some time. The "Nancy" does not amount to much
in her present condition.[2]

---

1. Blockade tactics placed two cordons of ships around a Confederate port; the
inner blockade consisted of ships with shallower draft that could get in close to the
inlets; the outer blockade consisted of larger and (sometimes) faster ships to pursue
blockade runners that evaded the inner cordon. Ships on the inner and outer blockade
signaled each other with colored rockets. Some blockaders also cruised far from American shores along the known routes to Bermuda or Nassau. The *Gettysburg* with its
great speed was indeed more suitable for this duty or for the outer blockade.

2. The USS *Fort Jackson* was a sidewheel steamer built in 1862 and fitted with 11
guns. She was capable of 14 knots and participated in the capture or destruction of
five blockade runners. The USS *Glaucus* was a screw steamer built in 1863 and armed

It seems to me that the blockade is very poor just now.

I am retaining my important vouchers &c for your approval.

I read an account of your proceedings in the N.Y. Herald—you must have been in some pretty sharp brushes.—At times I feel as though I should like to participate in these great battles, more particularly when I read, or hear of some heroic examples but at other times I feel as though I am glad to be out of them. I have seen the time I would much more willingly risk my neck, than at the present time. I feel now as though I should almost *flinch* were I brought into line for a hard fight. You will have a grand opportunity to judge of Butlers military skill—So far as I have read of his movements he is rather rising in my estimation—Mr Sands just came along & asked me if I was writing to you. I said yes—Well he clapped me on the shoulder, and asked me to tell you that he was living on the hope of seeing you back to your command soon. He also sends his most respectful regards & so do all the officers. I have taken the liberty to help myself to books in your library—I hear from home often and all send kind regards to you. . . .

Roswell to Flora

> USS *Delaware*[1]
> 9 miles below Richmond
> June 3, 1864

. . . We are still here opposite Gen'l Butler's lines, awaiting most impatiently for him to move,—or for Grant's army to reach the river so that we can move up with them for no one here has any confidence in Butler's doing anything. He evidently is not the man for the field.

We have had information for some days that the rebel fleet was ready to come down and Gen'l Butler sent Admiral Lee word yesterday that he had information that President Davis had ordered it to attack us at once, and that the fleet would certainly be down within a day or two. Now that Grant is getting so near the James River it becomes a matter of vital importance to the rebels to obtain control of the river

---

with 11 guns. She caught fire while chasing a blockade runner on May 28. The "Nancy" was a nickname for Lamson's former ship *Nansemond*, which was damaged in a gun battle with the CSS *Raleigh* May 6–7, 1864.

1. A sidewheel steamer carrying three guns.

to prevent its being used as a line of supply for Grant and Butler, and a matter of equal importance to us to hold it. The rebel fleet consists of the ironclads Richmond, Fredericksburg and Virginia as large as our Monitors and carrying four guns each (our Monitors carry two each but of larger caliber), six or eight gunboats and about a dozen fire-ships loaded with all sorts of combustibles and large quantities of powder and shell. Their ironclads and gunboats all carry torpedoes ahead, and this is their most formidable feature; we have never used torpedoes and our vessels are not fitted with them. I have made some torpedoes out of the best materials at hand here, and have each of my vessels armed with one containing 120 pounds of powder, and so arranged that we can explode them with great precision. The Admiral expressed himself very much pleased with them and is having some made for the other vessels. As my vessels lie ahead of the fleet we may have a chance to test their efficiency. I am about three fourths of a mile above the fleet and at night have ten heavily armed boats with grapnels and lines, just ahead of the gunboats, to prevent surprise and to grapple their fire ships and tow them ashore before they can reach the fleet, board their smaller vessels, torpedo boats &c. The Stepping Stones keeps under way near the boats to cover and assist them, and the others lie within supporting distance.

I go out with the boats at dusk, station them, give them their instructions and remain till 12 o'clock, when I pull alongside of the Stepping Stones, throw myself on a sofa and sleep till 3 o'clock a.m. when I am called and go to the boats to be ready for the rebs if they should come at day light, which would be their most favorable time. The boats have signals so they can communicate any suspicion of danger to me at once. If the rebs do come we will have one of the most singular fights in the history of naval warfare: ironclads, torpedoes and wooden vessels, large and small, fire ships and rams, a combination never yet brought together in action. If the fight should be at night it will be worth seeing. I have never believed, myself, that the rebels will attack us where we now are, and prepared as we are to receive them; but the Admiral and Gen'l Butler seem sure they will, so of course I do not put my judgment against theirs, only I wagered a box of Havanas with the Fleet Captain that they will not attack us *here*—when we move up they certainly will have to fight, and I have no doubt but we will find them ready.[1]

1. Lamson was right; the Confederate James River Fleet did not try to challenge

Last night and this morning we had some picket firing and I had one man wounded. This afternoon and evening we have been listening to Grant's guns in the direction of First Grove Church.[1] Oh, that we could do more to help him and his soldiers. Our prospects look bright now, and if Butler would only break through the very small force that is in his front and cut the Petersburg railroad again and more effectually, Lee's army could not stay in Richmond ten days if half that time.

I had a letter from the Gettysburg this evening—Mr McGloin (in charge) writes me that she is in fine order, but had not yet had a chance to chase a prize—he had received one letter from me which he had read on the quarter deck at General muster. His letter conveyed the kind wishes of the officers and crew that I would come back to them, and I am getting real homesick to be with them again. . . .

Roswell to Flora

USS *Delaware*
June 5, 1864

. . . Everything here remains as when I wrote you last except that the enemy have been withdrawing more men from before Gen'l Butler's front and sending them to oppose Grant, where guns grow more distinctly audible every day. I have been perfectly satisfied that the enemy has had no real force in our front for the last ten days or more. They have a strong picket line, attack our pickets and outposts at all times, and by so doing prevent any reconnoitering except in force, and that has not been attempted. The other night Gen'l Butler sent word that

---

Union control of the river below Trent's Reach, and except for some ineffective long-range shelling did not fire a shot in anger. But the Union fleet on the James River never moved upriver beyond Fort Chaffin. Once the contending armies moved to Petersburg, the Union navy played no further significant part in this campaign except to patrol the lower James and protect the huge Union supply depot at City Point. In March 1865 the Confederate fleet did make an abortive foray toward City Point.

1. These were the guns at the battle of Cold Harbor, a costly Union repulse in which the Army of the Potomac suffered 7000 casualties, most of them in the first half-hour of the unsuccessful assault.

the enemy had opened fire from all their batteries. I was with the upper line of picket boats at the time, directly abreast of the rebel lines, and we could see that they had only a few pieces of field artillery, probably not more than one battery, which they put in position in one part of their line, fired a few rounds, then limbered up and galloped off to another position where the same thing was repeated and so on along the entire line, with the occasional variation of scattering the pieces so as to fire from several points at once. I reported the facts.

It is too bad that while Grant and his brave men are fighting so hard that we should lie within sound of their guns and not be able to help them. Yesterday I got my first glimpse of Richmond from a treetop—we are now about nine miles from the City. I have several officers and men sick and wounded but the general health of the fleet is very good, though we do not get any fresh provisions. My health is excellent: I sleep from 12 to 3 at night and take a nap after dinner when nothing prevents. Grant has done splendidly has he not—he "fights it out in the same line," and steadily drives back the hitherto invincible Lee. . . .

Kate to Roswell

Mt. Vernon, Ohio
June 8, 1864

I have your dear, long, loving letter of the thirtieth of May this evening to fill my heart with renewed happiness and sweet thoughts. Your dear *dear* letters I cannot tell you how very precious they are to me—and this is the first one I have had since leaving New York, having to wait till it could be forwarded. But I must tell you what a busy day I have spent. This morning, right after breakfast I started out on a collecting expedition. I am a "gatherer" in a new system called the "Five Cent Collection." I have ten subscribers who pay me five cents a week for foreign missions. Nine other gatherers do the same and every two weeks the money is paid to a "receiver" (and sent to New York). I am getting my accounts straightened for the time I was away. That expedition occupied me till half past ten and I was very successful. Then I came home and sewed till dinner-time.

After dinner Mother and I started for the Aid Society meeting. . . . We had a busy afternoon, making and rolling bandages. It is sad work but I am glad to do any thing I can to help the soldiers. It seems that all I can do for the sailors is in trying to help and cheer *you*. You are the only sailor I can help. I wish I could do more for them.

On our way home we got the evening paper and read the doings of the Baltimore Convention as far as published. It looks very much as though Lincoln would be our next President. Fremont ought to be—sent to the Penitentiary any man who is willing on account of a personal enmity to divide the Northern vote at this time ought to be sent to keep forgers of proclamations in countenance.[1] But we need not fear God has kept our nation through too many dangers to desert us now—That will all come out right. . . .

Mother and I have been beautifying our front-hall this week. We have made and put down a pretty velvet carpet and draped the wall with a large flag—suspended from a shield. We want the "Stars & Stripes" where we can see them all the time.

Father writes that they are watching the progress of Grant hoping yet trembling—"But why should we tremble, when we know *God directs it all*?" And does it not seem as though He was fighting on our side—Oh, we surely must win the victory *this* time, and be indeed "a nation saved." We must pay a dear price for it but it is a noble glorious cause and not one drop of blood is wasted that is shed now. . . .

I want to be willing to have you where you are but sometimes I can not be quite willing. I am trying though and it is by remembering *your* courage and devotion to our country that I can have courage. I must not by repining prove myself unworthy the love of your loyal heart. . . .

1. On June 8, 1864, the National Union Convention (the Republican party had renamed itself the Union party in an effort to attract War Democrats) renominated Lincoln for president. On May 31 a splinter group of radical Republicans and disaffected War Democrats had nominated Major-General John C. Frémont for president on a third-party ticket calling itself the Radical Democratic Party. Frémont had been the first Republican presidential nominee in 1856; he was angry at Lincoln for giving him no military appointment since he had resigned his small command in 1862 when John Pope was appointed over him to command the Army of Virginia. Some mainline Democrats secretly encouraged the Frémont movement as a way of dividing the Republican vote. In September Frémont bowed to Republican pressure and withdrew from the contest. "Forgers of proclamations" refers to a forged proclamation supposedly issued by Lincoln calling for 300,000 more troops which was published in two anti-administration New York newspapers. These papers were temporarily shut down and their editors arrested, but they were soon released when it turned out that the proclamation had been a scam by two speculators to create a panic and make a killing on the gold market.

Roswell to Kate

USS *Agawam*[1]
James River
June 12, 1864

. . . I have been so very busy during the past week that I have not had time to write to any one—several officers have been sick, five more small steamers came for my division, and had to be organized and fitted out and I have had the entire charge of the picket boats at night, as usual. . . .

Gen. Gillmore made a reconnoissance toward Petersburg last night, and returned to-day, found the enemy in force but had no fighting. The *prospect* is now that the hardest fighting will be on the south side of Richmond, and that Grant will cross over a large portion of his troops.

All has been quiet for several days except the occasional report of artillery from Butlers lines, the gun boats, or Grant's batteries.

The rebel fleet lies under the guns of Fort Chafin, and occasionally makes a short excursion down the river.

We are lying at the lower end of Trent's Reach, the most difficult place in the river to cross—we shall be obliged to lighten our Monitors as much as possible to get them over at all, and even then it will probably take some time to accomplish it.

I have had some of the large torpedos we seized on our way up refitted and put down in the channel above the fleet, and have made a small bombproof ashore for the galvanic battery.

I have quite a fleet now, eight steamers, two launches carrying howitzers, eight armed boats and four hundred men. . . .

I had two letters from the Gettysburg yesterday—they do not seem to be getting along very well on board, and numerous complaints are made against Mr. McGloin the Executive officer in charge—with what foundation of course I cannot tell, but I will straighten them out when I get back to her. The officers all express the kindest wishes for me to come back, and as soon as I can do so consistently I will ask the Admiral to let me rejoin her. I sent Mr. McGloin an order some days

1. A ten-gun sidewheel steamer launched in 1863.

since to cruise off shore where he will be much more likely to pick up a prize than where he now is. . . .

Roswell to Kate

> USS *Delaware*
> James River
> June 15, 1864

. . . Things are changing here very rapidly, and you will probably hear of some fighting in this quarter soon. Grant has crossed most of his army over the James, and is marching on Petersburg with 80,000 men. Lee is hurrying over at Richmond to meet him, and to-day long trails of dust, moving down the roads from Richmond have indicated that the rebs were on the march. Last night we could hear their artillery moving down, and this morning at day-light their drums and bugles were sounding the march along the river, and further inland.

Yesterday Gen Grant was at Gen Butler's head quarters near us. If Grant gets the Petersburg R. R. Lee must drive him from it, very quick, or evacuate Richmond for it is the main line of supply for his army, and the only road for which they have a sufficient amount of rolling stock. The Danville & Lynchburg Roads are of different gages, and the cars from the Petersburg road cannot run on them.

The success of the campaign now depends on Grants getting that road, and on our holding the river. Yesterday the Admiral ordered a boom, made of logs lashed together to be made to place across the channel in front of the monitors to protect them from fire-ships and torpedos, but to-day Gen. Grant sent up five vessels to be sunk in the channel for the same purpose, and I was directed to put them in place and sink them, which I have just got accomplished. I not only have the duties of my division to attend to but whenever anything of this kind is to be done, I am always sent to do it. I like to be busy, though, and am always ready for anything, day or night.

Never, probably, in the history of the world did so much depend on a naval force, as is now depending on this fleet.

My division has been increased to nine steamers with between four and five hundred men, and my advance is about three fourths of a mile ahead of the fleet during the night, and a little nearer during the day.

I have been learning the army code of signals lately and can now communicate quite readily with their signal officers ashore which is of great advantage to us.

The Delaware is a very nice comfortable vessel, and her captain a very pleasant man; the cabin quite large enough for two so I am as well situated as I could hope to be out of my own ship, and my health is excellent.

The Gettysburg was at Hampton Roads day before yesterday, having towed in an ordnance vessel she found at sea in a sinking condition—she will go out again immediately. I have letters from several of the officers.

Do not fear, dear, but we shall be successful in this campaign and certainly decide the war, if not finish it all together, I do believe God is on our side, and that the right will triumph. . . .

Kate to Roswell

Mt. Vernon, Ohio
June 15, 1864

. . . I have been rather busy since Sunday with getting ready for Anniversary.[1] Yesterday I took tea at the Rectory and Mr Reese [the rector] and I made out a programme of the exercises, and arranged the order of the music. At seven we adjourned to the church to practise with the children. There was a very full attendance and they sang very well considering they had no one but myself to lead them most of the time. Mr Beardsley will help us on Sunday. I would not want to undertake it alone. We intend having plenty of flags in the church and to sing "America." Wouldn't you like to be here and hear us?

How very quiet it would seem to you here now, after being in the midst of war and excitement. I often think how quiet all the things I tell you of must appear don't my letters lack excitement? But all the little things which seem so tame when written are really quite exciting to us here and make a variety which causes the days to pass much more rapidly than they would without them. Mother and I have been at the Aid Society all the afternoon rolling bandages—to bind up some

1. Of the Episcopal Church in Mount Vernon, where Kate taught Sunday School, played the organ, and directed the choir.

poor soldiers' wounds, perhaps sailors too. I would like to work for the sailors if I could. Do I help *you* any? I think I do, but I want you to tell me again. . . .

The papers do not give us any news this evening except the defeat of Morgan's forces in Kentucky.[1] He did not get as far as Ohio this time. A letter from Fortress Monroe says "the Navy have done nothing thus far in the campaign but fish for torpedoes." No wonder when they haven't had a chance, but never mind your turn will come yet, it may have come even now. Have you heard any thing from the Gettysburg since you left her?

It is time to get ready for church and I must go. . . .

Roswell to Kate

USS *Delaware*
June 19, 1864

. . . The Admiral gave me permission to be absent part of the day [June 18] and getting horses from a New Jersey Battery near us I started with two Midshipmen from the Naval Academy who came here during their vacation to see war, and rode through Gen. Butlers lines to his head-quarters: a couple of his staff officers joined us there, and we crossed the Appomattox on a pontoon bridge and took the road that led towards the heavy artillery firing in the direction of Petersburg, about seven miles distant.

On the route we passed immense trains of waggons, ambulances, and vehicles of all kinds, and I counted one-hundred and twenty-five waggons waiting to cross the bridge.

As we approached the front the sound of the firing grew louder and we could soon see the smoke from the guns showing the position and direction of our lines.

---

1. Confederate Brigadier-General John Hunt Morgan (1825–64), a daring cavalry commander who had led several raids behind Union lines in Kentucky, including one across the Ohio River into Indiana and Ohio in July 1863, during which he and many of his men were captured. He escaped from prison in Ohio and returned to the Confederacy. In May and June 1864 he led another raid as far as north as Lexington, Kentucky, but was defeated on June 12 and forced to retreat into southwest Virginia. Later in the year he was killed during a raid in Tennessee.

Riding to Gen. Meade's head quarters we learned that an assault on one of the rebel lines had been ordered and was to take place in a short time—so after taking a look at Meade, Hancock, Williams and the other heroes of the "Grand Army" we gallopped about a mile to the front where we found Gen. Birney forming the columns of his division for the assault.[1]

We took a position on a high point in a rebel redout from which we could see the field very well, except where the line was in the woods. Martindale[2] was on the right, Birney on the left and several Generals in the centre.

The rebels were in a line of works on the crest of a ridge in our front, and had a battery that partly enfiladed our position further right.

Our artillery opened first and it was soon evident that our force of that arm was very much greater than the enemy's—an occasional musket shot from the skirmish line told where they were.

After giving the rebels a good dose of shell and schrapnel, our line advanced and two columns moved up the hill at double quick and were soon lost to our sight in the woods, but an instant after the sharp quick vollies and the whizzing of musket balls, told that the work had commenced.

This continued for over half an hour more we were at least partially successful in taking the works, and I understand that the rebels were driven entirely from there this morning. This is the *third* line of defences taken around Petersburg, and there are several more to take— the rebels fortify every point, and when driven from one position fall back into another fighting for every inch of ground.

I could not learn what our loss was, but it was not very heavy. It is reported to-day that Meade has possession of the rail road below Petersburg, and was within half a mile of the town—we could see it very well from our position yesterday. Gen. Grant was at Bermuda Hundred so I did not see him.

This afternoon the rebel fleet came down, and we had a few shots

---

1. Major-General Winfield Scott Hancock (1824–86), commander of II Corps in the Army of the Potomac; Brigadier-General Seth Williams (1822–66), Adjutant General of the Army of the Potomac; Major-General David B. Birney (1825–64), commanding a division in II Corps.

2. Brigadier-General John H. Martindale (1815–81), commanding a division in XVIII Corps.

at them at long range but they went back under cover of Fort Chafin again. I have never believed they would attack us where we are now and I have not changed my opinion.

Gen. Grant paid the Admiral a visit this afternoon, and I was asleep and did not see him.

Butler is doing nothing as usual except insisting that the rebels are very strong in his front where they probably have but a handful of men. Grant has one-hundred thousand infantry. . . . There is no other news of interest—everything is progressing in our favor and I have no doubt but we shall take Richmond this campaign.

I hope you will hear of our being nearer Richmond before long—now is our time—now every man should do his utmost for Union and Liberty—God grant that the right may triumph *soon*. I dreamed of you last night. . . .

Roswell to Kate

> USS *Delaware*
> James River
> June 22, 1864

. . . Yesterday morning the rebels commenced taking away the brush in front of their batteries at "Howlets," just above our position, and on a high bluff that entirely commands the river—so much above it that we can with difficulty elevate our guns enough to reach it.

As they unmasked the works we could see the black muzzles of the guns, and gave them a shot or two by way of a reminder that we observed their movements and knew what was coming—they soon replied, and sent shot and shell whizzing and splashing around us but not doing much damage. We replied from this vessel, the Agawam (wooden) and the iron clads, and our fire, especially from the monitors was the finest artillery practice I have seen for a long time. The rebel iron clads also came down but kept a point of land between us and themselves, over which they fired at our wooden vessels.

We paid no attention whatever to their attack though they threw shells all around us but directed our fire at the batteries, and soon saw plainly that we had dismounted one of their guns—what other injury we did them we could not tell.

Our damage was slight—this vessel only had some rigging shot away.

The monitors always have to be attended by wooden vessels to furnish them with supplies and to act as advanced guards and the rebels perhaps thought they could drive our wooden vessels away and compel the monitors to drop further down the river—if so they were mistaken.

I dined with the Admiral on board the "Malvern"—just before we sat down to dinner a man was struck just over our heads, but not much hurt—we had music (in the air) and baked beans and fried chicken.

I had been quite unwell for a couple of days, and yesterday morning was scarcely able to sit up, but went to each of my vessels and placed them in position.

In the afternoon I was so tired that I went to sleep on deck, in the midst of the firing, and slept soundly for more than an hour in spite of the heavy guns discharged over me, and the whistle of the shells falling around us.

To-day the rebs have been perfectly quiet, probably they saw we were not much damaged by their fire and have concluded to save their ammunition for closer quarters.

I am much better this evening and shall be quite well again by to-morrow—if I could only see *you* I should be *instantly* well.

The hot sultry days and damp chilly nights are very trying to those out at night, and we have quite a number of people sick—but my health has been excellent till this slight attack, which is over now.

This morning President Lincoln, Asst. Sec. Fox, Gen. Butler, Gen. Barnard[1] and other officers paid us a visit. Father Abraham came up in a steamer, and Gen Butler met him here.

They visited some of the vessels with the Admiral and then all the commanding officers were sent for to be presented to the rail splitter who made some funny remarks and then rode over to Point of Rocks with the Admiral and Gen. Butler. Mr Lincoln looks much better than when I saw him last in Washington.

Gen. Grant has crossed a small force back over the James River—and is fortifying some points on the banks—his army at Petersburg is gaining ground steadily, but slowly and with considerable loss—this however must be expected where the enemy must be driven out of

---

1. Brigadier-General John G. Barnard (1815–82), chief engineer of the armies in the field.

one line of works after another. Lee is now in our front with probably all his forces.

We must be patient and not expect too much at once, and be willing to make sacrifices and meet with losses to obtain our *grand object*—and secure it we surely shall if we are not discouraged by difficulties that courage, and perseverance can entirely overcome. . . .

Roswell to Kate

USS *Delaware*
James River
June 26, 1864

. . . You ask the prospect of Grant's spending 4th of July in Richmond—he has lost over twelve thousand men trying to take Petersburg, and it will take some time yet—certainly two weeks—to drive the rebels out of that place, and then he will have to fight for every inch of the ground from there to Richmond (twenty-two miles) unless by cutting their communications he starves them out, which is highly improbable for the rebs eat little and fight hard. If driven from Petersburg Gen. Lee will no doubt take up the "Swift Creek" line, which is a very strong one.

I was out to Petersburg yesterday all day and rode along our entire front; there was no fighting, only the usual skirmish fire of the picket lines and an occasional discharge of artillery. On Thursday [June 23] we lost two regiments and four guns taken. We are gaining ground surely but slowly and at a heavy expense of men. No doubt we will succeed finally but it looks now like a long job, and if Grant gets Richmond any time this season he will do well.

The rebels are doing gloriously, and it must be a long hard fight yet.

I am sorry we cannot do more, but it would be useless for us to advance without the army; so we can only hold the river, protect Butlers flank, and be ready to move up when the time comes, which will probably not be very soon. The Admiral will not remain much longer here but will return to Hampton Roads the interests of the Squadron requiring his presence there, and there being no prospect of anything to do here. When he goes down I shall probably go also and rejoin the Gettysburg.

Just above where we are now is a part of the river that must be deepened some before our vessels can pass, and even if they were above it they could not accomplish much. The Admiral does not deserve the censure thrown upon him by the [New York] Herald recently, but there are things connected with this campaign that I will tell you, but which I would not like to write now.

I do not see any prospect of our doing anything for some time but to lie here in this hot muddy river so I am quite willing to go to the "G" and do what I can to cut off the rebels supplies.

I shall try to arrange it to come back if there is anything for us to do. . . .

Roswell to Kate

> USS *Delaware*
> James River
> June 29, 1864

. . . Yesterday evening the rebels opened again from the battery just above us, and sent a few shot splashing amongst us, which we returned, and all was quiet again.

Some days since Gen. Grant sent a small force to the left bank about six miles below us to hold a point at Four Mile Creek, the rebels sent down a force to meet [them] then threw up some batteries, and today have been firing on our supply and mail steamers as they passed—one small steamer belonging to the army was disabled. We are going down in the morning with a couple of gun boats to see if we can drive them away as they will soon be shelling the camps of our troops there.

Heavy artillery firing has been heard in the direction of Petersburg during the last twenty four hours, but what it amounts to we have not learned—probably our batteries are shelling the town, and theirs shelling our camps, and the rear of our lines, which they can do. I see the papers pass *very* lightly over our losses on last Thursday. . . .

I have a letter this evening from the Gettysburg—she has not done much yet, and there has been some difficulty among the officers—I am anxious to get back to her to straighten things out. If there is no prospect of some advance being made soon I shall probably rejoin her. . . .

Kate to Roswell

Mt. Vernon, Ohio
June 29, 1864

I am not sad this evening, but in a very sober quiet mood. How I wish this war was over, and you could be here with me, and talk to me, instead of being away off there in Virginia so many miles between us, though *our hearts* are not so far apart, no miles can separate them. But I do want to see you so much—to be near you and hear your voice again. The papers tell us of an attack on Chapin's [Chaffin's] bluffs by Gen Foster and the *gunboats,* so you must have been in that.[1] I trust you are safe and well. You *must* be safe and I know I shall soon hear so from your own hand. What a crisis this is! We must and will win the victory—and God grant it may be soon—this dreadful work cannot continue much longer.

All the churches have united and hold a prayer meeting for the country every Monday, Tuesday and Friday evenings. Earnest fervent prayers are offered at every one that we may have the victory this time, that our rulers and officers may be blessed and guided that our Army & Navy may be strong in the right and nerved for conquest over this unholy rebellion. I always pray for *you* there in my heart as well as at many other times. . . .

You don't know how much good your letters do me. I rely more on your assurance that this campaign will decide the war than on all the newspaper reports for or against that fact. Your letters make me braver and more earnest in trying to be patient and strong to bear this time of trial as *your* betrothed should. I would not be worth your true love if I could *wish* to keep you at home in such a time as this. I am proud of having you where you are. I am proud of your courage and patriotism and I will never knowingly keep you back from any duty. *Dear* Roswell I do love you—more than I can ever tell you— you are very dear to me. I could not live without you. My whole heart is yours. My life and happiness is bound up in yours. My heart has grown to yours so I could not tear it away. Goodnight dear.

---

1. A false report occasioned by the exchange of gunfire described in Lamson's letter of June 22. Brigadier-General Robert S. Foster (1834–1903) commanded a division in X Corps.

God bless, strengthen and comfort you—and bring us together soon. . . .

Roswell to Kate

USS *Malvern*
City Point
July 3, 1864

. . . I wrote you some time since that I might not stay here much longer—the obstructions ordered by the government to be placed in the river, being now complete, and there being no immediate prospect of Grant's getting Petersburg or of the navy being able to move any further up the river the Admiral is going down to Hampton Roads, and probably from there all along the coast to attend to the other interests of the Squadron, and will return whenever his presence is needed.

Capt. Melancthon Smith is left in command in the river.[1] I expect to rejoin the Gettysburg soon, and shall be very glad to do so till there is a prospect of our being able to accomplish something here.

Yesterday Fleet Capt. Barnes[2] went home on a short leave, and he and the Admiral proposed that I should come on board and occupy his room, and this morning, the Admiral again inviting me to do so I brought my traps from the Delaware, with some regret at leaving Capt. Eldredge[3] who has been very hospitable and kind.

This evening a part of my division was sent down the river, being no longer needed, and I turned over the remainder, and came down with the Admiral in a tug the Malvern having preceded us.

We are now lying opposite Gen. Grant's head quarters and near the point where the supplies for his army are landed—the river looks quite like New York harbor at night there are so many vessels of all kinds with lights at their mast heads.

We will celebrate the "Glorious 4th" here, and I presume go down to Hampton Roads to-morrow evening or next day.

There is no news of interest—our losses during Wilson's Cavalry raid are not so great as first reported—not over four or five hundred men,

---

1. Captain Melancthon Smith (1810–93), a 38-year veteran of the navy.
2. Lieutenant-Commander John S. Barnes.
3. Acting-Master Joshua H. Eldredge, captain of the USS Delaware.

and ten pieces of artillery—he damaged their rail-roads considerably.[1]

Everything at Petersburg is as it was when I wrote last, and it may take Grant all Summer to take it.

During the past week the rebels opened batteries on our vessels at different points along the river to prevent our supply boats coming up, but were driven away without much trouble.

Capt. Smith asked the Admiral to let me remain up the river with him for a while, but he refused; I said nothing, as I am willing to stay or go as I can be most useful.

The Navy Dept. and the Naval Committee of the Senate have called the Admirals' attention to the large amount of cotton the rebels succeed in getting through the blockade, and with which they purchase supplies for their army, and, if possible, a stronger effort than ever will be made to break up the trade; he is going to visit the Squadron off Wilmington for this purpose.

I do not know yet whether I shall go down in the vessel or in the Newbern: it will depend on which [goes] first.

Thank you for the confidence you express in the *Navy*, and I hope it will always merit your approbation; I am only sorry the rivers here are not wider and deeper so as to give us an opportunity to do more for the Country I am sure we wish to serve, and the ladies I *know* we are devoted to—if we only had a chance on blue water. . . .

The campaign will undoubtedly end in our favor, but we may not accomplish all we hoped to do *this* summer; and there may remain a little more for us to do *next*. . . .

Kate to Roswell

                                    Mt. Vernon, Ohio
                                    July 5, 1864

. . . Your letters have made me a little less sanguine in my expectations dear, but I am glad to know just how things really are, one can

---

1. A raid by 5000 of Sheridan's cavalry June 22–July 1 commanded by Brigadier-General James H. Wilson (1837–1925) to break up Lee's vital rail supply line between Petersburg and Lynchburg. They did put the railroad out of commission for a couple of weeks, but at the cost of 1500 Union troopers (three times Lamson's estimate), most of them captured by Confederate cavalry.

never tell how much of what is told in the papers is to be believed, or can know how much is left untold for fear of discouraging the people. Like you I have no doubt of the result, for how could it be other than the triumph of the *right*, but it does require a great deal of patience to wait for the end. How I wish I could do something to help. I hope they will call for more men—draft—or do *anything* to bring them in, that this may be ended as speedily *as possible*, that we may be spared more suffering in our country. I only wonder the call has not been made long ago and the men prepared. It takes so long to get a new army ready. I hope it will be done soon. I always want to know all that you are doing and that I can only get from your letters. Every occurrence interests me when it concerns you in any way. I should think you would want to be on the Gettysburg again, it must be very trying to be obliged to stay so long in the river with no prospect of soon being nearer Richmond. I think too you will be better out at sea than in the river. I do not know much about the weather climate &c in blockading but I am sure you could do more good there and would very soon settle those refractory officers.

Perhaps we had better change. I go and keep them straight—and you come and keep house, lead the choir, take care of the children and teach my Sunday School class. What do you think of such a plan? . . .

Kate to Roswell

Mt. Vernon, Ohio
July 13, 1864

Probably this trouble at Baltimore and Washington[1] will prevent us from receiving each other's letters for a while, but I will write any how, you may get them sometime, and it comforts me to feel that I have you *some where* to write to. . . .

What do you think of the prospect for rebeldom capturing Wash-

---

1. A raid down the Shenandoah Valley, across the Potomac, and to the very outskirts of Washington on July 11 by a small Confederate army under the command of Major-General Jubal A. Early (1816–94). Union reinforcements drove Early away from the capital and back to the Shenandoah Valley, but this raid disillusioned many people in the North with the prospect that they could ever win this war.

ington before we capture Richmond? Perhaps it is not very patriotic, but I cannot help the feeling that even such invasions are better than stagnation. They will at least keep us active and awake to the dangers surrounding us. I do hope they will manage to capture the whole force. At any rate I don't believe they will succeed in diverting Grant from his purpose. He has paid too great a price for his present position to give it up now. I trust there may not be more than "a little" left to be done next summer. . . . You know it is said to be "always darkest just before day." Do you not think it is almost as dark now as it very well could be and that the "day" must be coming soon? . . .

CHAPTER 8

I AM GETTING TIRED
AND WEARY

JULY–OCTOBER 1864

URING LAMSON'S TWO months' absence from the *Gettys-burg* that ship had not lived up to its potential for catching blockade runners. Many hints in Lamson's letters suggest that the reason for this failure lay in the lack of aggressiveness shown by her acting commander, William McGloin. Dissension among the officers seems to have developed, which undoubtedly hurt the ship's efficiency. Ironically, just as Lamsom left Hampton Roads on his way to the Union coaling base at Beaufort, North Carolina, to rejoin his ship, the *Gettysburg* finally caught a blockade runner on the high seas off the North Carolina coast, on July 9. She was the *Little Ada,* a fast steamer built in Scotland in 1862 expressly for blockade running. The *Gettysburg* returned to Beaufort on July 14, when Lamson came on board and resumed command.

———•◆•———

Roswell to Katie

USS *Gettysburg*
Beaufort, N.C.
July 17, 1864

Your kind letter of the 6th deserves a longer answer than I returned the other day, but I had just got on board again, and had my hands and head full, and the steamer came alongside quite unexpectedly for the mail, so I just sent you a line to let you know that I was here, again on board my own ship.

I wrote you from the James River that I had gone on board the Malvern at the Admiral's invitation, and as I had nothing to do except amuse myself I had a good rest for several days.

On the evening of the 3rd the obstructions being completed, and part of the fleet sent down the river, the Admiral turned over the immediate command to Capt Melancthon Smith, and we came down to City Point. On the morning of the "4th" I went on shore with Adml Lee and called on Gen. Grant at his head quarters. While he and the Adml were having a confab I got a horse and rode out to the camp of Gen. Sheridan Com'dg the Cavalry Corps took lunch and came back in time to come down to Hampton Roads in the Malvern that evening. I knew Gen Sheridan quite well some seven years ago when he was a 2d Lieut of Infantry—he was in Oregon, and had seen my fathers family since the war commenced.

From Hampton Roads we went to Norfolk to have some slight repairs made, and came down to the Roads again on the evening of the 8th; then came the news of the Florida's presence on the coast and the Admiral was busy sending off all vessels he could that were able to cope with her.[1]

The "Fort Donelson" was about to sail for this place and fearing the Malvern might be still longer detained I requested permission to come down at once, and the Adml said I might do as I chose—so I came, arriving last Tues. morning.

---

1. The CSS *Florida,* a fast screw steamer built in England in 1862. Armed with nine guns, she was the most feared and successful Confederate commerce raider next to the CSS *Alabama.* The *Florida* destroyed or captured 33 American merchant vessels before she was captured in October 1864.

The Gettysburg came in on Thursday for coal.

Mr McGloin sent the gig for me, and I went on board immediately. The officers all seemed glad to see me, and the crew in defiance of regulations and discipline broke out with three roaring cheers that quite took me by surprise.

I found things in a great mess, but the ship looks as well as I expected things are getting straight now, however, and I have have heard the officers remark that she seemed a different ship, I hope she will be still more "different" before a month more.

My share of the prize "Little Ada" should amount to three or four thousand dollars. . . .

I have orders from the Adml to leave the ship and come to Hampton Roads if I hear of any probability of a move up the James River again— I should like to be there if there is to be a determined advance of the Army and Navy towards Richmond, otherwise not.

Your photograph hangs over the head of my berth, and I often look at it longing for the time when I shall look again in your sweet face, and see your eyes tell me again how truly you love me. . . .

Roswell to Flora

USS *Gettysburg*
Beaufort, N.C.
July 22, 1864

. . . The officers of the Gettysburg did not get along very happily while I was away, but I have got them pretty well straightened out now and the ship begins to look more as it should. On the 9th the G. captured the rebel steamer "Little Ada," from Bermuda to Wilmington with a cargo of lead and drugs for the Confederate Army. The chase lasted 4 hours and the Gettysburg sustained our expectations in regard to speed—she is a splendid ship. I expect to go to Norfolk in two or three weeks to put the ship in dock to paint the bottom,—will be there four or five days. I sail this afternoon on a cruise; the dark nights of this month are just commencing, and I hope to fall in with some of the rebel supply vessels—intend to cruise on and near the Bermuda line. . . .

Roswell to Kate

USS *Gettysburg*
Beaufort, N.C.
July 31, 1864

. . . Since writing you last I have been out cruising, and came in yesterday morning for coal and supplies—shall go out again to-morrow at noon.

On the 26th we sighted a blockade runner which we chased all day, and although we did not catch her, I was not at all disappointed in the speed of the Gettysburg. They have some vessels that none of ours can catch, and I am quite sure the one I chased was the "City of Petersburg" one of their fastest.

The Gettysburg showed her great speed, and in a heavy gale we had during two days proved a much better sea boat than I expected.

I hope to fall in with something this time out, and am quite confident they cannot have many vessels that can run away from us.

Things were in a worse state than I thought possible when I came on board but I hope you will soon hear that the Gettysburg is one of the happiest as well as best regulated ships in the Squadron. . . .

The Admiral came in yesterday in the "Malvern," the fleet is divided into four divisions—that of the "James River," the "Sounds of N.C.," East Bar and West Bar off Wilmington. I belong to the division off East Bar or New Inlet and am an outside cruiser. The Divisional officer is Capt. O. S. Glisson of the "St Iago de Cuba."[1]

This evening I went on board to see the Admiral but he was ashore; while waiting for him, the officer of the deck reported that he was going to my ship. Immediately returned and found him in the cabin; he said he had been in my state room to see what he knew he should find there, a portrait of the lady whose letters came to his care—and he said many things about *your sweet face* that I will *tell* you some time, but may not write. He wished to be remembered to you, and said you must already consider him one of your friends. . . .

---

1. Captain Oliver S. Glisson, commander of the USS *Santiago de Cuba*, a large sidewheel steamer built in 1861 and carrying 10 guns.

Kate to Roswell

Mt. Vernon, Ohio
July 31, 1864

. . . What do you think of the idea of Gen Grant's "blowing Peters-burg up?"[1] There seems to be a prospect of some work to do on the river soon. I do hope Sherman will succeed in capturing Hood and his army, instead of their "retreating" again—though Hood does not seem to admire Johnston's style of fighting. I trust we shall hear good news from there soon. It is amusing to read the quotations from rebel papers claiming such a grand victory at Atlanta. It is not hard to make people believe what they want to be true.[2]

The coming draft will clear Mt Vernon completely—there are more to be drafted from this ward than are in it. I hope some of the cop-perheads will have to go now. It would do them good.

Well, here it is the first of August, summer will soon be past—this summer that I have dreaded so much. It is very nearly three months now since we said "Goodbye," and I watched so long to see the Get-tysburg pass. It may be three more months and perhaps longer before I will see you again, and as long as I know you are safe and well I can bear it better and I will not expect you or ask you to come, when you can be doing any thing for the cause where you are, but I do hope it may not be *very* much longer that it will need you. . . .

1. A reference to the ill-fated battle of the Crater on July 30, when units of IX Corps tunneled under the Confederate lines at Petersburg, exploded a mine, but failed to exploit this extraordinary opportunity to break through the resulting gap in the Confederate defenses.

2. As Sherman closed in on Atlanta, Jefferson Davis removed General Joseph E. Johnston (1807–91) from command of the Army of Tennessee and replaced him with Lieutenant-General John Bell Hood (1831–79) on July 17, 1864. Hood counterat-tacked but was repulsed in three bloody battles from July 20 through 28.

Roswell to Kate

> USS *Gettysburg*
> Norfolk, Va. August 13,
> 1864

We arrived here day before yesterday evening from our cruising ground for some repairs, and to have the ship put in the dock—when iron ships have been at sea four or five months a kind of sea grass begins to grow on the bottom which lessens their speed very fast, and it has grown so long on the Gettysburg that she does not run as fast as when we left New York by at least two knots per hour.

During the last ten days we were out I sighted *four* blockade runners, three of which we chased, and if the ship had been in as good running order as when we left New York I should certainly have caught two fine large steamers loaded with cotton, as it was one of them was obliged to throw over his cargo to escape, and we picked up fifteen or twenty-thousand dollars worth. The coal we got at Beaufort last was very poor, so that we were not able to carry as high a pressure of steam as usual.

I have learned the track of the blockade runners pretty well, and fell in with these four just as I had calculated. I chased one more than half way to Bermuda.

Although we did not catch them we all have as much confidence in the ship as ever, for had it not been for poor coal, and the grass on the ships bottom we should have caught two of them. They have some of the fastest steamers in the world in the trade now, and some that none of our vessels can catch, and I do not expect them all to run away from us.

We had a very exciting cruise with pleasant weather except one heavy gale from the North East during two days which the "G" rode out like a duck in a mill pond.

If I had time I would give you all the incidents and particulars, but we have so much work going on, and my attention is needed in so many different directions that I must wait till I see you.

I found it necessary to make some changes in my officers on my return, and I am glad to tell you that the "G" is now one of the happiest ships in the Squadron—every one contented and all anxious to remain in her. I have on board now one hundred and thirty officers and men.

We will go in the dry dock this afternoon, and will probably be here a week leaving in time to get back to our cruising ground for the next dark nights. Yesterday I gave the Paymaster leave to go home for four days, but I shall not be able to leave the ship at all. Some of the officers will probably go for three or four days. I have not heard from you for some time now, but suppose my letters have gone to Beaufort. My prize money will not count up so fast as you think I fear, for the new prize law passed through the influence of the N.Y. people will probably deprive us of our share of this vessel [i.e., the *Gettysburg* ex *Margaret and Jessie*], and if I get two or three thousand dollars from the *Little Ada* I shall be fortunate. By the time we get our prize money it has become beautifully less.[1] All that is nothing however if we could only stop the rebel supplies that are constantly going in to their army through Wilmington. . . .

Roswell to Kate

USS *Gettysburg*
Beaufort, N.C.
Aug. 31, 1864

We came in here again, yesterday for coal, and as usual I found several of your dear letters awaiting me. You *deserve* an answer to each one but as I am going to sea to-day I will answer them *all* generally now, and make up deficiencies when I can.

1. As commander of a vessel on blockade duty, Lamson was entitled to one-tenth of the amount of prize money due to that vessel as captor of the prize, as adjudicated by a prize court. All navy ships within signal distance of the vessel making the capture, and in condition to render aid if required, were entitled to share in the prize money. On the basis of the 10 percent formula, Lamson did earn about $5,270 for his share in the capture of the *Margaret and Jessie*. His share for *Little Ada* was $4,290 if he received one-tenth, but in that case he may have had to share with William McGloin, who was actually in command of the *Gettysburg* at the time of the capture, in which case Lamson's share would be half of this amount. Altogether during the war, ships under his command (the *Nansemond* and *Gettysburg*) took four prizes (and destroyed two others) and picked up jettisoned cotton bales from two blockade runners that escaped. Lamson's total wartime share of prize money should have been approximately $25,000. There is no indication in his papers what amount he actually received, but judging from his complaints about miserly prize counts it was probably less.

Last cruise was a very successful one, and the "G" did what I never doubted she could do under proper circumstances, caught one of the finest and fastest vessels in the Confederate service; with a cargo of cotton and Confederate Cotton Bonds bound for England.

On the morning of the 24th Inst. we sighted black smoke to the S & W from us and immediately started in pursuit. We soon made out a blockade runner chased by one of our vessels (the Keystone State)[1] the blockade runner being evidently much the fastest. We soon left the Keystone State astern and it became a chase between this vessel and the stranger, who was evidently very fast and ably commanded for she made use of every manoeuvre known to sailors to evade us, and took advantage of every circumstance in his favor & they soon began to throw over cotton to lighten the vessel more. I put the "G" in her best sailing trim, and she went through the water beautifully from fifteen to fifteen and a half knots (sea miles) per hour and at times went even faster.[2] In two hours I had him within range of my guns and yawing the ship a little gave him a shot which fell very near him— another shot struck a bale of cotton on deck, and another took effect in the bow causing the vessel to leak some still he held on most gallantly till he saw I was coming alongside when he surrendered.

The prize proved to be the "Lilian" one of the most beautiful ships I have ever seen, and as her captain remarked when he came "as good and as fast a ship as they had" except perhaps one or two lately built. We went on board and had some difficulty in stopping the leak, but finally succeeded in doing so. She came out of Wilmington the evening before and at the time of the capture had over five hundred bales of cotton on board, the vessel cost $175,000 in gold in England last March and with her cargo is now worth more than $600,000—the finest ship by far, and the most valuable prize ever captured on this blockade.[3]

She was until recently commanded by John Newbern Moffet[4] who

---

1. USS *Keystone State*, a sidewheel steamer built in 1853 and acquired by the navy in 1861, carrying 11 guns but rated at only 9.5 knots.

2. Fifteen and one-half knots is equivalent to 18 miles per hour.

3. The *Lilian* was a fast steel-hulled ship built expressly for blockade running in Glasgow in 1864. As usual with captured fast blockade runners, the navy converted her into a two-gun blockader, this time keeping the same name.

4. Lamson got the name garbled; it was Captain John Newland Maffitt (1819–86), one of the best Confederate naval officers.

formerly commanded the Florida, privateer; she was named for one of his daughters, and I am sure the lady cannot be much prettier.

After the Captain came on board he said—"if I am a sailor, you handled your ship beautifully." I told him I had admired his maneuvering during the chase, and the gallantry with which he held on after we had him within range.

The Keystone State was in sight at the time of the capture and will share in the prize though she would have been out of sight in a very short time more, and just before the "Lilian" surrendered another vessel hove in sight which proved to be the USS Massachusetts, the supply vessel for Admiral Dahlgren. She will put in a claim but I do not think she will share as she was not at all within the distance prescribed by law.

Capt. Crosby (Adml Lee's fleet captain when I was flag Lieutenant) is a real nice gentleman and I am quite willing to share with him, but after such a splendid chase to have a slow old beef boat share is rather too much, especially as she does not belong to our Squadron—however I am satisfied, that the Gettysburg's reputation is established, and there is nothing talked of in the fleet but the chase and the way the two vessels were maneuvered—there is not another vessel in the fleet could have caught him.

It is only when I think of *you*, dear, that I wish at all we had been alone, but we still get along as it is I doubt not.

Capt. Crosby had a splendid gig built for him at the Phila. Navy Yard & the finest boat I have ever seen in the Navy—the other day he agreed that if I chased a cotton loaded steamer, and caught her and he shared in the prize he would give me the boat—it is coming this morning, and I have now a gig that will match your pennant beautifully. The Admiral said he would rather have caught the Lilian than any other vessel they have. Capt. Crosby is to command her as soon as she can be fitted out as a blockader. . . .

My share of the prize will certainly be about $10,000. $15,000 if the Massachusetts does not share.

Roswell to Kate

> USS *Gettysburg*
> Navy Yard, Norfolk
> Sept. 14, 1864

Here we are again for some overhauling that will keep us during this week, and perhaps part of next.

When I rejoined the ship last July I found that many things had been neglected, and I have been trying to get her in good order again ever since as stormy weather is coming and I told the Admiral I thought we had better come in now, and complete the repairs necessary for the Winter cruise.

We had a beautiful run from Beaufort making one of the quickest passages I have heard of, and shall soon be back again, I hope to capture another "Lilian." . . .

Kate to Roswell

> Mt. Vernon, Ohio
> Sept. 14, 1864

. . . How cheering all the war news is now. I am sure we have cause for rejoicing, and hope for the future. I am glad to see the blockade at Wilmington proving so effective—last evenings papers announced the capture of the "A. D. Vance" and "Eliza."[1]

I am looking every day for another capture by the Gettysburg—What a blessing it would be if Wilmington could be as effectually stopped up as Mobile is now. Well perhaps it will before long—When we can spare the men to go and take it—as I trust they will soon take Mobile. We will wait with much interest the further development of Sherman's

1. The cheering news was Farragut's victory at Mobile Bay on August 5 and the subsequent capture of the Confederate forts guarding the entrance to the bay, which closed Mobile to blockade runners, and Sherman's capture of Atlanta on September 2. The *A. D. Vance* was a fast blockade runner owned by the state of North Carolina which had made many successful trips before she was captured by the USS *Santiago de Cuba* on September 10. She was subsequently converted into a blockade ship the USS *Frolic*. The *Eliza* was a privately owned blockade runner.

plans, as he emphatically declares the campaign is only fairly begun—
If *this* one could only end it! but just wait till after the election and
we'll see. I didn't mean to give you "national" news tonight but you see
I couldn't help it. . . .

Roswell to Kate

USS *Gettysburg*
Beaufort, N.C.
Sept. 25, 1864

I arrived here yesterday evening from Hampton Roads, and by order
of the Admiral am getting ready to go to sea again this afternoon. . . .

I wrote you on our arrival at Norfolk: we completed our repairs in
the time anticipated by the Admiral and are now in fine order for the
Winter. I scarcely left the ship at all while we were at the Navy Yard,
and was heartily glad to get away.

The blockade runners seem to be running mostly to Halifax now
and I shall cruise on that route while out this time. . . .

I have no idea when I shall be able to come North again—the exi-
gencies of war and of the service can alone determine it—I might ask
for leave, but have no idea I should get it. The Admiral says no other
ship does as much as mine does, and has made the most flattering
reports to the Department in regard to her activity and efficiency; but
I am getting tired and weary; and my health is not at all good I should
be glad to have a little rest somewhere, but cannot ask for it under
the circumstances. . . .

To-day is Sunday and a day of rest in most parts of the Christian
world, but is not that here. . . .

Roswell to Kate

USS *Gettysburg*
Beaufort, N.C.
Oct. 3, 1864

We have been out on another cruise, but only sighted one runner
and as it was just sundown at the time we lost sight of him soon after
in the darkness.

I came in at daylight yesterday morning, and sail again to-day hoping to have better luck.

Two vessels were destroyed by the fleet off New Inlet last week—the "Night Hawk" and the "Lynx."[1] The Adml told Capt. Crosby yesterday that they were beginning to guard the bar "as the Nansemond used to do."

The cotton in the Lilian sold the other day for little more than half what we expected it to bring, and what it should have sold for.

I have dates from you to the 21st ulto, and Aunt's kind invitation to come to Mt. Vernon—it will not be possible for me to come for I am *sure* I *could not get leave* if I asked for it; and under present circumstances I should not like to ask. I fear I gave you unnecessary uneasiness in regard to my health—I am not *sick* but do need a little rest which I shall get no doubt when I have earned it; do not be in the least anxious about me—I am used to hard work and when it is all over I shall get well quicker than if I neglected my duty now. . . .

---

1. The *Night Hawk* was a privately owned blockade runner; the *Lynx* was a fast steel-hulled vessel built in Liverpool in 1864 expressly for blockade running and owned by the Confederate government.

CHAPTER 9

WE HAVE TAKEN

FORT FISHER

OCTOBER 1864–APRIL 1865

O N SEPTEMBER 17, 1864, the Navy Department removed
Samuel Phillips Lee from command of the North Atlantic
Blockading Squadron and appointed David G. Farragut in his
place. Farragut declined, citing poor health, so the Department named
David Dixon Porter (1813–91) instead. As commander of the Mississippi Squadron, Porter had worked with both Farragut and Grant in
campaigns to gain control of the Mississippi River, including the capture of Vicksburg on July 4, 1863, for which Porter was rewarded with
promotion to rear admiral. Lee was named commander of the Mississippi Squadron to succeed Porter, so in effect the two men exchanged
places. But the switch was something of a demotion for Lee, for the
Union's complete control of the Mississippi made it a quiet theater,
while the plan to attack Fort Fisher turned the North Atlantic Squadron into the theater of greatest naval activity.

Lee's removal from command of this fleet may have had more to do
with politics than with his naval record. His brothers-in-law Francis P.
Blair, Jr., and Montgomery Blair had fallen out of favor with the Republican party, and Montgomery had been forced to resign from the
Cabinet at about the same time Lee was removed from his command.
With respect to naval strategy, Lee had endured much criticism for
his failure to shut down blockade running into Wilmington. The prob-

lem, as Lamson frequently pointed out, was that the numerous shoals and channels at the mouth of the Cape Fear River below Wilmington were extremely hard to patrol even with the large number of ships available by the latter part of 1864. The solution was a combined army–navy attack to capture the huge earthwork Fort Fisher, guarding the main entrance into the Cape Fear River. Lee had recommended such an attack, but Secretary of the Navy Welles did not think he was the man to lead it. Because of his earlier capture of New Orleans and his "damn the torpedoes" attack at Mobile Bay on August 5, 1864, Farragut had enormous prestige. When he turned down the command, Porter seemed a logical alternative—especially because Grant had gained a favorable opinion of him during their joint campaign against Vicksburg. So Porter came east and Lee went west in October 1864. Lamson naturally wondered what Lee's departure would mean for his own future. But his abilities and energy soon won Porter's respect, and Lamson found himself called on for even more important and dangerous duty than before.

———•———

Roswell to Kate

USS *Gettysburg*
Beaufort, N.C.
Oct. 13, 1864

Many thanks for your kind letters of the 2d & 3rd Insts, which have been received since coming in from our last cruise.

Generally when we come in we coal all night and go out the next day, but this time I am giving officers and men, and myself too a couple of days rest, and shall not sail till Sat. or Sunday, though I am all ready for sea now. Most vessels take a week to coal, and it is so unusual to see the "G" in port so long that many ask what is the matter.

We came in on Monday morning early, and just as we anchored the Admiral's boat came alongside to ask me to breakfast with him, which I did, and received the first positive information in regard to his removal from this Squadron to the West Gulf Squadron. I cannot say I was very much surprised for I have seen by the way the Department was treating him for some time that something was brewing. He showed me all the Correspondence between himself and the Department, and I think they have treated him very badly, and without the least indication of that consideration or kind feeling that he shows so often to those serving under him (of course this is for *you* alone). *No one* can *blockade* Wilmington better than he has done with the vessels furnished for that purpose and he has repeatedly urged the government to place at his command the means of capturing the place and of ending the blockade running in that way. Undoubtedly Farragut is sent here for that purpose, and the means that were with-held from Lee will be granted to him. As Admiral Lee remarked they have sent the greatest Naval Commander of this or of any age to succeed him, and he added that if Farragut could command the resources of the government or enlist its cooperation more fully than he could he was perfectly willing to relinquish the command at once.

Our Navy Department does many unjust and arbitrary things now days of which there have recently been some marked instances in this fleet, and no matter how hard an officer may try to do his duty or how faithfully devote himself to the service he is as likely to receive censure as praise.

There are many things connected with this change that I cannot write that would explain it more fully, and which I will tell you when I see you. I say nothing about it here.

Admiral Lee will take with him the love and respect of all the better portion of the Officers of the Squadron, and will leave many who will never forget his kind consideration.

You ask if my position will be changed by his removal; not unless Farragut brings some officer with him who takes a fancy to the fastest ship in the fleet, and who has political influence enough at Washington to get her.

I do not anticipate anything of the kind, however, and only mention it as a possibility. . . .

My health is improving and I begin to feel more like myself again. I have not been so *sick* as you seem to think—only a little weary. My great happiness now is in sailing my new gig: the fastest boat in the fleet. I have been taking some of my officers out sailing occasionally, but they do not seem to be so fond of dashing about in the surf or the bar or of carrying sail till the boat is half under water, and now decline my invitation unless the breeze is gentle last night it blew so hard that I lost my foremast but had a new one made first thing this morning. If you will come down I will give you a sail and you shall see what a splendid boat I have, and how *gently* and safely she will carry a *lady* over the water.

Last cruise I did not see a blockade runner, but picked up the crew of a vessel that foundered in a gale of wind we had; they were in a small boat half full of water and with nothing to eat but a little salt codfish, and nothing to drink. I saw the boat first, and ran for it sometime before we made out what it was.

We also brought in a large steamer bound to N.Y. that had her sails all blown away, smoke pipe blown away and was entirely disabled. I hove-to to windward of her, and one of my officers volunteered to go in a boat and carry a hawser which was done safely though the sea was running very high and we towed her in. There was one old lady on board who was sadly frightened. . . .

Roswell to Kate

> USS *Gettysburg*
> Norfolk
> Oct. 26, 1864

. . . Last Wednesday I chased a blockade runner in the direction of Nassau and on Thursday chased another in the same direction. We gained on them about a mile an hour, and at sundown had them almost under our guns, but the nights were so dark that we lost sight of them.

The last one we chased threw over board all of his cargo.

We should have caught them had it not been for the grass that has grown on the Gettysburg during the last two months, and which impeded her progress at least two miles per hour. On examining her at Beaufort I decided to come here to have the ship put in dock, and the grass scraped off, which will be done to-day and I will sail to-morrow.

You have heard no doubt of Admiral Porter's orders to this Squadron and of the immense preparations making for an attack somewhere (If I could *talk* to you I would *tell* you all about it, but I may not write it).

I have just received a General Order announcing the "Divisions" of the Fleet and the Divisional Commanders—Five Divisions each commanded by a Commodore, and the Iron Clad Division under Commod Radford[1] consists of seven of our best Iron vessels. I doubt if any Naval

---

1. Commodore William Radford (1809–90), commander of the USS *New Ironsides*, the largest ironclad in the Union fleet.

Commander ever commanded so formidable a fleet before in the history of the world. All our large frigates are in the fleet as flag ships of Divisions, and the fleet numbers over *one hundred* ships, most of them carrying powerful batteries. I belong to the 2d Division, Commo. Lanman.[1]

As I came into Hampton Roads, and saw such a splendid fleet anchored in "line ahead" by Division I felt a new pride in belonging to such a Navy. As soon as we were near enough I made the private signal of the "G," and as soon as it was answered from the flag ship ran up my divisional flag.

Divisional flags, and Pennants of Divisional Commanders were flying from every ship but I could not see *the* pennant so I hailed the guard ship and learned that Adml Porter was at Norfolk and that Com. Thatcher[2] was the Senior officer.

He was anchored at the head of the line, and as the "G" dashed up between the lines of the 2d & 3rd Divisions every glass was directed to the prettiest and *swiftest* ship in the fleet. I stopped alongside the Com and went on board to report. I never met him before but found him a very pleasant old gentleman; he invited me to breakfast with him, but as the "G" was not anchored but lying-to with some danger of drifting foul of the other vessels I returned on board, and soon after anchored near the Admiral who had come down in the "Malvern."

I reported to Admiral Porter and received an order to have what I wanted done and come up at once.

Everything is very much changed on board the "Malvern" but I found several of my old friends still there, and passed a few minutes very pleasantly with them. The flag ship was completely surrounded by "Gigs" with occasionally the "barge" of one of the Commodores, and their flags and pennants made the scene look bright and lively as well as stirring.

When my gig was called up all the officers went to the side to see her and all admired the boat and pennant very much.

We are as busy as we can be, and all working hard to get away to-morrow.

I had hoped to get a few days leave next time we came in, but of course I can not think of such a thing now, and I could not get it even if I asked. So dear we must do our duty bravely and live in hope. . . .

1. Commodore Joseph Lanman (?–1874).
2. Commodore Henry K. Thatcher (1806–80).

Roswell to Kate

> USS *Gettysburg*
> Beaufort, N.C.
> Nov. 6, 1864

We came in yesterday and I found *five* of your dear letters awaiting me—from the 12th ulto to the 23rd inclusive.

I need not tell *you* how much pleasure they have given me, and I am sorry I cannot make a better return, but my stays in port are very short and exceedingly busy ones, and I cannot write much at sea; I have to be on deck almost every hour of the day and night, and devote all the time I can get to rest.

. . . I saw Admiral Porter on leaving Hampton Roads got one of my Officers promoted and a son of Admiral Dahlgren was ordered to the vessel.

The last four days out were the stormiest I have seen even in the Gulf Stream, but the Gettysburg rode out the gale finely.

Friday morning I fell in with a vessel disabled and in a sinking condition, and though the gale was at its height and sea running very heavily succeeded in saving the Captain and crew.

I came near losing some of my own men who volunteered to go to the sinking vessel.

I saw no blockade runners during the cruise, but the inshore vessels were more fortunate two or three fine prizes having been taken by the fleet off the bar. . . .

Adml Porter treated me with great kindness while at Hamtpon Roads invited me to breakfast with him, and allowed me to choose my cruising ground.

He admired the Gettysburg very much and I ran down through the fleet as we passed out to show him her speed.

My health is still improving.

I hope I shall be with you on Christmas but of course I cannot say positively when I shall come North again.

We hear that Lieut Cushing has blown up the ram at Plymouth with a torpedo boat—it was a gallant thing and should insure him his promotion.[1] . . .

---

1. Lieutenant William B. Cushing was indeed promoted to Lieutenant Commander

Roswell to Kate

USS *Gettysburg*
Beaufort, NC
Nov. 13, 1864

... I am sure, dear Katie that you cannot need my prayers as much as I do yours for my heart has been very cold lately, and has gone far from that Savior who is so loving and so lovable, and who has never deserted me in the time of need.

There are so many things and influences in a life like this to draw one away that nothing but *constant* watchfulness and prayer can insure safety: I fear I have not used these means as unceasingly as I ought; but your prayers dear Katie are always with me constantly drawing me back, and shedding their sweet influence over my spirit when perhaps *nothing else* would reach it. . . .

The attack on Wilmington is postponed indefinitely the army were not ready too many men having been sent home to vote for Mr. Lincoln—and Admiral Porter was informed that no reinforcements could be expected till after the election—We hear that Father Abe is reelected, and I hope it is true, and that he will hurry up the troops now, and not keep such an immense fleet doing nothing.[1]

I had no opportunity to vote being at sea—if I could I should have voted for Mr. Lincoln though I do not think he has a *single* qualification for the head of a nation—except that he is pledged to continue the war till a lasting peace is established.

Last week I had two chases but they commenced too late in the day to give us any chance of catching the vessels.

---

for his daring exploit in sinking the feared CSS *Albemarle* at Plymouth, North Carolina, with a spar torpedo carried on a small boat on the night of October 24, 1864.

1. Lincoln was decisively reelected with the electoral votes of all but three Union states. While winning about 55 percent of the civilian votes, he carried nearly 80 percent of the soldier votes. Soldiers from Illinois, Indiana, and New Jersey were furloughed home to vote because the Democratic legislatures of those states had refused to make provision for absentee voting by soldiers, but those of all other states could vote in camp by absentee ballot. The reason for postponement of the attack on Fort Fisher was not so much the election as it was the operations of the Army of the Potomac and Army of the James at Petersburg and Richmond, which prevented Grant from detaching troops for the Fort Fisher attack. By December these troops became available.

If we sight a vessel at twelve miles distance and gain a knot an hour, and this is a great difference in the speed of two fast vassels it must be ten hours before we are within range of our guns, and we frequently make blockade runners out from our mastheads fifteen or sixteen miles off.

I chased the "Hope"[1] from noon till dark gaining about a mile and a-half an hour, and at dark had her almost within range, and gaining rapidly but lost her in the darkness; next night she tried again to get into Wilmington and ran close to one of our small vessels near the bar without seeing her, and was captured without trouble. The Captain said he threw overboard two-thousand sacks of coffee and a large quantity of machinery to escape from the Gettysburg, and that if there had been an hour more of daylight he would have been compelled to surrender—his men were so much exhausted by their efforts that they would make no effort when they found themselves close to the vessel that captured them. The "Hope" was the largest of all their vessels.

I am ordered now to go off the Western Bar at the mouth of the Cape Fear River for a chaser so that if a vessel gets out past the bar blockaders I am to chase off shore while they resume their stations shall go out to-morrow or next day. . . .

To-day the Newbern came in with fresh beef and vegetables for the fleet; her arrival twice a month is the great event in this harbor; the yellow fever has abated very much at Beaufort. . . .

I cannot tell when I shall come North now that the plans for the Squadron are so much deranged, but will write you as soon as can form any estimate as to the time no doubt it will be before the Winter is over. My health is not at all good but I think it is improving.

Roswell to Kate

USS *Gettysburg*
Beaufort, N.C.
Nov. 25, 1864

We are in port again for coal, and again your kind letters have met me, and made me both sad and happy—happy to hear from you, and

---

1. A fast steel-hulled ship built in Liverpool in 1864 expressly for blockade running and rated at 16 knots.

sad that I may not see you as soon as you anticipate and that you may have to spend Xmas without me: I cannot tell certainly—I may be in Hampton Roads in a week perhaps not for many weeks but I have been expecting orders to go there for some time. Well, it cannot be *much* longer before I come North, at all events, so we will have courage till then. . . .

Yesterday was Thanksgiving I suppose "at home:" it had but a slight tendency that way here—enough, however to recognize it by. . . .

No person, I think will be so glad to have the war end as those on this blockade.

Last week I chased a very large blockade-runner two hundred and fifty miles, but he was as fast as the Gettysburg and I was no nearer at the end of the chase than when we first sighted him distant about six miles.

It was blowing pretty heavily during most of the chase, and both vessels plunged and rolled badly in the heavy sea.

Coming in we had another gale off the Frying Pan shoals; this is the rough season and it is quite rough enough I assure you.

I am stationed now off the Western Bar, just outside the vessels that blockade the bar, to chase whenever a signal is made that a vessel has got out.

The Tallahassee went in over New Inlet bar last Sat. night. I do not think the blockade has been as poor as it is now for a long time.[1] The Gettysburg is in good order yet and officers and men all well. I will write you as soon as I can conjecture anything in regard to the time when I shall come North. . . .

---

1. The CSS *Tallahassee* was built in London as a fast cross-channel steamer in 1863, purchased by the Confederate navy in 1864, armed with five guns, and turned loose on American fishing boats and merchant ships, of which she destroyed or captured thirty-nine in four months before the fall of Fort Fisher denied her a home port and forced her to sail to Liverpool, where she was sold to a British shipping company. In his comment on the weakness of the blockade, Lamson meant to imply a criticism of its management under Porter's command compared with Lee's, but there were other

Roswell to Kate

USS *Gettysburg*
At sea
Dec. 5, 1864

This cruise has been longer than usual and it is over a week since I have written to you.

My station was off West Bar, you know as a chaser the Admiral did not understand the position of things or he never would have placed me there; so as soon as half an excuse offered for a chase I dashed off towards Nassau, and the next day fell in with a blockade-runner, but so late in the day that although I gained on him he escaped at night.

The next day I saw nothing, but yesterday sighted a blockade runner being chased by one of our cruisers "U.S.S. RR Cuyler" from whom, however he was getting away finely till the Gettysburg appeared and caused his capture in three hours.

The prize proved to be the "Armstrong" with a cargo of cotton from Wilmington, and a fine prize.

During the latter part of the chase we sighted the U.S.S. Mackinaw which also joined in the chase, but was left astern.[1]

The Armstrong tried to gain the weather gauge, but I luffed up to defeat his intention, and force him near to the Cuyler passing across the bows of the Mackinaw, and giving the chase a shot which forced him to relinquish his intention, and kept him between the Gettysburg and the Cuyler.

This maneuvre decided the chase and he soon surrendered, but not before a shot from the Cuyler had struck the vessel.

When we passed the Mackinaw the Gettysburg was dashing through the water so gracefully and swiftly that she elicited the admiration of every one, and as soon as it became evident that I should out maneuvre the chase Capt. Beaumont ran up the signal "Good Boy" I replied

---

reasons as well: the short days and long nights of November and the stormy weather typical of that time of the year were ideal for blockade runners.

1. The USS *R. R. Cuyler* was a screw steamer rated at 14 knots built in 1859, chartered by the navy in 1861, and armed with 12 guns. The USS *Mackinaw* was a 10-gun sidewheel steamer launched in 1863 and rated at 13 knots. The *Armstrong* was privately owned.

"Thank You;" I thought of giving him a more impertinent reply for I did not fancy being called a "boy" by even one of the oldest Commanders in the service.[1]

The Captain of the prize said pointing to the "G" "that is the only vessel that could have caught me alone, and I should not have been captured but for her."

The Cuyler and Gettysburg will share in the prize, and perhaps the Mackinaw—her distance astern at the time of the capture making his claim somewhat doubtful.[2]

The Armstrong threw overboard a large quantity of cotton during the chase and to-day we have picked up about one-hundred and forty bales—we may get some more to-morrow morning, but I have but little coal left and must bear up for Beaufort to-morrow evening or sooner if bad weather should come on.

To-day I received an order from the Admiral directing me to cruise off just as I have done it was dated three weeks ago.

The prisoners say Sherman is within twenty-five miles of Savannah that every effort is made to keep it a secret but that it was well known in Wilmington.[3]

Dec. 6   5:30 a.m.

I was unable to finish your letter last evening, dear, so you see I am up bright and early to have it ready for the prize to take to Hampton Roads—We have had the most beautiful bright, warm sunny days during this cruise. . . .

1. Commander John C. Beaumont (1821–82), who had been in the navy since 1838.

2. The *Mackinaw* did share in the prize. Lamson's share should have been between six and seven thousand dollars.

3. On December 5 Sherman's army was indeed nearing the end of its famous march from Atlanta to the sea, closing in on Savannah, which surrendered to him on December 21.

ON CHRISTMAS EVE 1864 the army–navy task force launched its long-awaited campaign to capture Fort Fisher, chronicled in Lamson's subsequent letters. Before the naval bombardment of the fort began on December 24, however, Lamson played a key role in a dangerous effort to damage the fort by filling an old ship with gunpowder and exploding it in shallow water as near the earthen walls of the fort as possible. This bold enterprise was the brainchild of Major-General Benjamin F. Butler, who would command the army troops in the attack on Fort Fisher. Having read about the explosion at the British port of Erith of two gunpowder barges, which destroyed nearby buildings, Butler conceived the idea of packing a shallow-draft ship with two hundred tons of gunpowder and running it into the shallows in the expectation that the explosion would have a similar impact on the fort. Commander Alexander G. Rhind, captain of the USS *Louisiana*, was selected to blow up his own ship for this purpose. He would be assisted by Lamson's Naval Academy classmate Samuel W. Preston. And Admiral Porter selected Lamson to command the ship to tow the *Louisiana* into position and bring off Rhind and Preston after they had set the fuses. If this scheme had worked, Rhind, Preston, and Lamson would have been heroes almost equal to William Cushing, who had blown up the CSS *Albemarle*. The *Louisiana* exploded as intended, but it did so about six hundred yards from the fort, allowing the open air to absorb the force of the blast and doing the fort and its garrison virtually no damage, contrary to Lamson's assertion in his letter of December 29.

Lamson to Kate

> USS *Gettysburg*
> Off Frying Pan Shoals
> Dec. 24, 1864

I have had much to write you during the past week, but circumstances have not permitted me to do so, but I must now write you an outline of what I have been doing, and I will give you the particulars as soon as I can. Enclosed I send you a letter commenced on the 15th so you see I intended to write to you.[1]

The powder ship of which I wrote arrived at Beaufort with Commander Rhind and Lieut. Preston in charge of her; and on last Sat. morning Admiral Porter sent for me, and said he wished me to go in with Capt. Rhind to assist in getting the vessel in position under Fort Fisher and to bring off Capt. Rhind and those with him after everything had been arranged to ensure the explosion. Capt. Braine[2] had told me that the Admiral had spoken of my going in with the vessel, but the first intimation I had of it was his saying, "You are going in with the powder ship, you know; any vessel in the squadron is at your orders, so make your own arrangements to accompany Capt. Rhind and bring him out."

Of course I had but one answer to give him, and selected the Nansemond as the vessel most suited for such a desperate service, but she not reaching me in time I took the Wilderness, a vessel much like her.[3] It was intended that the powder ship should steam in under Fort Fisher at night; and that when in the right position the fuzes should be lighted and Capt Rhind should come on board of the Wilderness which was to follow him in and steam off to a safe distance before the explosion; on trial, however it was found that the powder ship (the Louisiana) could neither steam nor steer and that the attempt to destroy the forts in this way must be abandoned, or I must tow her to her position under the guns of the fort. We were to have made the attempt last Sunday evening but the Louisiana was not quite ready, and on Monday a heavy storm came up which blew with great violence till yesterday morning. The fleet which was awaiting the explosion to make the attack was obliged to run off shore, and we had great difficulty in keeping the Louisiana afloat at all. Capt Rhind Preston and myself were up day and night, till we were so worn out that even the desperate chances of getting her in afforded a relief. Last night the arrangements having been perfected I took the powder vessel in tow and steamed in for the batteries soon after dark. It was a much too clear and starlight night for such a purpose, but the Admiral had writ-

1. This letter has been lost.

2. Lieutenant-Commander Daniel Laurence Braine (1829–98).

3. USS *Wilderness*, a sidewheel steamer built in 1864 and carrying four guns. Ironically this ship, like the *Gettysburg*, was named for a great Civil War land battle in which the navy had played no part.

ten us during the afternoon, that he should attack to-day and that he depended on its being done. After getting pretty well in I lay to to see if it would not get a little darker when a *blockade runner* came dashing by, and steering directly for the forts.

We followed him in; he answered the challenge from the forts and they showed the lights that guided him in over the bar and that served to guide us in under the forts. We now ran *boldly* in with our fearful tow till the breakers were close to us, and the parapets and embrasures of the fort loomed up almost as distinctly as in the day time.

The water was shoaling up on the beach very rapidly and I gave the signal to Capt. Rhind to cast off the hawser, which was done, and he passed in still nearer the fort, while I slacked an anchor down easily to make no splash in the water, and anchored with a spring on my cable so that I could turn the vessels head off shore, and waited for Capt. Rhind. He had a boat in readiness to which was attached a long line by which he was to be pulled quickly alongside of the Wilderness. It took some twelve or fifteen minutes for him to start the clocks, and adjust the fuzes, which being done he gave the signal, and we pulled him alongside. The rebels now discovered us and challenged us from the beach, but we cut the hawser by which we were moored and the little Wilderness dashed forward to seaward as if she too knew the value of every moment of time till we were out of range of the guns of the fort and clear of the powder ship which a single shell from the forts would have exploded prematurely.

We had just reached a safe distance when the Louisiana blew with a terriffic explosion.

An immense column of flame rose towards the sky, and four distinct reports like that of sharp heavy thunder were heard and a dense mass of smoke enveloped everything.

There is no record of such a mass of powder ever having been exploded before, so its effect could only be conjectured.

The vessel was fitted by the Navy Department, and if they had tried they could not have selected a worse vessel or made worse arrangements for such an affair.

It was a perilous enterprise but we were more than willing to undertake it in the hope of being of service to our country and of saving the lives of our men by at least partially destroying the works before the attack. God took care of me, and saved me from the danger for your sake, and in answer to your prayers, I firmly believe.

Early this morning we ran out to the flag ship when Admiral Porter invited us to breakfast with him, while the lines of battle were forming, and I got on board the Gettysburg again just in time to hoist your pennant at the main and to take her into action in the first line of battle instead of with the reserve of the 2d division where I had been directed to take my station. . . .

Roswell to Kate

USS *Gettysburg*
Off Fort Fisher
Dec. 27, 1864

I had commenced a letter giving you a detailed account of the actions here, but am suddenly ordered off Cape Fear and have not a moment to finish it so will send it just as it is.

We fought the batteries two days and completely silenced them when Gen Butler landed part of his troops and some of them got into the forts but they were not supported and from some cause not apparent he reembarked all his men instead of taking the battery as there is no doubt he might have done. We can silence the forts, but cannot take them without a *soldier* to command the troops.

Roswell to Kate

USS *Gettysburg*
Beaufort, N.C.
Dec. 29, 1864

. . . I tried to write you an account of the two days fight with Fort Fisher and the batteries at the mouth of the Cape Fear River, but was kept so *constantly* on the move night and day that I was obliged to send it unfinished or send you no news at all.

The explosion of the powder ship took place as I wrote you on the night of the 23rd (Friday night) and the fleet went into action the next morning.

We have since learned the effects of the terrible explosion, and although it did not destroy the forts as many supposed it would it did an immense amount of damage and killed or disabled almost the entire

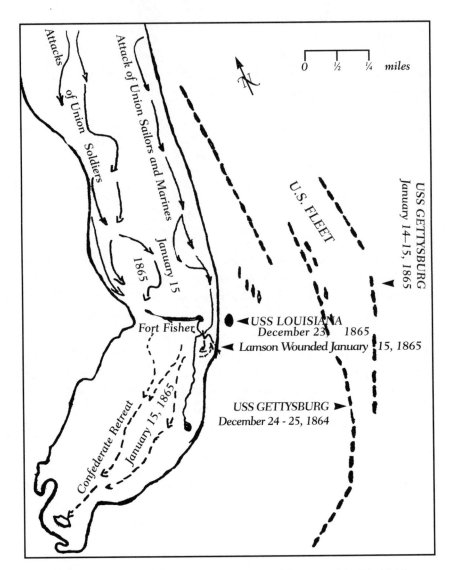

Fort Fisher, December 23–25, 1864, and January 14–15, 1865

garrison, so that the forts had to have a new garrison the next morning. This undoubtedly saved us the lives of many of our men, and some four ships, for the old garrison was well drilled at the guns and the *new* one did not know anything about them—the inaccuracy of their fire was noticed at once. It was the grandest sight I ever beheld, the fleet going into action under the fire of the forts; each vessel swinging into her position as coolly as though coming to anchor in port: to the sound of a salute, the different colored signal flags thrown out by the Admiral, and the flag ships of divisions made it seem all the more like a gala day till the rushing of the shot and bursting shells showed the work that was to be done and reminded each one of his duty to the sacred cause for which we are fighting, and for which our country is suffering.

The fleet was soon all closely engaged, and before sundown had silenced the rebels completely.

Soon after the commencement of the action a rush of steam from the Mackinaw showed that her boilers had been struck, and she soon signaled "disabled" a little while after the "Osceola"[1] was struck through the boilers so near the Gettysburg that I could almost have jumped on board, and soon after she signalled "sinking." The Admiral sent a vessel to her assistance, and as she drew out of the line I ran in and took her place; the guns that had disabled her exploded water over us and one shot just missed our flag but a kind Providence watched over the Gettysburg for your sake, and we were not struck during the action, although no vessel in the line was nearer or more exposed to the enemy's fire. The position assigned us was with the reserve 2d Division, but after going in with the powder ship I got permission to go into action in the first line between the Brooklyn[2] and the Osceola.

After sundown the signal was made to "retire for the night" and I was directed to go around the Frying Pan Shoals with orders for the vessels on the other side; this took all night, and we got back just in time for the next day's fight, which was similar to the first except that a number of vessels (the "G" among them) were sent to *cover* the landing of Gen. Butler's troops, which had arrived during the night. Four or five thousand were safely landed, and his skirmishers had advanced quite near the fort, when to the surprise and dismay of every one he gave an order for them to reembark again.

The fleet had *completely silenced the batteries*, and were ready to *renew* the assault, which was expected every moment, and which would *undoubtedly* have succeeded when the order came for the troops to fall back and reembark. Before falling back, however, *four* of the brave fellows *mounted the parapet of Fort Fisher and brought away the rebel flag*. If Gen Butlers cheeks did not tingle with shame when he heard of this, he is indeed the shameless coward the southrons call him.

1. USS *Osceola*, a sidewheel steamer launched in 1863 and armed with nine guns.
2. USS *Brooklyn*, a 24-gun screw sloop of war launched in 1858.

Words are too weak to express a proper indignation at such conduct, but if I could only have him to deal with I would as certainly hang him at the yard-arm to-morrow morning as the sun rose.[1]

He alone is responsible that the lives lost in this attack have been lost for nothing; that they have been lost without benefit to the cause to which they were devoted. The country, too, must bear the immense expense of the expedition without receiving anything but shame for recompense.

The rebels of course discovered the weak points to their works and our mode of approach, and are certainly working day and night to strengthen the one and guard against the other. Gen. Butler makes some excuse about reinforcements on the way to the fort and bad weather, but it made no difference if the whole Confederacy had been enroute for the fort for they could have been taken before any assistance could have reached it; and during almost a year on this coast I have never seen less surf on the beach or finer weather for landing troops: and if the weather was too bad to land troops how *could* he reembark them, an operation *infinitely more difficult*.

The Admiral has protested against Gen. Butler's having any further connection with the expedition and sent the Fleet Capt. this evening to Gen. Sherman to see if he cannot come up with or send troops enough to assist in taking the works. Gen. Butler went to Hampton Roads some days since.

If we had succeeded as we hoped, the Gettysburg was to bring the despatches home, and I should have got a short leave so you see I am suffering under two disappointments.

I came up to-day for coal, and have some repairs to make that will detain us a couple or three days when I suppose we will resume our station on the blockade till the preparations are made to renew the attack. The fleet are at anchor here and in "Lookout Bight" awaiting the troops that are to cooperate.

I hope the Gettysburg will carry your pennant through an action soon that will [be] of more benefit to our country than the last has been. Our loss is sixty killed and wounded. I do not know the loss

---

1. History has been almost as hard on Butler as Lamson was for his timidity and incompetence in this affair. Grant did not hang Butler from the yardarm, but did secure his removal from command. Grant named Brigadier-General Alfred H. Terry (1827–90) to command the ground troops in a renewed effort to take Fort Fisher, which succeeded on January 15, 1865.

among the troops, but it must be small. That the powder ship saved many lives in the fleet there is no doubt, and that is a sufficient recompense for the desperate risk we ran in taking the vessel under the fort and blowing it up.

Kate to Roswell

Mount Vernon, Ohio
Jan. 8, 1865

. . . Of course you know, and I know you cannot help it, but it is almost *four weeks* since I have had a word from you. I try to comfort myself with the thought—perhaps you are coming, but as it is only "perhaps" and the uncertainty is so great there is not very much comfort in it. But I am *sure* I shall have a letter, or yourself, this week. Oh, how I wish you could come, if you cannot now, I fear you cannot all this winter, and I cannot bear to think of that possibility. I *do* want you, more than I can tell you—and I do think you need a little rest.

But you know better than I whether you can come, and if it is not *right* you know I would not ask it, but I cannot see why it would not be right. Indeed dear, it is very difficult to be unselfishly patriotic all the time, I try not to complain—but I fear I do sometimes. It is not easy to see always that it is best. Write to me as often as you can dearest Roswell, though I know I need not urge you—but do tell me again *you love me*—Not that I have *any* fear or doubt, but I want so much to see the words again—if indeed I may not hear them soon as I so long to do. . . .

Roswell to Kate

USS *Gettysburg*
Beaufort, NC
Jan. 10, 1865

Since writing you last, the fleet have been here and off the harbor making preparations to renew the attack and awaiting the arrival of the troops who came two days since under command of Maj. Gen. Terry.

The weather has been so unfavorable since that nothing could be done and we are awaiting a change.

I have received orders to proceed to New Inlet and as soon as the bar is sufficiently smooth to cross it with safety I shall go to sea.

New Years evening after sundown the Admiral ordered me to Hampton Roads with important despatches; but it was so dark when I received them that the pilots would not attempt to take the ship out, there being no lights here; the Admiral told me to try to take her out which I did; but we struck heavily several times, only got off the reef after great difficulty.

By lowering my boats and sending them ahead to sound I managed to follow them out, but it was anything but a pleasant New Years evening—after delivering my despatches and executing some orders at Norfolk for forwarding ammunition I returned and have been lying at anchor since.

Everyone is confident that this attack will be successful and I have no doubt of it myself, but the rebels are better prepared and will probably give us a warmer reception. Butler lost *the* opportunity to take Wilmington and we must repair the mistake as well as we can.

I see in some of Butler's papers the most plausible collection of falsehoods in regard to the affair some even going so far as to attempt to throw the blame on Admiral Porter. When I read the papers I doubt if I was at Fort Fisher at all—. . . .

We have been having quite pleasant times during the last few days— many of my classmates and friends are here in the different vessels, and have been on board to see me and we have visited each other generally, with an occasional oyster supper in the evening. A party of us sailed out in my gig the other day and visited several of the vessels lying outside—They have not been having so pleasant a time.

I finished a letter home [to Oregon] this morning giving them an account of the attack &c., and containing some complimentary (?) allusions to Gen. Butler who is to receive a leather medal from the fleet with appropriate inscriptions.

I hope to be able to tell you soon of a success that will do very much towards ending the war; in the meantime you must give yourself no uneasiness for me for the same kind Father who has cared for us both will take care of us still. . . .

Kate to Roswell

Mount Vernon, Ohio
Jan. 11, 1865

Yours of the 24th and 27th Dec. came yesterday evening, and I need not tell you were joyfully welcomed. I particularly needed it then for I was half sick with headache and had been looking forward all day to the hope of a letter in the evening. I am quite well again this morning and more hopeful and happier than I have been for several weeks, just the sight of your writing does me *so much* good, and I am sure another is on the way to me now. . . .

I had no idea until I read your letter of the dangerous part you have had to do in the expedition, though I felt all the time that you were in some great peril, and indeed I did pray that you might be kept safely through it, that our Father's arm would be around you to shield you from any harm, and I cannot be thankful enough that he has so answered my prayer. . . . When I read the accounts of the explosion of the Louisiana I little thought *who* commanded the little "Wilderness," nor did I realize how great the danger to which he was exposed. You did not say anything about coming now, I shall hope for that in the next one. You must be nearly worn out. . . .

Mother sends kindest love, and says she hopes you won't tow any more powder ships for we aren't ready to lose you yet. . . .

Roswell to Kate

USS *Gettysburg*
Off Fort Fisher
Jan. 15, 1865

We have taken *Fort Fisher* by a bombardment and a combined assault of soldiers and sailors.

It has been a dreadful Sunday, but we have done *something* toward ending the war.

I led one of the divisions and was shot through the left arm and shoulder on the edge of the parapet under which I lay with the other wounded till dark. Am on board again wounds which are not severe dressed and quite comfortable.

We assaulted the sea face, which is casemated at the same time that the army assaulted the rear. Our men were driven back with heavy loss nearly all the leading officers being killed or wounded. Preston of my class was killed near me and several classmates wounded.

God and your prayers and love were with me during those dreadful hours.

I love you more even than ever, and will come to you as soon as I can. . . .

Roswell to Commander Alexander Rhind[1]

USS *Gettysburg*
Off Fort Fisher
Jan. 16, 1865

You will no doubt learn the good news of our victory and the sad, sad tidings of Preston's death before this reaches you; but as he was shot by my side I thought you would like to know some of the particulars of the fall of one whom we all loved and admired so much, and whom I knew was sincerely attached to you.

The storming party from the fleet was landed about 2 miles from the fort before noon, and Mr. Preston had charge of an advanced force with shovels to throw up some rifle pits so that we could approach as near as possible without being exposed to the enemy's fire. About 3 p.m. the signal was made for the assault, and Mr. Preston was near the head of the column. We advanced along the beach near the water till we had reached the palisades, where we turned straight for the sea face of the fort, the army assaulting on the left flank and rear of the fort about the same time.

The fleet now ceased firing, and in an instant the entire front of the fort was lined with riflemen, who, secure behind the breastworks, poured a terrible fire into us, and we received grape and canister at the same time from the Mound and the other batteries.

The men still pressed forward, and when near the palisades Mr.

1. Although this was a personal letter, it was later published in *O.R. Navies*, ser. I, vol. 11, pp. 450–51.

Preston was struck in the left thigh or groin, the femoral artery being severed. He fell forward, and one of the men stooped to assist him and was shot, falling on Mr. Preston. Some one pulled him off, and Mr. Preston turned over on his back and soon expired. I had got forward some twenty paces more, when I was knocked down by a shot through the left arm and shoulder. I arose again and got up nearer the parapet, when I fell from loss of blood and exhaustion.

The officers were all doing their utmost to get the men forward, but the hopelessness of attempting to get over the palisades, ditch, and the steep parapet was apparent, and the men fell so fast that every formation was instantly broken; still I think we would have made a more desperate effort if so many of the leading officers had not been killed or wounded. Our men fell back, taking many wounded with them, but leaving the ground covered with the dead, dying, and wounded. As soon as I could get a bandage round my arm to stop the flow of blood I started to crawl to Preston to see if I could do anything for him, but a wounded man near him called to me that he was dead. Poor fellow, it made my heart sick to see him stretched out on the sand, and I mourned him, not only as a dear friend lost, but as a loss to the service of the most superior young officer I have ever seen in it.

In the meantime the army carried almost without resistance five traverses on the left, for Colonel Lamb says he thought ours the main attack and had most all the garrison to meet us.[1]

The fleet opened fire again over us, who were lying under the parapet, and the army took one traverse after another till the rebels surrendered. The army officers say freely that they never could have got into the fort had it not been for our assault on the sea face drawing the garrison to that side. Looking down from the parapet now I do not wonder we did not get up, especially as we had no sharpshooters to cover us to keep the rebels from using their muskets so freely . . .

---

1. It is true that the attack on the sea face of Fort Fisher, which occurred a short time before the army troops launched their assault on the land face of the L-shaped fort, drew the attention of the defenders to the sea face and made the army's task easier. But it is not true that the army took the first five traverses "almost without resistance." In fact the fighting on the land as well as the sea face was fierce. Army troops suffered a total of 955 casualties in the attack, and the navy suffered 386. Some navy casualties occurred on shipboard from shell fire, but most came in the assault which was carried out by marines and by volunteers (of whom Lamson was one) among the sailors. The *Gettysburg* lost six men killed and six wounded, including Lamson, from 70 that Lamson led onto the beach.

Roswell to Kate

New York
Jan. 29, 1865

I arrived here safely last evening, and my wounds are doing very well.

The Admiral wished me to remain at Fort Fisher if I could, but I was prostrated with fever and being unable to move he gave me two weeks leave with permission to write to the Dept. for more leave. I came to Fortress Monroe, was stopped by the ice, and reached here via Washington last evening pretty well used up. This morning I felt quite well again and have made my way to Mr. Goodnows in Brooklyn where I am now writing. As I wrote you the evening of the battle I was wounded in the arm and shoulder—no bones broken and only a pretty severe flesh wound which is already healing. The wounds were badly burned which made them quite painful and induced fever, but I suffer very little now except when they are being dressed which is once or twice a day.

As you have no doubt learned from the papers Paymaster Gillette and Act. Ensign Laighton of the Gettysburg are killed by the explosion of the magazine in Fort Fisher.[1] I sent an officer home in charge of their remains the next day. This accident cost more gloom and sadness over the vessel, and fleet than the death of all those who fell in the battle. . . .

Every one here and in Washington thinks the assault of Fort Fisher one of the most desperate fights and one of the most gallant and important achievements of the war. It was even a more fearful struggle than they think and it was God who gave us the victory. How much I wish to see you and tell you the story of the fight—How *much* I wish to look in your dear eyes again. As soon as I am well enough to travel I will come to Mt. Vernon if my leave can be extended long enough. . . .

---

1. On the morning after Fort Fisher was captured, a careless Union marine carrying a lighted torch wandered into the main powder magazine containing 13,000 pounds of gunpowder and blew up himself along with at least another 130 men killed and wounded.

Kate to Roswell

> Mount Vernon, Ohio
> Jan. 29, 1865

Yours of the 10th, and also the one written after the dreadful 15th was over, came to me this evening telling me the first I knew of your wound. I cannot tell you all there is in my heart of thankfulness to our kind Father that He keeps you from that other fearful peril—Oh, *how good* He is that He spared your *life* to me. But I do not forget dearest that you were struck in the deadly conflict—that you were so long without care, and that you are now suffering. It makes me faint when I think of that terrible day. I *cannot* think of it—but trust you may *soon* be with me, and I will take such good care of you. *Do* come just as soon as it is safe. I *wish* I could go to *you*, but you know I cannot do that.[1] I hardly know where to send a letter but will try sending to Mr Goodnow. . . .

Dear Roswell it made me very sad to hear of Preston's death I well know what a trial it will be to you for you loved each other so much.

My prayers have followed you wherever you were and God has answered them very graciously.

Roswell to Kate

> Windsor, Vermont
> Feb. 8, 1865

I wrote you day before yesterday that Commodore Rodgers had telegraphed for me by direction of the Admiral, and that I should go by the next train after I wrote—my trunk was at the depot, but just before the train came I received a telegram from the Department that my leave had been extended twenty days as my health is such that I really thought I ought not to go just yet. I telegraphed to Commodore Rodgers that I should not come unless there was something of more than ordinary importance to be done, in which case he could telegraph me again and I would come immediately at all hazards.

---

1. It is not clear why she could not come to New York.

I do enjoy the rest and quiet and my Aunt's kind care *so* much that I am quite sad when I think of leaving it again, but as soon as I can put a coat sleeve on my arm I shall return to my duty—How much I would like to see you, dear, before I go but it scarcely seems possible unless you reach Irvington before I leave New York. God hasten the time when we can have a home of *our own* and when these long separations shall be over. It would be a great trial to me to leave the Navy—the profession I love above all others, and in which I have so many pleasant friends and, I think, bright prospects—but if it is to be always as it has been during the past two years, I must leave a service that however desirable in itself, keeps me away from you. I have received but one letter from you since the fight I suppose they are being detained on the Gettysburg or in New York. . . .

Katie we will appreciate being to-gether, and prize each other's society the more, perhaps, for our long separation. . . .

Roswell to Kate

USS *Gettysburg*
Norfolk
Feb. 27, 1865

I am again on board my own ship, after a leave that was very pleasant in some respects, and in others very unpleasant; it was a great disappointment to me not to see you, and a deep regret that I could not obey your earnest summons to Mt. Vernon.

Your letters, written just before and just after the battle are beginning to reach me, and I thank you just as much for them as though they had come sooner, though I was anxious at their non-reception.

Every body seemed glad to see me on board again, and the officers welcomed me warmly, and I am glad to be again with those who have given me such tokens of affection, and who have stood by me so bravely. . . .

I expect to take the Gettysburg to N.Y. the latter part of next week—about the time I suppose that you will reach New York, so I hope to see you very soon. I hear unofficially but direct from the Dept. that the Gettysburg is to be fitted out for Admiral Goldsborough's yacht and despatch vessel, to accompany the Colorado on her European cruise, and that I am to command her. I shall know certainly in a few days, and will let you know at once. The Admiral has offered me a position on his staff if I wish it.[1] . . .

Roswell to Gideon Welles

USS *Gettysburg*
Norfolk,
March 13, 1865

Sir:

I have the honor to acknowledge the receipt of the Department's order of the 9th Inst. detaching me from the command of this vessel on the reporting of my relief, and directing me to report to Rear Adm'l Pauling at the Brooklyn Navy Yard on the 10th April next for duty on the U.S.S. Colorado as Fleet Lieutenant of the European Squadron.

Jeremiah Lamson to Roswell

Willamina, Ore.
April 8, 1865

It is with pleasure that I now write you, because I am assured of your safety.

We learned by the papers that you was severely wounded at the taking of Fort Fisher, but not hearing any thing from you we feared that your wound had proved mortal, mail after mail and no news from you. I wrote to your uncle E. G. Lamson to write me, at last the long looked for letters came from you giving an account of your first and second attack on Fisher, and that you was safe, it was a day of rejoicing with us. How thankful we ought to be to God that your wounds were not mortal.

1. Rear-Admiral Lewis M. Goldsborough was appointed to command the European Squadron in the spring of 1865. His flagship, the USS *Colorado,* was a 52-gun screw frigate launched in 1856. Lamson went to Europe, not as commander of the *Gettysburg,* which remained in the United States, but as Flag Lieutenant of the fleet with his headquarters on the *Colorado*. It was a gesture of the navy's high regard for him, but it also postponed his marriage to Kate. The main function of the European squadron was to show the flag in various European ports.

We have just received the news that Richmond is taken. On the reception of the news there was a great gathering at Salem. Gov. Gibbs made a speech in which he alluded to your services, cheer after cheer was given for you.

If you should come back to Oregon she would bestow her best gifts upon you. You could have your choice in positions in Oregon if you should leave the Navy. As you say you have fought and worked hard to obtain the position that you now ocupy, and if you resign you give up in part what you have been striving for.

It looks like this rebellion is near its end and peace must soon come and then your duties will be much easier than in times of war. You have a shure thing for life with a salery that will pay a little more than your expences.

If you leave the Navy you may make more money and you may not of this you must be the judge. In a social point of view a private life is far preferable to that of the Navy.

For the last five years all kinds of business in Oregon has been overdone.

I had considerable money loaned out, which has been paid to me in green backs at pay worth but fifty cents on the dollar in gold which is the basis on which we do buisness.

So you see that I have sustained quite a loss in greenbacks. As opportunity presented I have invested in real estate thinking that would be safe if it did not bring me much income. We now have 2500 acres land and a large herd of sheep and cattle. Prospects for business in Oregon looks better than it has done should I make sails I could let you have some money but dare not promise you.

When are [you] coming hom? All well and join in sending much love.

EPILOGUE

L IKE SO MANY Civil War heroes who survived the conflict, Lamson found life in the postwar era to be an anticlimax. Nothing in peacetime could equal the stimulation of war that kept the senses on constant alert and made each moment of life precious because it might be the last. Having looked forward to a career that combined his two passions, the navy and Kate, Lamson decided that he must sacrifice one for the other. Anticipating many decades of marital bliss and an old age telling war stories to his grandchildren, Roswell buried five of his seven children plus Kate one after another, had no grandchildren, and suffered excruciating pain from a mysterious malady that left him crippled during the last decade of his life.

The postwar years began on a hopeful note. Sailing for Europe as flag lieutenant on the USS *Colorado*, Lamson had every reason to anticipate an illustrious career in the navy. His letters to Kate from exotic-sounding European ports were full of cheer. By the end of 1865, however, unrest and dissatisfaction crept into their correspondence. Rapid demobilization chilled the chances for promotion in the peacetime navy. A lieutenant's pay seemed inadequate to support a family, and the prize money Lamson expected materialized slowly or not at all. The long separations from wife and home that sea duty would entail grew less and less appealing.

In the spring of 1866 Lamson resigned from the navy to accept an offer from his uncle Ebenezer G. Lamson to become managing director of the Windsor Manufacturing Company, of which Ebenezer was president and chief stockholder. This factory, located on the Connecticut River in Windsor, Vermont, produced machine tools, sewing machines, saws, drills and bits, and other hardware. During the Civil War it also made rifles for the Union army. Building on that experience, Ebenezer Lamson hoped to find a market in the armies of North America and Europe for his "Balls Patent Repeating and Single Loading Rifles." After resigning from the navy, Roswell stayed on in Europe for another year (to Kate's consternation) trying to sell this rifle to European armies. Their ordnance officers were polite but noncommittal. Roswell returned home in June 1867 with few contracts. After further delays to build a house in Windsor, he and Kate were finally married on November 14, 1867.

For two years their life in Windsor was busy and happy. Their first child, Roswell Buckingham Lamson, was born on September 27, 1868. But in 1869 things began to go sour. Roswell had some kind of falling out with his uncle, and they parted company in 1870. Having evidently lost the money he invested in the company and suffered a flareup of malaria contracted during the war, Lamson took his wife and infant son to Oregon, where he arrived in the fall of 1870 "much enfeebled and poor both in health and pocket."[1]

For several years Roswell tried to make a living farming a portion of the family homestead that his father gave him. Two children born in 1873 and 1875, Frederick and Mary, died in infancy. For one year, 1873–74, Roswell served as county clerk of Multomah County (Portland). Another year, 1876–77, he taught mathematics at Pacific University in Forest Grove, twenty miles west of Portland. Roswell must have wondered often during these years what had become of the good will of Oregonians that his father had so often mentioned in wartime letters: "If you should come back to Oregon she would bestow her best gifts upon you. You could have your choice in positions in Oregon if you should leave the Navy."

In 1877 Roswell finally called in some of those chips by securing appointment as clerk of the U.S. district court in Portland, a position he held for seventeen years during which he watched his son Roswell grow up and become a lawyer who would ultimately practice before

1. From the obituary of Lamson in the Portland *Morning Oregonian*, Aug. 15, 1903.

that same court. In most other respects, however, those were years of sadness. Kate and Roswell's fourth and sixth children, Alice and Ethel, born in 1877 and 1882, lived only one and three years, respectively. Their fifth, Helen, was healthy and grew to adulthood. But their seventh and last child, Gertrude, was born in 1885 and lived to the age of twelve. At least Kate was spared the sadness of this death; she had died of a tumor of the spleen and liver in 1892 at the age of forty-nine. Of the five children who did not live, Alice died of whooping cough and Gertrude succumbed to a heart disorder. The cause of death for the other three children is unknown. Both Roswell Jr. and Helen married, but neither had children. Whether this lack of issue and the infant deaths of so many of Kate and Roswell's children could have been the consequence of their consanguinity (first cousins) will never be known.

In any event, several years before Kate's death Roswell's own health began to deteriorate. He experienced liver and stomach problems that he attributed to recurrent bouts of malaria. More serious was a debilitating illness diagnosed as "locomotor ataxia," a spinal disease that caused partial paralysis of feet and legs. By 1890 his weight had dropped to 111 pounds on a frame nearly six feet tall. In 1894 he could walk only with a cane or crutches and was forced to resign as clerk of court. In his application to President Grover Cleveland for a disability pension, Lamson stated that "during the past thirteen years [I have] not drawn a conscious breath without pain, and [my] life has been and is a burden to be borne only from a sense of duty."[1] In 1895 the navy reappointed him lieutenant and placed him on the retired list.

Lamson eked out eight more years of life on a lieutenant's pension, burying his twelve-year-old daughter Gertrude in 1897. On August 14, 1903, he died in Portland and joined Kate and four of their children

---

1. From a copy of Lamson's pension application in the Lamson Papers. Lamson's disease may have been the consequence of a youthful indiscretion, perhaps during his two years in Europe after the Civil War. The more common term for locomotor ataxia is tabes dorsalis, which is normally caused by syphilis. Its symptoms are those experienced by Lamson—including gastric and visceral pain, for which malaria seems an unlikely cause. The incubation period for tabes dorsalis generally ranges from five to twenty years. If Lamson was unfaithful to Kate and contracted syphilis, he paid for it dearly—and so perhaps did Kate and the children. We are indebted to Dr. Maurice S. Albin of the Department of Anesthesiology at the University of Texas at San Antonio for information and references on tabes dorsalis, both as it was understood in Lamson's time and as it is understood today.

at Riverview Cemetery. His casket was wrapped in the American flag that had flown on the USS *Mount Washington* when it was shot nearly to pieces on that April day forty years earlier when Roswell's life and prospects stood at their zenith.[1]

1. Portland *Morning Oregonian,* Aug. 17, 1903.

INDEX